PHILOSOPHICAL PROBLEMS

PHILOSOPHICAL PROBLEMS

An Introductory Text
in Philosophy

PETER ALWARD

broadview press

BROADVIEW PRESS – www.broadviewpress.com
Peterborough, Ontario, Canada

Founded in 1985, Broadview Press remains a wholly independent publishing house. Broadview's focus is on academic publishing; our titles are accessible to university and college students as well as scholars and general readers. With over 600 titles in print, Broadview has become a leading international publisher in the humanities, with world-wide distribution. Broadview is committed to environmentally responsible publishing and fair business practices.

The interior of this book is printed on 100% recycled paper.

Library and Archives Canada Cataloguing in Publication

Alward, Peter Wallace, 1964-, author
    Philosophical problems : an introductory text in philosophy
/ Peter Alward.

Includes index.
ISBN 978-1-55481-285-1 (softcover)

    1. Philosophy—Textbooks. 2. Textbooks. I. Title.

BD21.A49 2017   100   C2017-905495-3

Broadview Press handles its own distribution in North America
PO Box 1243, Peterborough, Ontario K9J 7H5, Canada
555 Riverwalk Parkway, Tonawanda, NY 14150, USA
Tel: (705) 743-8990; Fax: (705) 743-8353
email: customerservice@broadviewpress.com

Distribution is handled by Eurospan Group in the UK, Europe, Central Asia, Middle East, Africa, India, Southeast Asia, Central America, South America, and the Caribbean. Distribution is handled by Footprint Books in Australia and New Zealand.

Canadä Broadview Press acknowledges the financial support of the Government of Canada through the Canada Book Fund for our publishing activities.

Edited by Martin R. Boyne
Book Design by Em Dash Design

PRINTED IN CANADA

For my parents, John and Judith

CONTENTS

ACKNOWLEDGEMENTS

I would like to thank my colleagues at both the University of Lethbridge and the University of Saskatchewan for their support during the time I spent working on this project. I would also like to acknowledge the support and encouragement I received from Broadview Press. In particular, I would like to single out the efforts of Stephen Latta at Broadview, without whom this project would not have come to fruition.

INTRODUCTION
FOR INSTRUCTORS

Like many post-secondary philosophy instructors, I have spent much of my career teaching historically based introductory-level philosophy courses. The readings for these courses have consisted largely of primary-source materials, written by the philosophical greats themselves. On numerous occasions I have asked first-year university students to read such works as Plato's *Meno*, Hume's *Dialogues Concerning Natural Religion*, Descartes's *Meditations on First Philosophy*, and Berkeley's *Three Dialogues Between Hylas and Philonous*, and the results have been largely successful. Nevertheless, a few years ago I decided I wanted to try teaching an introductory course using a textbook. I was motivated in part by the desire to mix things up a bit, having taught the same basic version of the course on more than twenty occasions. But I had also become convinced, through my encounter with Jaegwon Kim's wonderful text *Philosophy of Mind*, that it was possible to deliver a credible philosophy course using a textbook, rather than an anthology, as the main source of readings. My view had always been that textbooks lacked the philosophical depth required for the serious philosophy I aspire to achieve in the classroom. Kim's book demonstrated to me that the breadth and clarity characteristic of a textbook could be combined with the depth and rigour of primary-source material.

What remained to be done was to find a text that shared the virtues of Kim's book but was designed for the introductory level. Alas, my search proved fruitless. Despite soliciting texts from the various publishing representatives who found their way to my office and engaging in countless web and library searches, all the candidates I found seemed to me to be too thin or too superficial or too obscure or too idiosyncratic. Doubtless in many cases the fault was mine, my own idiosyncrasies being what they are. Nevertheless, rather than abandoning the project of a text-based introduction to philosophy, I decided to write the textbook myself. One might worry that it was a mere conceit on my part to suppose that I could successfully pull this off, and time will tell if I have actually done so. But I believe I have two features that provide grounds for optimism. First, I am an extremely clear writer and, as a result, am able to make even difficult ideas accessible to philosophical novices. An anonymous referee once went so far as to charge me with "unusual clarity" in his/her report on a paper involving technical issues in the philosophy of language. And second, I am an extremely broad philosopher. I have published on issues in the philosophy of language, the philosophy of mind, metaphysics, the philosophy of art and literature, biomedical ethics, and environmental ethics, and have taught courses in all these areas and in epistemology, logic, business ethics, and the philosophy of law, among others. As a result, I consider myself well placed to write a textbook that competently covers a range of topics one might hope to find in an introductory text.

Although I suspect I am not unusual in this regard, my central pedagogical goal is not to get students to learn about philosophy but rather to engage in the practice of philosophy itself. More cautiously, I should say that my goal is not merely to get students to learn about philosophy—that is, to learn what questions philosophers have asked, what answers they have given these questions, and what arguments they have offered in support of their own answers and against the answers of others. After all, to engage in the practice of philosophy—or at least to do it well—one has to know something about philosophy. But one needs to do more than this. Among other things, one needs to adopt a critical attitude toward the answers and arguments that other people have given to philosophical questions and to attempt to develop and defend one's own answers to them. One disadvantage of using primary sources in an introductory philosophy course is that doing so puts a kind of roadblock in the path of student engagement in philosophical practice. The ideas contained in primary-source material are often complex and sophisticated; the language used is often technical or archaic; the formulation of issues often varies from reading to reading. As a result, students often find themselves ill-placed to figure out even what questions, answers, and arguments are expressed in a reading, let alone to critically evaluate them. A corresponding advantage of using a clearly written textbook as the main source of readings in an introductory philosophy course is that this kind of roadblock is removed: students can focus their energy on critical work rather than spend a large portion of their time on interpretation. One might, of course, object that making students read difficult material is good for them. No doubt, but other things might be better: for example, spending their time critically evaluating ideas and arguments. Alternatively, one might point out that the instructor can step in and help when students have difficulty understanding the readings in a course, and, in fact, that is the instructor's job. But not only does this involve using scarce classroom time on things that can be done outside the classroom, but it also provides a disincentive toward student reading. After all, what is the point if the instructor is just going to explain it in class? I do not mean to overstate the case here. Of course, a credible introductory course can be delivered using primary sources. But there are grounds for thinking that an introductory philosophy course delivered using a textbook can be credible as well.

The book consists of fourteen chapters, one of which is a self-standing introduction to philosophy, and the remainder of which are divided into two fairly standard sections: metaphysics and epistemology, and ethics and political philosophy. The first section, on metaphysics and epistemology, covers a lot of what are generally considered to be core topics: mind and body, knowledge and skepticism, free will and determinism, personal identity, and the nature and existence of God. It also includes less standard fare, however, including chapters on modality and causation, and on truth and fiction. The second section, on ethics and political philosophy, is divided into two subsections, one focused on more general issues in these areas and the other focused on the applications of general principles to specific problems. Included in the first subsection are chapters on moral skepticism, moral realism, justice, and liberty; included in the second subsection are chapters on punishment and abortion. In each chapter, basic concepts and central problems are carefully introduced, followed by a number of approaches to those problems. In addition, a number of objections to each of the approaches considered are sketched. It is worth emphasizing that the views considered do not systematically line up with views that particular philosophers have defended. Rather, they are designed to characterize a variety of important approaches to the problems at issue. Moreover, they are intended to be first passes at the approaches they instantiate. Instructors and students should expect to need to develop and revise them in light of the objections that are presented to them. And the objections, which are typically sketches rather than full-blown arguments, are designed to be developed and revised as well. Rather than treating it as a finished product, instructors and students should view this text as a launching-off point for engaging in the practice of philosophy.

1

PHILOSOPHY

Philosophy courses are Increasing

For most introductory students at the college or university level, philosophy is an entirely new discipline. Although the numbers of high-school philosophy courses are increasing, they nevertheless remain relatively rare. As a result, many students have little idea of what to expect in their first philosophy course. The term "philosophy" is, of course, a familiar one, but many of its uses have little to do with what goes on in the philosophy classroom. One common use is to characterize a person's or organization's guiding principles. When someone says something like "My philosophy is to live and let live," or "Our philosophy is that the customer is always right," they are using the term in this sense. And although such guiding principles might be based on philosophical reasoning or even entailed by a philosophical theory, in general they are of little concern to the practice of philosophy.

It is one thing to say what philosophy is not; it is another thing to say what it positively is. This is difficult to do because the nature of philosophy is itself a philosophical question—and a difficult one at that. In order to get a handle on this question we will have to get some clarity on the concepts of truth and reason, as well as on the difference between empirical and conceptual questions. And in order to begin to engage in the practice of philosophy, we will have to acquire a competence with logic, which lies at the core of philosophical reasoning.

Philosophical reasoning

1.1 What Is Philosophy?

The first thing to note is that rather than merely being a body of knowledge, philosophy is, in addition, a practice. A body of knowledge is a collection of facts, perhaps unified by certain overarching principles. Chemistry, human anatomy, geography, and other disciplines count as bodies of knowledge in this sense. A practice, in contrast, is a way of going about doing something, a method or series of related methods directed toward some end or goal. Activities such as yoga and whittling count as a practice in this sense. It is worth emphasizing that many academic fields consist of both a body of knowledge and a practice: chemical knowledge is grounded in various kinds of chemical research; and mathematical reasoning yields knowledge of mathematical theorems of various kinds. Similarly, there is a lot of philosophical knowledge to be had: knowledge of the theories defended and arguments deployed by philosophers past and present, knowledge of important distinctions that are widely made, knowledge of fallacious forms of argument, and so on. But unlike other fields, the truth of such theories, arguments, and distinctions is itself a matter of controversy. Nevertheless, knowledge of them serves to better enable one to engage in philosophical practice.

In its most basic form, the practice of philosophy consists in the pursuit of truth by means of reason. Both of these notions require some comment. The first thing to note is that truth is not some object "out there" to be sought after but rather a property of claims, beliefs, or propositions. Some claims and beliefs have the property of truth whereas others lack this property, being instead false or even indeterminate. As a result, what the pursuit of truth consists in is determining which claims, beliefs, or propositions are true. For example, "The 2012 Olympics were held in London" is true, "Russia is a country in South America" is false, and "Humans will have a colony on Mars by 2100" is (arguably) indeterminate. There is nothing mysterious or impractical about an inquiry into the truth of these claims, and one shouldn't be alarmed or confused by the very idea of pursuing truth. Now the nature of the property of truth is itself a matter of philosophical controversy. The most common view is what is known as the "correspondence theory" of truth. According to this view, a belief, claim, or proposition is true just in case it "corresponds to the facts." Beliefs, claims, and propositions describe or represent the world as being a certain way. The belief that pigs can fly represents the world as being one in which pigs have the ability to get airborne. And a belief, claim, or proposition corresponds to the facts just in case the world in fact is as it is represented as being. Because as a matter of fact pigs cannot fly, the belief that they can do so is false; but if pigs could fly then the belief in question would correspond to the facts and, hence, would be true.

Reasoning is the attempt to work out what follows from what one believes, the claims one makes, or the propositions one endorses. If the beliefs, claims, or propositions you start from are true, or likely so, and your reasoning is good, the products of your reasoning—your conclusions—will be true, or likely so, as well. Logic is the study of good reasoning and, in particular, the conditions under which particular claims, beliefs, or propositions in fact follow from certain other beliefs,

Logic lies at the centre of philosophical Practices. (handwritten)

claims, or propositions. As a result, logic lies at the centre of philosophical practice. It is worth emphasizing that not all questions can be settled by reason alone. Some questions are, instead, partially or primarily empirical, requiring observation or experimentation to be settled. To the extent a question is empirical, it is not the proper target of philosophical investigation but rather is better suited to scientific or social-scientific investigation. Nevertheless, the boundaries between philosophy and the empirical disciplines remain vague, and there is much blending between the two: not only are empirical results often germane to philosophical questions but philosophical issues also often arise within predominantly empirical disciplines.

It is worth (handwritten)

As characterized here, philosophical practice presupposes the ideal of objective truth, that is, that at least some claims, beliefs, and propositions are true independently of the beliefs and values of those who make, hold, or endorse them, and other claims, beliefs, and propositions are false in this same sense. Relativism, in contrast, is the view that the ideal of objective truth should be rejected in favour

Truth Bearers

It is one thing to characterize what conditions have to be satisfied in order for something to have the property of truth, but it is another thing to specify what sorts of things are potentially capable of having this property. One common view is that truth bearers include both statements or claims and beliefs. So, for example, the claim that the planet is roughly spherical and the belief that it is not are each candidates for truth or falsity. Another view is that **propositions** are the only primary bearers of truth, where propositions correspond to what people claim or believe, and that claims and beliefs are truth bearers only in a secondary or derivative sense. For example, on this view it is the proposition that the planet is roughly spherical that is a candidate for truth and falsity. And whether the claim or belief to this effect is true depends on whether this proposition is true.

The ideal of objective truth should be rejected in Favour (handwritten)

Relative Truth

Although the claim that truth is relative is commonplace, it is not always entirely clear what it amounts to. In particular, it is not clear what it means to say that a claim is true for one person and false for another, but neither objectively true nor objectively false. One suggestion is that for a claim to be true for someone is for that person to believe it, and for it to be false for someone is for him or her to disbelieve it. The trouble with this suggestion is that it is compatible with objective truth. After all, a claim could be true for me in the sense that I believe it despite its being objectively false. A second suggestion would be to couple the idea that for a claim to be true for someone is for her or him to believe it with the hypothesis that the world lacks any kind of determinate nature. However, not only does the suggestion that people have beliefs presuppose that the world has some kind of nature—it is inhabited by psychological subjects who have beliefs and make claims about it—but also, insofar as it is natureless, any claims made as to its nature are objectively false. Finally, a third suggestion would be that each psychological subject literally occupies a distinct world, and for a claim to be true for someone it must be true in the world that he or she alone inhabits. The trouble with this is that it seems to suggest that distinct psychological subjects never communicate or otherwise interact with one another; after all, to do so they would have to occupy a common world.

of the claim that truth is always relative to an individual's or group's beliefs and values. As a result, beliefs, claims, and propositions are never simply true but only ever "true for" someone or other. Moreover, if there is no objective truth, then there is no fact of the matter of what follows from particular beliefs, claims, or propositions. As a result, relativists often also reject reason in favour of **rhetoric**—discourse not designed to discover the truth of things but rather to persuade in the absence of truth. It is important to note that many philosophers consider the wholesale rejection of the ideal of objective truth and the use of rhetoric instead of reason to be antithetical to the practice of philosophy. Still, there is room within philosophical practice for a variety of attitudes toward truth and logic.

1.2 A Philosophical Taxonomy

There is a wide variety of distinct areas of philosophy. In fact, in almost any subject matter philosophical questions arise. For example, the philosophy of art, the philosophy of science, the philosophy of language, and the philosophy of psychology, among many others, are well-established branches of philosophy. Nevertheless, there are a number of core areas whose results are often taken up in the more specialized branches of philosophy. The core areas in question are metaphysics, epistemology, ethics and value theory, social and political philosophy, and logic. We will consider each in turn.

Metaphysics is the study of reality, of how things are. Now, of course, the nature of things is also the subject matter of the various empirical disciplines. What distinguishes metaphysics from physics, chemistry, and biology, for example, is that it is concerned with very general, abstract questions that are amenable to philosophical treatment. One example is causation. Physics can tell us what the particular causes of various physical phenomena are; a metaphysical question, in contrast, is the nature of causation itself—what it is for one thing to cause another. Another example is the human mind. Neuroscience can tell us how the brain works; a metaphysical question would be whether or not the mind can be identified with the human brain. An important branch of metaphysics is **ontology**. The concern of ontology is with what sorts of entities there are, or with the basic categories into which the various existent things fall.

Epistemology is the study of knowledge. Rather than being focused on what the world is like, the concern of epistemology is with whether and how we can acquire knowledge of it. One central epistemological concern is with the nature of knowledge: how does a thinking and perceiving subject need to be related to things in the world in order to count as having knowledge of them? One question is what knowledge is; another is whether we have any. Skeptics sometimes argue that certain sorts of knowledge—of morality, or of a world external to one's mind, for example—or even knowledge in general, is impossible. Hence, another epistemological concern is whether such skeptical claims are well grounded. Other epistemological concerns include the kinds of evidence that count as adequate justification for our beliefs and epistemic responsibility, that is, the kinds of evidence we need to gather in order to have fulfilled our epistemological duties in the circumstances in which we find ourselves.

Ethics is the study of morality: what makes an action right or wrong. Rather than being concerned with how things are, ethics is focused instead on how things ought to be. Value theory—the study of what makes things valuable—is related to ethics because rightness and wrongness are often understood in terms of the value of an action or its consequences. A central ethical concern is with whether there are objective moral facts or whether morality is relative to culture in some sense. If morality is objective, then an account needs to be given of its ground or basis. And if morality is not objective, then an account needs to be given of our moral talk, reconciling its importance and meaningfulness with the fact that it is, in effect, talk about nothing. Other ethical concerns include the relation between a supreme being of some kind and morality, and whether acting morally is in one's rational self-interest. In ethics, we also ask specific practical questions, such as "When is physical violence permissible?" "Is euthanasia / abortion / genetic enhancement ever acceptable?" and "How should we respond to issues of discrimination?"

Social and political philosophy is the study of collective enterprises, including, but not restricted to, political and economic systems. As with ethics, social and political philosophy is primarily normative: concerned with the sorts of institutions we ought to have rather than what we in fact have. Central concerns of social and political philosophy include the sorts of political systems that are morally defensible, as well as what counts as a just distribution of societal goods. Other questions include the limits of liberty (in what range of activities should individuals be free from government interference?), the justification for punishment, and state interference in child-rearing.

Finally, **logic** is the study of reasoning. As with ethics and social and political philosophy, logic is a normative discipline: it is not concerned with how people in fact reason but rather with what counts as good and bad reasoning. The study of logic not only provides basic tools for engaging in philosophical practice but is also a subject of philosophical interest in its own right. The next section will consist of a brief introduction to logic designed primarily for the former purpose.

1.3 Logic

A central concept in logic is that of an argument. In the logical sense, an argument is not an angry dispute but rather a written or spoken stretch of discourse, or sequence of sentences, which is structured in a certain way. First, at least some of the sentences that make up the discourse must be statements; that is, they must be used to make claims and must either be true or false (or at least believed to be so by the speaker). Examples of statements include the following:

Professor Alward is wearing brown shoes.

It is currently 7 p.m.

A tiger peed on Professor Alward's nephew.

Examples of non-statements include:

What time is it?

Please pass the salt.

Stop thief!

Second, in addition to containing statements, in order for a stretch of discourse to count as an argument, one or more of its constituent statements must be offered as reasons or evidence for one or more of the others. Consider, for example, the following discourse:

Since Professor Alward teaches logic and all logic teachers have mean streaks, it follows that Professor Alward has a mean streak.

Since it contains three statements—"Professor Alward teaches logic," "All logic teachers have mean streaks," and "Professor Alward has a mean streak"—and since the first two statements are offered as reasons for accepting the third, this stretch of discourse is an argument. Note: the statements offered as reasons or evidence are the **premises** of the argument and the statement they are offered as reasons or evidence for is the **conclusion**.

It is worth emphasizing that it is not always obvious whether a stretch of discourse is an argument, or, if it is, exactly what the argument is. The presence of logical indicator words—"since," "because," "hence," "it follows that," and so on—is reasonably good evidence of the presence of an argument, but in their

Types of Statements

Three important distinctions can be drawn between types of statements worth mentioning here. First, we can distinguish between objective and subjective statements. A statement is objective just in case there is a fact of the matter regarding whether it is correct or incorrect; a statement is subjective, in contrast, just in case it is a mere matter of opinion and hence neither true nor false. Judgements of taste—"Brussels sprouts are terrible," for example—are normally thought to be subjective. Second, we can distinguish between descriptive and normative statements. A descriptive statement makes a claim about how things actually are, whereas a normative statement makes a claim about how things ought to be or whether how things are is good or bad. Statements that make moral claims—"Breaking your promises is wrong," for example—are a familiar kind of normative statement. And third, we can distinguish between necessary and contingent statements. A statement is contingent just in case even if it is in fact true it nevertheless could have been false, and vice versa; a statement is necessary just in case, if true, it must be true (and if false, it must be false). Mathematical statements are often thought to be necessary in this sense.

[handwritten: Deductive Inductive ☐ Deductive ☐ Inductive]

absence one has to rely on such things as actual inferential relations between statements (what in fact provides evidence for what), the context in which the stretch of discourse occurs, and background knowledge of various kinds. Reconstructing the argument in a stretch of discourse can also be difficult because, in many cases, one or more of the premises, or even the conclusion, may be simply assumed but not stated.

There are a number of different kinds of arguments, but for our present purposes we will focus on just two: **deductive** arguments and **inductive** arguments. The difference between deductive and inductive arguments is in the kind of support their premises are designed to give their conclusions. Deductive arguments are designed to guarantee their conclusions, to make their truth a certainty. Inductive arguments, in contrast, are designed only to make their conclusions likely. Let us consider each in turn.

A good deductive argument is one that has two independent features: it is valid and all of its premises are true. A valid argument is one whose premises

Standard Form

Before evaluating the argument in a stretch of discourse as good or bad, it is often useful to put it into **standard form**. This involves creating a list of statements in which the premises of the argument occur first, labelled as premises, and the conclusion or conclusions occur last, labelled as conclusions. Sentences that play no role in the argument are omitted from the list, and any unstated premises or conclusions are added to it. Finally, any extraneous language, including logical indicator words, is eliminated. Consider again the following stretch of discourse:

> Since Professor Alward teaches logic and all logic teachers have mean streaks, it follows that Professor Alward has a mean streak.

The argument in this passage can be put into standard form as follows:

PREMISE 1: Professor Alward teaches logic.

PREMISE 2: All logic teachers have mean streaks.

CONCLUSION: Professor Alward has a mean streak.

and conclusion are related in such a way that if the premises are all true, then the conclusion must be true as well, or, equivalently, it is not possible for the premises to be true and the conclusion false. It is worth emphasizing, however, that this condition can be met even if one or more of the premises is in fact false. Consider the following example:

PREMISE 1: All pigs have wings.
PREMISE 2: All winged things can fly.
CONCLUSION: All pigs can fly.

[handwritten: Deductive = guarantee their conclusions. Inductive = conclusions likely]

Although both premises are in fact false, if they were instead true, the conclusion would have to be true as well. If, however, an argument is valid and all of its premises are true, then the relation between the premises and the conclusion guarantees the truth of the conclusion. An argument that meets these two conditions is sound. The following is an example of a sound argument:

PREMISE 1: All dogs are mammals.
PREMISE 2: All mammals are animals.
CONCLUSION: All dogs are animals.

As with the prior example, since it is not possible for the premises to be true and the conclusion false, the argument is valid. But since both premises are in fact true, the argument is sound as well. It is worth emphasizing that although a good deductive argument must be sound, many unsound arguments are nevertheless deductive. What is required for an argument to be deductive is not that it in fact be sound, but rather that it be intended or designed to be sound by its originator.

A good inductive argument also has two independent features: it is strong and all of its premises are true. A strong argument is one whose premises and conclusion are related in such a way that if the premises are all true then the conclusion is likely or probably true. As with validity, this condition can be met even if one or more of the premises is in fact false. Consider the following example:

PREMISE 1: Most dentists desire only to inflict pain on others.
PREMISE 2: Justin Trudeau is a dentist.
CONCLUSION: Justin Trudeau desires only to inflict pain on others.

If the premises of this argument were true, the conclusion would probably be true as well. Hence the argument is strong, despite having false premises. It is worth emphasizing that, unlike validity, the strength of an argument comes in degrees: the more likely the premises make the conclusion, the stronger the argument.

As with validity, inductive strength concerns the relation between the premises and the conclusion of an argument. But if the premises of a strong inductive argument are in fact true, the conclusion is in fact probably true as well. An argument that is both strong and has only true premises is cogent. The following is an example of a cogent argument:

PREMISE 1: Most tenured professors teaching at Canadian Universities have PhDs.
PREMISE 2: Professor Alward is a tenured professor teaching at a Canadian University.
CONCLUSION: Professor Alward has a PhD.

Since the premises make the conclusion likely, the argument is strong; and since the premises are, in addition, true, the argument is cogent. It is worth emphasizing that since the conclusion of a cogent argument is only probably true, it could turn out in fact to be false.

One final note: in philosophy courses, students are often asked to critically evaluate arguments. Introductory philosophy students, however, often have little idea of how to proceed when faced with such instructions. The characterizations of deductive and inductive arguments on offer here provide two distinct strategies. For simplicity, we will simply focus on deductive arguments, but similar points could be made regarding inductive arguments. Since a good deductive argument is sound—it is valid and has only true premises—to criticize a deductive argument requires showing either that is invalid or that at least one of its premises is false. First, a valid argument is one in which the truth of the premises guarantees the truth of the conclusion; hence, to show that an argument is invalid requires showing that it is possible for the premises to be true and the conclusion false, by thinking up possible or imaginable circumstances in which this is so. Second, although there are a number of ways of showing a statement to be false, one useful way is the method of counter-examples. If a premise makes a universal claim attributing a property to all members of a certain class, one can show the claim to be false by identifying just one member of the class that lacks the attributed property. Consider, for example, the universal statement

All Canadian university professors vote NDP.

In order to show this statement to be false, one need only identify a single Canadian university professor who votes for a different political party.

Reading Questions

1.   What is the difference between a practice and a body of knowledge?

2.   What is the ideal of objective truth?

3.   What is the difference between reason and rhetoric?

4.   What is the difference between a sound and a cogent argument?

Reflection Question

1.   Try to think of a number of scenarios in which it would be important to persuade someone of something. Would it be appropriate to use rhetoric rather than reasoning to convince your audience in such circumstances?

Further Reading

Students interested in reading more about logic might look at William Hughes and Jonathan Lavery, *Critical Thinking*, 7th ed. (Peterborough, ON: Broadview P, 2015).

PART I

Metaphysics and Epistemology

2

MIND AND BODY

[handwritten: metaphysics = mind + Body are one?]

[handwritten: Bodies and minds]

The mind–body problem is one of the oldest and most venerable issues in philosophy. The question concerns the relation between bodies and minds. In particular, the issue is whether the human mind is something over and above the physical human body, or whether it can be identified with the body or some part of it, such as the brain. This is an important question because our minds and mental attributes are what define us as persons. If the mind is distinct from the body, this has implications not only for the possibility of survival after bodily death but also for the moral appropriateness of treating one another in certain ways.

The mind–body problem, at its core, is a metaphysical one. As a result, in order to come to grips with it, we will need to develop some fundamental metaphysical distinctions. Of particular importance will prove to be the distinction between properties or universals, on the one hand, and substances or particulars, on the other. In addition, we will need to address the phenomena of consciousness, mental representation, and mental causation.

CHAPTER CONTENTS:

- the concepts of mind and mental properties are introduced;
- the metaphysical distinction between monism and dualism is drawn;
- substance dualism—the view that the mind is distinct from the body—is discussed;
- a variety of physicalist accounts of mentality are distinguished; and the problem of consciousness is addressed.

[handwritten: Of particular importance will prove to be]

27

2.1 Mentality

In order to address the relations between bodies and minds, we need to get clear about what we mean by the mind. A simple, although perhaps not very informative, answer is that the **mind** is the subject of mental states, that it, it is what mental states are states of. Just as bodily states—such as size, shape, or mass—are states of a body, mental states are states of a mind. Characterizing the mind in this way is useful for our purposes because it is neutral between various accounts of the mind. If the mind is the brain, then mental states are states of the brain; if the mind is an immaterial soul, then mental states are states of the soul; and if the mind is the whole human body or the person, then mental states are states of the body or the person.

Though it may be useful, characterizing the mind in this way is informative only if we know what mental states are. The first question is what we mean by a state of any kind. Consider, for example, a bodily state like a body's having a certain size or shape. All this amounts to is the fact that a subject—in this case a body—has a property—a certain size or shape. So mental states consist in the fact of a mind's having certain specifically mental properties or attributes. The second question, then, is what mental properties are. This question will be addressed in two stages: first, a taxonomy of mental properties will be developed; and second, the issue of what such properties have in common will be considered.

WHAT KINDS OF MENTAL STATES AND PROPERTIES EXIST?

Although there are a number of different ways to categorize mental states and properties, for present purposes we will consider three basic categories. The first category consists of **experiential states**—states of seeing, hearing, and feeling various things, for example. Seeing the computer screen in front of me is a current experiential state of mine, for example. When one is in an experiential state, one has a sensation of something. Moreover, such states typically have a **subjective qualitative character**: there is something it is like to be in them. Being in pain, for example, feels a certain way to the subject of pain, the person whose pain it is. The subjective qualitative characters of experiential states—what they are like—are sometimes referred to as **qualia**. The second category consists of **thoughts**, such as beliefs, desires, hopes, wishes, intentions, and the like. What is characteristic of such mental states is that they are representational or meaningful. The belief that most snow is white, for example, represents the world as being a certain way, in particular as containing snow predominantly of a certain colour. Because the meanings of thoughts are normally taken to be propositions, they are often referred to as **propositional attitudes**. The third category consists of **moods** and **emotions**—anger, love, melancholy, boredom, and so on. Like experiential states, moods and emotions often have a characteristic subjective qualitative character. Anger, for example, feels a certain way to the angry person. And some, but not all, such states are, like thoughts, representational. One might, for example, be angry that the Habs lost a recent hockey game; but one might also simply be melancholy without being sad about anything in particular.

[handwritten: The mind is the subject of mental states]

WHAT DO MENTAL STATES HAVE IN COMMON?

As it stands, our account of mental properties is something of a mishmash. One might hope that there is a common feature that unifies the mental and distinguishes it from the non-mental or physical, but it is far from clear that any such unified account of mentality is forthcoming. In particular, not only do the candidate unifying properties fail to be satisfied by all mental properties but they are often satisfied by non-mental properties as well. One suggestion might be that all and only mental states are conscious in the sense that they are states that the subject is aware of. This excludes the now-familiar notion of subconscious beliefs from mentality, and we are also often conscious of physical states of our bodies in this sense. I am currently conscious of the fact that there is dirt under my fingernails in the sense of being aware of this fact; but the state of there being dirt under my fingernails is not, for that reason, a mental state of mine. Another suggestion is that all and only mental states are representational. But some mental states arguably are not representational—moods, for example—and some other non-mental states are representational. This very sentence is representational despite being a state of a document rather than a state of mind. Although there may well be other candidate properties offered to unify the mentality, it is far from clear that they will fare any better than those considered here.

[handwritten: one might hope that there is a common feature that unifies the mental and distinguishes.]

2.2 Monism and Dualism

In order to adequately assess the various accounts of the relationship between minds and bodies, a number of metaphysical distinctions need to be introduced. The first distinction is between particular things, on the one hand, and properties or features, on the other. Consider, for example, a brown table. The table is a particular thing and brownness is a property or feature of it. One distinguishing mark of properties is that they are universal: the same property can be wholly present in a number of distinct particulars. The same shade of brown can be shared by a number of distinct tables. Another distinguishing mark is that an occurrence of a property is dependent on the particular thing in which it is present in a way in which the particular is not dependent on the property. The brownness of a particular table—in contrast to brownness in general—depends for its existence on the existence of the table; but the table does not depend for its existence on its brownness. After all, the very same table might instead have been black, and, moreover, it might subsequently become black.

The second distinction is between monism and dualism (see Figure 2.1). In certain areas of discussion, the question sometimes arises as to how many different kinds of things are being talked about. When such a question arises, one can offer a monist or dualist answer: the **monist** claims that there is really only one kind of thing (such as physical matter), whereas the **dualist** claims that there are in fact two distinct kinds of things (such as matter and non-physical minds). In the philosophy of mind, the question of how many things there are arises both at the level of particular things and at the level of properties. The former question concerns whether the mind is a physical entity of some kind—identical to the brain, the body, or the person, for example—or whether it is some kind of non-physical entity. **Substance dualism** is the view that there exist both physical and non-physical entities, and that while the human body and brain (among other things) fall into the former category, the mind falls into the latter. **Substance monism**, according to which there exists only one kind of entity, has a number of variants. According to **physicalism** (or, more precisely, physicalist substance monism), the only kind of particular things that exist are physical things; hence, the mind just is some kind of physical entity, such as the brain. According to **idealism**, in contrast, the only entities that exist are mental entities; hence, the mind, as well as the human body and brain, are mental entities of some kind. Idealism has never been a widely shared view, and we will ignore it in the remainder of this discussion.

Even if one accepts physicalism at the level of particular things, the question still arises as to how many basic types of properties there are. Consider, for example, a mental state such as being in pain or believing that most snow is white. Now all physicalist substance monists might well agree that the mind is the physical brain (or the body or the person) and, hence, that such mental states are states of the physical brain. But they might disagree over whether mental states are just one kind of physical state of the brain or a fundamentally different non-physical kind of state of the brain. The (physicalist) **property monist** claims that all properties are physical properties; hence, being in pain and believing that most snow is white are just certain sorts of physical states of the physical brain, perhaps neurophysiological states. So, for example, a property monist might identify being in pain with being in one kind of neurophysiological state and identify believing that most snow is white with being in another kind of neurophysiological state. The **property dualist**, in contrast, claims that there are both physical and non-physical mental properties and that being in pain, believing that most snow is white, and the like fall into the latter category. So, for example, a property dualist might deny that mental states are identical with any neurophysiological (or other physical) states and instead insist that being in pain and believing that most snow is white are states of the physical brain over and above its neurophysiological states.

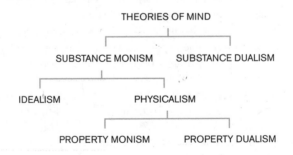

FIGURE 2.1 • *Theories of Mind*

[handwritten: Property monist = All properties are physical]

2.3 Substance Dualism

Substance dualism is the view that there are two distinct kinds of particular things: non-physical minds and physical objects, including the human body and brain. There are a number of versions of substance dualism, differentiated by how they distinguish between minds and physical objects, as well as by how they take minds and physical things to be related to one another. Within the philosophical literature at least, the most prominent version is **Cartesian dualism,** so named for its originator, René Descartes (1596–1650). According to this view, minds are essentially thinking things—to be a mind is to be the subject, or thinker, of thoughts. Consider, for example, the belief that most snow is white. Whatever it is that has that belief is a mind, on the Cartesian view. Physical objects, in contrast, are extended things—that is, things that occupy regions of space-time. Since, for example, rocks, trees, chairs, and human bodies take up space, they count as physical objects. Now on the Cartesian view, minds are not extended things—things that take up space. As a result, they are distinct from physical objects such as human bodies and brains, which do take up space. What then is a human person, such as myself, which has a human body and is capable (at least after my morning cup of coffee) of thought? On this view, a human person is a composite entity consisting of two very different kinds of parts: a thinking mind that occupies no space and an unthinking human body that takes up space.

[handwritten margin note: Minds do not take up space]

There are two remaining questions that the Cartesian picture needs to address concerning how the mind and the body, which make up a human person, are related to each other: how they are joined with each other, and whether they influence each other. First, although minds take up no space, they can nevertheless occupy spatial locations. One might think of them on the model of mathematical points in space. As a result, minds can be joined with bodies in virtue of being located in them and moving with them. Second, according to Cartesian dualism, despite being distinct entities, the mind and the body stand in causal relation to each other: physical states of the physical human body can cause changes in the mental states

[handwritten margin note: Mind and Body in causal Relation to each other]

of the non-physical mind; and mental states of the non-physical mind can cause changes in the physical states of the physical body. So, for example, damage to bodily tissue can cause the mind to enter into states of pain and distress; and the desire to alleviate pain and distress can cause the physical body to make motions and noises designed for the purpose.

Many different arguments have been offered in support of substance dualism. For our present purposes, we will focus on just one: the **conceivability argument**. This argument relies on two metaphysical principles: the conceivability principle, and the **necessity of identity**. According to the conceiv-

Essences

The essence of a thing is the property or collection of properties that make it the kind of thing that it is. The essence of gold, for example, is being an element with 79 protons and electrons. Although something can undergo a change in its non-essential properties, to change its essential properties is to destroy it or to make something entirely different out of it. Moreover, while objects do not exist without possessing their essential properties, it is also not even possible for them to do so.

ability principle, whatever one can imagine or conceive is possible—even though it may not in fact be the case, it could be so. So, for example, even though pigs cannot in fact fly, the fact that you can imagine them doing so entails that there are possible circumstances in which they do so, or equivalently, the supposition that they fly, although false, is not self-contradictory. It is worth noting that according to some versions of this principle, what is required to establish the possibility of some proposition is a more stringent kind of conceiving or imagining than we often engage in. And according to the necessity of identity, if an object A is the same thing as an object B, then A and B must always be the same thing, or, equivalently, it is not possible for A and B to be different things. Since, for example, George Eliot is numerically identi-

> ## Numerical Identity
>
> **Numerical identity** concerns the number of objects—people or rivers or cars—that are under discussion. If you are discussing one and the same person rather than two distinct people, then you have an instance of numerical identity. So, for example, since a conversation about George Eliot and Mary Anne Evans is a conversation about just one person, Eliot and Evans are numerically identical. This is to be contrasted with **qualitative identity**, which requires only that the objects under discussion share all properties. Qualitatively identical objects can nevertheless be numerically distinct. Consider, for example, identically manufactured chairs.

cal to Mary Anne Evans, the necessity of identity entails that the former is necessarily identical to the latter: there are no possible circumstances in which George Eliot and Mary Anne Evans are two distinct people (although there are, of course, possible circumstances in which Mary Anne Evans was not called "George Eliot").

The conceivability argument can be represented as follows:

PREMISE 1: The mind can be imagined to exist without the body.
PREMISE 2: Whatever can be imagined is possible (conceivability principle).
SUB-CONCLUSION: It is possible for the mind to exist without the body.
PREMISE 3: If the mind is identical to the body, then it is not possible for the mind to exist without the body.
CONCLUSION: The mind is not identical to the body.

First, it is noted that you can imagine your mind existing without your body (including your brain). This can consist in imagining having a distinct body from your actual body or imagining existing as a disembodied mind. From the conceivability principle, it follows that it is possible for your mind to exist without your body. But if your mind is identical to your body or your brain, then from the necessity of identity it follows that it is not possible for your mind to exist without your body. Finally, since we have already established that it is possible for your mind to exist without your body, it follows that your mind is not identical to either your body or your brain. Hence, the mind and the body are distinct entities.

There are a number of ways in which one might go about critiquing the conceivability argument. First, one might object to the necessity of identity by pointing to examples of true identities that are nevertheless possibly false. Consider, for example, the following identity: the 44th president of the United States was Barack Obama. Although this is in fact true, had the 2008 presidential election turned out differently it would be false. Similarly, the mind may really be the body without it being the case that the mind is necessarily the body, and so the very conceivability of a mind without body doesn't entail that the mind is not the body. And second, one might object to the conceivability principle on the grounds that one can conceive of impossibilities. For, example, one might argue that we can conceive of round squares despite the fact that they are impossible. Similarly, it might be impossible for the mind to exist without the body despite the fact that we can imagine it existing without the body.

> ## Modus Tollens
>
> **Modus tollens** is a commonly used rule of inference. Consider a conditional statement of the form "if p then q." According to this rule, if it can be established that the consequent of this conditional, q, is false, then one can conclude that the antecedent, p, is false as well. Suppose, for example, it is true that if it is snowing, then it is cold. According to modus tollens, if you can establish that it is not cold, you can conclude that it is not snowing. This is the reasoning that governs the inference from the Sub-conclusion and Premise 3 to the conclusion in the conceivability argument.

In addition to criticizing the argument for substance dualism, one might also criticize the view itself. First, one might argue that there is no independent reason to believe in the existence of non-physical minds in the first place. Insofar as they are non-physical, they arguably cannot be experienced; and if they cannot be experienced, it is unclear what kind of evidence can be offered for their existence. As a result, substance dualism is just unmotivated. Second, one might argue that, other things being

> ## Non-Interactionist Substance Dualism
>
> There is a systematic correlation between metal states or events and physical states or events that is most naturally explained by causal relations between mental states and physical states. So, for example, the best explanation of why my arm rises after I form the intention to raise it, and why I have a sensation of pain after my finger gets injured, is that my intention causes my arm to rise and the damage to my finger causes a sensation of pain. But it appears that the substance dualist cannot avail herself of this kind of explanation, given the problems for mental–physical causation that arise for this view. There are, however, a number of alternative explanations of mental–physical correlations that have been offered by substance dualists. According to **parallelism**, the mental and physical realms are causally isolated from each other. Nevertheless, the realms have been set up in such a way that when I intend to raise my arm, my arm rises. The mental and physical realms are like two perfect eternal clocks originally set at the same time: they always show the same time despite having no influence on each other. And according to **occasionalism**, although the mental and physical realms are causally isolated from each other, God can influence both realms. Even though tissue damage in the physical realm cannot cause anything to happen in the mental realm, whenever God detects tissue damage he causes a sensation of pain in the corresponding mind. And although an intention to raise one's arm can have no influence in the physical realm, whenever God detects some such intention he causes the relevant person's arm to rise.

equal, simpler theories are preferable. Since it posits two basic kinds of particular things, substance dualism is more complex than physicalism, which posits only one. As a result, unless substance dualism has compensating theoretical advantages over physicalism, the latter is to be preferred. But, the argument continues, despite its greater complexity, substance dualism has no such advantages over physicalism. In particular, there are no observable phenomena for which the appeal to non-physical minds offers a better explanation than the physicalist can appeal to. And third, one might wonder by what mechanism mental events can cause physical events and vice versa if, as the Cartesian dualist has it, physical entities occupy regions of space and minds do not. Consider, for example, causation in the game of pool. In pool, one ball can cause another ball to move only in virtue of contact between them. And pool balls are able to have contact with one another only because they both occupy regions of space. But since, on the Cartesian picture, human bodies occupy regions of space while minds do not, they cannot interact by means of contact. What is required—and what is missing—is an alternative account of how they do interact, given these putative facts about them.

2.4 Physicalism

In this section, we will consider alternatives to substance dualism: behaviourism, the identity theory, and functionalism. What unifies these views is that they all take the only kind of particular things to be physical objects. As a result, they all either deny the existence of the mind or identify it with some physical entity or other. **Behaviourism** is the view that mental states are behavioural states. A behavioural state is either actual behaviour or a behavioural disposition. Behaviour consists of bodily movements, like the upward or downward motion of an arm or the swivelling motion of a head. Because behaviourists typically invoke speech in their accounts of mental states, behaviour should here be understood broadly to include both bodily motions and the production of certain sorts of noises. In addition to actual behaviour, behavioural states include dispositions to engage in certain sorts of behaviour when subjected to the right kind of stimuli. Salt, for example, has the disposition to dissolve in water in the sense that if it were placed in water it would dissolve; and it retains this disposition even if it is never placed in water. Similarly, a subject might have the disposition to quickly crouch upon hearing someone yell "Duck!" even if he or she never hears this. So, according to behaviourism, to be in a mental state of a certain kind is either to behave in a way characteristic of that state or at least to be disposed to do so. For example, a behaviourist might identify a state of pain with pain behaviour, in the sense what it is to be in pain is just to wince, groan, and the like. And a behaviourist might identify believing that most snow is white not with any actual behaviour but rather with the disposition to answer "yes" if asked "Is most snow white?" Finally, since the behavioural states with which mental states are identified are states of the body, it remains open to the behaviourist to identify the mind with the body, although behaviourists more characteristically simply deny that there is such a thing as the mind.

There are, however, a number of reasons to balk at the behaviourist rendering of mental states. First, there are grounds for thinking that the connection between mental states and their characteristic behaviour is contingent, that one can be in a mental state without engaging in its characteristic behaviour, or being disposed to do so, and one can engage in behaviour characteristic of a mental state without being in that state. Someone conditioned from a young age not to respond to tissue damage with pain behaviour, for example, might nevertheless find herself in pain despite not being in the corresponding behavioural state; and an actor on stage might behave as if he believes that the sky is falling despite not believing any such thing. Second, mental states do not individually yield behaviour but only do so when combined with other mental states. Someone who believes that most snow is white, for example, and who is asked "Is most snow white?" will answer "yes" only if in addition she minimally understands the questions and desires to reveal her snow-colour beliefs to her interlocutor. As a result, no single mental state can be identified with a person's current behaviour or behavioural dispositions. And third, certain mental states, such as pain, have characteristic feelings that are at least arguably essential to them. Behaviourism, however, has no room for feelings in its account of mentality.

The second physicalist theory of interest here is the mind–brain identity theory. According to the identity theory, mental states are not behavioural states but rather internal states of a subject. And given that it is a physicalist theory, the internal states with which the identity theory identifies mental states are typically neurophysiological states of the brain. Exactly which brain state is identified with which mental state is an empirical question. If, for example, empirical investigation reveals that a certain brain state causes pain behaviour—wincing, groaning, and the like—or combines with other internal states in the requisite way in so doing, then that brain state is pain. It is important to note that this view does not simply identity particular instances of mental states with particular instances of brain states; rather, it identifies types or kinds of mental states with types or kinds of brain states. For this reason, the mind–brain identity theory is sometimes called the type–identity theory. Finally, since the brain is the subject of brain states, identity theorists typically identify the mind with the brain.

Although there have been numerous objections raised against the identity theory, many of them are too technical for an introductory-level course. As a result, we will focus on just one important objection here: the multiple realizability objection. In order to understand this objection, one has to realize that, according to the identity theory, a (type of) mental state just is a (type of) human brain state. The view is not that there are two states—a mental state and a brain state—that happen to be correlated with each other. Instead, there is just one state, which is at the same time both a mental state and a brain state. Consider, by way of analogy, a glass containing water. Given the identity between water and H_2O, it is also true of the glass that it contains H_2O. But it does not follow from this that there are two liquids in the glass: water and H_2O. Rather, there is just one liquid, which is at the same time both water and H_2O. The upshot is that according to the identity theory, mental states just are human brain states. As a result, in order to be capable of having mental states,

Case Study 2.1: Artificial Intelligence

Two firms—FrankenCorp and DataTech—are competing to produce the first artificially intelligent robot. FrankenCorp's strategy is to artificially produce a biologically human brain to put into a robot body. DataTech's strategy, in contrast, is to create a genuinely intelligent computer to put into its own robot body.

QUESTION: Is there any in principle reason to believe that only FrankenCorp's strategy could be successful?

an entity needs to have a human physiology and, in particular, a human brain. But, the objection goes, mental states are multiply realizable: that is, creatures with very different physiologies can, at least in principle, be in the very same mental states that human beings find themselves in. Like us, at least some non-human animals are capable of pain and other sensations, as well as mental representations of their local environments. And it is at least in principle possible for there to be intelligent aliens, as well as robots with computer brains, capable of the more sophisticated psychological states we find ourselves in. But according to the mind–brain identity theory, insofar as such entities lack human brains, they are entirely incapable of mentality.

Functionalism is currently the most widely held philosophical theory of mind. It is designed to reconcile physicalism—the view that the only particular things are physical—with the multiple realizability of the mental. Mental states, on this view, are internal states that have characteristic causes and effects and which thereby mediate perceptual inputs and behavioural outputs. Pain, for example, is roughly a state that is caused by tissue damage and that causes winces and groans, among other things; and the belief that most snow is white is, again roughly, a state that is caused by observations of snow and that, when accompanied by knowledge of English and the desire to express one's snow-beliefs, will cause the subject to answer "Yes" in response to the question "Is most snow white?," among other things. Although human brain states occupy these causal roles in human subjects, different kinds of states can occupy these roles in subjects with different physiologies. So, for example, as long as a subject has some internal state that is caused by tissue damage and that causes wincing and groaning, it is capable of being in a state of pain, even if it lacks a human brain and hence cannot find itself in the kind of brain states that occupy this causal role in us. As a result, although each particular mental state is, according to functionalism, identified with a particular physical state of the subject, kinds of

Case Study 2.2: Functionalist Dualism

Suppose there was a composite being with a physical body, vulnerable to various kinds of tissue damage, and an immaterial mind, capable of entering into various immaterial states of mind. And suppose that one of these immaterial states was typically caused by damage to bodily tissue and typically caused the being's body to wince and emit groaning sounds.

QUESTION: According to functionalism, would this state of an immaterial mind count as a state of pain? If so, in what sense does functionalism count as a version of physicalism?

mental states are not identified with kinds of physical states: since subjects with different physiologies can be in the same kind of mental state, this kind of mental state cannot be identified with the kinds of physiological states that either subject is capable of. For this reason, functionalism is sometimes characterized as a token identity theory. Finally, since human brain states are identified with mental states in the case of human subjects, the human mind can be identified with the human brain on the functionalist picture. The minds of creatures with different sorts of physiologies, however, will have to be identified instead with whatever functions in them in the way in which the brain functions in us. human mind

As with the mind–brain identity theory, many of the objections to functionalism are too technical for an introductory-level course. Nevertheless, there remains one important objection to functionalism that will be addressed here: the so-called **exclusion argument**. The issue is mental causation and, in particular, the role that mental states play in causing physical events—such as bodily movements—to occur. It is commonplace to suppose that our thoughts and other mental states cause things to happen. For example, my desire for the delicious flavour of Alexander Keith's India Pale Ale—together with my belief that the glass on the table in front of me contains that beverage—has periodically caused my arm to reach and grab glasses in my vicinity. Moreover, the fact that the state in question has the mental properties that it does plays an essential role in the production of the behaviour in question. If my mental state were not a desire for the delicious flavour of Alexander Keith's India Pale Ale but rather a hope for a sunny day, it would not cause my arm to reach out and grab the glass. The problem is that on the physicalist picture, all physical events—including bodily behaviour—are wholly caused by prior physical events and states. So, in the case at hand, my arm-reaching and bottle-grabbing behaviour is wholly caused by neurophysiological (and other physical) states of mine that precede it. What this means is that insofar as the mental states and properties of a subject are distinct from his neurophysiological states and properties, the former make no causal difference in his behaviour. If my neurophysiological states and properties wholly cause me to reach for and grab a certain glass, and the property of being a desire for the delicious flavour of Alexander Keith's India Pale Ale is distinct from any neurophysiological properties I instantiate, then the property of being a desire of this kind is excluded from any causal role. And, as we have seen, functionalism is committed to the distinction between mental properties and physical properties. As a result, functionalism is incompatible with the fact that it was exactly because my mental state was a desire for the delicious flavour of Alexander Keith's India Pale Ale that it caused the behaviour that it does. This argument can be represented in standard form as follows:

PREMISE 1: My desire for the delicious flavour of Alexander Keith's India Pale Ale causes my arm-reaching and bottle-grabbing behaviour.

PREMISE 2: All of my behaviour is caused by my physical states.

SUB-CONCLUSION: My desire for the delicious flavour of Alexander Keith's India Pale Ale is a physical state of mine.

PREMISE 3: If functionalism is true, then no mental states are physical states.

CONCLUSION: Functionalism is false.

The upshot seems to be that, insofar as physicalism is correct, only a view that identifies mental properties with physical properties—such as the mind–brain identity theory—is compatible with the role that mental properties play in the production of behaviour.

2.5 Consciousness

Even if it is conceded that the mind can be treated as a physical entity—the body or the brain—and mental states can be predominantly treated as physical states of such entities—behavioural states, brain states, or functional states—many people still resist the idea that the phenomenon of **consciousness** can be incorporated into a physical picture of reality. In a broad sense, conscious mental states are those that the subject is aware of. My pain and my belief that most snow is white, for example, count as conscious states of mine insofar as I am aware of them. Now it is certainly true that not all of our mental states are conscious in this sense: unconscious states include not only motivations that might be hidden from the subject but also perceptual states when the subject is operating on "autopilot"—driving while thinking of something else, for example—and tacit beliefs—such as that the moon is devoid of giant ants at its centre—that one holds without ever specifically contemplating. The interesting conscious states for our present purposes are those with a subjective qualitative character, that is, states such that there is something that it is like to be in. Consider, for example, pain. Not only is pain a conscious state in the sense that the subject of pain is aware of her pain. In addition, pain has a subjective qualitative character: being in pain feels a certain way to the subject. And although believing that most snow is white is conscious in the first sense, having some such belief does not normally feel a certain way to the believer. Qualia are the subjective qualitative characters of conscious mental states, the phenomenal properties that such states have in virtue of what it is like to be in them.

THE ZOMBIE ARGUMENT

A number of different arguments have been offered to show that consciousness is incompatible with a physical picture of the world. For now we will focus on two of them: the zombie argument and the knowledge argument. By **zombies** is meant not the living dead but rather exact physical duplicates of human beings whose mental states lack qualia. Suppose, for example, that you are in a state of pain and that your pain feels a certain way to you. A zombie would be a molecule for molecule duplicate of you who lacks all qualia—although your zombie may, like you, have an internal state that is caused by tissue damage and in turn causes wincing and groaning, there is nothing it is like for it to be in this state.

The zombie argument proceeds in more or less the same manner as does the conceivability argument for substance dualism. First, it is noted that zombies are imaginable. Second, from the conceivability principle, it follows that zombies are possible. Third, it is claimed that if physicalism is true, then the physical properties of an entity determine all of its properties, including any phenomenal properties, or qualia, that any of their internal states might have; hence it is not possible for physically identical entities to differ in any of their intrinsic properties. But finally, since zombies just are physical duplicates of us with different intrinsic properties, physicalism must be false. It is worth noting that the conclusion of the zombie argument is not that there are non-physical particulars but rather that certain properties of physical entities—qualia—are non-physical.

Many of the objections one might raise against the zombie argument are similar to those considered earlier during our discussion of the conceivability argument. One might, as above, argue that the conceivability of zombies does not establish the possibility of zombies or that their possibility is compatible with physicalism. But, in addition, one might argue that the conclusion of the argument—that qualia are non-physical properties—runs into problems in its own right. In particular, one might argue that this kind of property dualism implies that qualia are causally inert. After all, the physical properties of our bodies are sufficient by themselves to explain our physical behaviour. As a result, if qualia are non-physical, they play no causal role in our behaviour. Even verbal reports that seem to describe qualia—"I have a feeling of pain in my leg," for example—could not be caused by qualia. Qualia would, in effect, be **epiphenomena**, entities that lack any causal power and, hence, make no difference to anything that happens in the world.

THE KNOWLEDGE ARGUMENT

The **knowledge argument** relies on the case of a hypothetical scientist, Mary, who was raised and educated in circumstances in which the only colours she experienced were black and white, as well as, presumably, various shades of grey. The rooms in which she lived—as well as all the objects contained therein—were coloured in this way, as were also her own body and clothes and the bodies and clothes of those with whom she directly interacted. And her only access to the world outside her room was through black-and-white video and internet feeds. Moreover, Mary is a kind of super-scientist: she has learned everything there is to know about the physical nature of the world, including all the facts of physics, chemistry, biology, and so on. Now suppose that Mary is one day released from the room and experiences a red object—an apple or a fire truck—for the first time. Upon having some such experience, she learns something new: what it's like to experience red. But since, by hypothesis, prior to this experience she already knew all the physical facts, by means of this experience she must have acquired knowledge of a non-physical fact. It follows that facts about qualia, and hence qualia themselves, must be non-physical.

There have been a number of responses to the knowledge argument, focused largely on different senses in which someone might be said to know something. One important approach of this kind involves distinguishing between propositional knowledge—or knowing *that*—and know-*how*. Propositional knowledge is knowledge of facts or propositions. Examples include knowing that 2 + 2 = 4 and knowing that the planet is roughly spherical. Know-how, in contrast, consists in having an ability of a certain kind, like knowing how to ride a bicycle or knowing how to speak French. Although it is certainly true that certain abilities may require a certain amount of propositional knowledge, in general no amount of knowledge is by itself sufficient for know-how. Consider, by way of illustration, the folly of trying to learn how to ride a bike by mastering the kinesiology of bike riding. According to the ability response, while it is certainly true that Mary learned something when she was released from the room, what she thereby acquired was an ability—know-how—rather than propositional knowledge. In particular, she acquired a new method of identifying red objects. Prior to her release, Mary could identify red objects only through the use of an optical spectrometer or by relying on the reports of others. But after her release she learned how to identify them by direct observation. And since she did not acquire propositional knowledge by means of her experiences of red things, according to the ability response there is no reason to suppose that she thereby acquired knowledge of non-physical facts.

In this chapter, we have investigated a number of different theories of mind, including substance dualism, behaviourism, the mind–brain identity theory, and functionalism. Although many historical philosophers and many modern religions adopt a broadly dualist perspective, functionalism and other varieties of physicalism tend to dominate current academic philosophy. Nevertheless, the issue remains unsettled, and the philosophy of mind more generally remains an area of active research.

Reading Questions

1.   What are the three basic categories of mental states? What features are characteristic of experiential states?

2.   What are two ways in which properties and particular things can be distinguished?

3.   How are minds and bodies related according to Cartesian dualism?

4.   What is the difference between interactionist substance dualism and parallelism?

5.   What is the difference between the two kinds of behavioural states?

6.   What does it mean to say that mental states are multiply realizable?

7.   What is the difference between functionalism and the identity theory?

8.   What are the two senses in which a mental state can be conscious?

9.   What are qualia? What does it mean to say that qualia are epiphenomenal?

10. What is the difference between propositional knowledge and know-how?

Reflection Questions

1. Think of a number of unusual scenarios. What would imagining or conceiving of these scenarios consist in? Can you imagine any scenarios that you think are impossible?

2. Think about the similarities and differences between a human being, a mouse, a cockroach, a tree, and a vending machine. How many of these are capable of consciousness? What features differentiate those that are conscious from those that are not?

Further Reading

A good general introduction to the issues discussed here:
Jaegwon Kim, *Philosophy of Mind*, 3rd ed. (Boulder, CO: Westview P, 2010).

Cartesian dualism:
René Descartes, *Meditations on First Philosophy*, ed. Andrew Bailey, trans. Ian Johnston (Peterborough, ON: Broadview P, 2013).

Behaviourism:
B.F. Skinner, *About Behaviorism* (New York: Vintage, 1974).

Mind–brain identity theory:
David Armstrong, *The Mind-Body Problem: An Opinionated Introduction* (Boulder, CO: Westview P, 1999).

Functionalism:
David Lewis, "Mad Pain and Martian Pain," *Readings in the Philosophy of Psychology*, Vols. 1 and 2, ed. Ned Block (Cambridge, MA: Harvard UP, 1980), pp. 216–22.
Hilary Putnam, "The Nature of Mental States," *Mind, Language, and Reality* (Cambridge: Cambridge UP, 1975), pp. 429–40.

Consciousness:
Frank Jackson, "What Mary Didn't Know," *Journal of Philosophy* 83 (1986): 291–95.
Thomas Nagel, "What Is It Like to Be a Bat?," *Philosophical Review* 83 (1974): 435–56.
L. Nemirow, "Physicalism and the Cognitive Role of Acquaintance," *Mind and Cognition: A Reader*, ed. W. Lycan (Oxford: Blackwell, 1990), pp. 490–99.

KNOWLEDGE AND SKEPTICISM

Knowledge is one of the most central and important subjects of philosophical inquiry. Many people aspire to it, both for the power it brings and for its own sake. Many people claim to have it, but often the knowledge claims of different people turn out to conflict with one another. Moreover, it is widely agreed that individual actions, as well as joint enterprises, based on knowledge rather than mere opinion are more likely to be successful. As a result, we must determine both what knowledge is and how one goes about acquiring it.

The central target of this chapter is what is known as propositional knowledge. Therefore, not only will we have to distinguish knowledge of propositions from other kinds of knowing but we will also need an account of what conditions have to be satisfied in order for someone to know a particular proposition. One question is what knowledge is; another is whether we have any. The epistemological skeptic claims that knowledge is impossible. In this chapter we will assess whether the skeptic has offered any good reason to believe this is true.

CHAPTER CONTENTS:

- a taxonomy of different kinds of knowledge is introduced;
- the traditional account of knowledge is investigated;
- alternative accounts of knowledge are considered;
- the requirements for justified belief are discussed; and
- the problem of philosophical skepticism is addressed.

43

3.1 A Taxonomy of Knowing

The central concern of this chapter is with **propositional knowledge,** that is, knowledge of facts or propositions of various kinds. Examples include such things as knowing that water boils at 100°C, knowing that the Montreal Canadiens have the most all-time Stanley Cup victories, and knowing that your mother loves you. There are, however, a number of types of knowledge other than propositional knowledge (see Figure 3.1). One such sense of knowledge, introduced in Chapter 2, is **know-how**. Know-how consists in having a practical skill, such as knowing how to ride a bicycle or knowing how to speak French. Although knowing how to do certain things may require some propositional knowledge, propositional knowledge by itself does not normally suffice for know-how. Consider, for example, someone with extensive knowledge about the grammar and vocabulary of French but who has never tried to speak the language.

A third sense of knowledge is **acquaintance**. Rather than a proposition, the object of this kind of knowledge—what one has knowledge of—is a particular person, place, or thing. One might, for example, know Paris or know Bob Dylan's music (in contrast to knowing Dylan himself) in the sense of being acquainted with them. This minimally requires some kind of direct contact with of the object of knowledge, as opposed to knowing of it only by reputation or the like.

Finally, a fourth sense of knowledge is **knowing who** someone is. Knowing who is clearly distinct from acquaintance: it is commonplace, for example, for people to know who Bob Dylan is despite not knowing him in the sense of being acquainted with him. The relationship between knowing who and propositional knowledge is, however, somewhat more complicated. In order to know who the murderer is, for example, one presumably has to know some proposition to the effect that the murderer is so-and-so. But knowledge of exactly which proposition is required may depend on the context. Suppose, for example, that the murderer is a person who is both the butler and the king's illegitimate son. In some contexts, knowing who the murderer is requires knowing the proposition that the murderer is the butler, whereas in other contexts this requires knowing that the murderer is the king's illegitimate son.

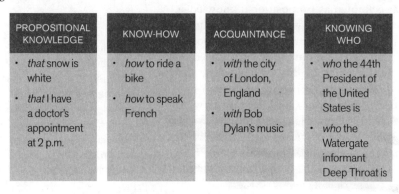

PROPOSITIONAL KNOWLEDGE	KNOW-HOW	ACQUAINTANCE	KNOWING WHO
• *that* snow is white • *that* I have a doctor's appointment at 2 p.m.	• *how* to ride a bike • *how* to speak French	• *with* the city of London, England • *with* Bob Dylan's music	• *who* the 44th President of the United States is • *who* the Watergate informant Deep Throat is

FIGURE 3.1 • *Types of Knowledge*

Propositional knowledge is, in part, a psychological state. In particular, it is a kind of **propositional attitude**—a psychological state in which a subject is related in a certain way to a proposition. And such states are distinguished not only by the proposition to which the subject is related but also by the attitude of the subject toward it, that is, whether she believes or doubts or hopes or fears that it is true. So, for example, not only is believing that most snow is white a distinct propositional attitude from believing that cats are superior pets to dogs, so too is doubting that cats make superior pets to dogs. And just as one can believe or hope or fear, for example, that the temperature of the planet is rising, one can also know this proposition. But unlike belief, desire, and the like, propositional knowledge is not a purely psychological state; rather, it is a mixed state involving psychological and non-psychological elements. In particular, in order to know something, the proposition to which you are psychologically related has to "correspond to the facts." Although one could believe or fear that the temperature of the planet is rising even if it were not, one can know that the temperature of the planet is rising only if the temperature is in fact rising. Some people are willing to claim knowledge for themselves on the basis of their own certainty, taking the fact that they are personally convinced of the truth of some proposition as sufficient grounds for the judgement that they know it. It is worth emphasizing, however, that certainty is a purely psychological state in the sense at issue: one could, after all, be certain that the temperature of the planet is rising even if it were not. As such, certainty cannot be identified with any mixed state like knowledge.

3.2 The Traditional Account of Knowledge

Although there are many accounts of propositional knowledge, the most prominent and widely held view is the so-called traditional account of knowledge. According to this view, knowledge is equivalent to justified true belief. More precisely, a subject S knows a proposition p if and only if S believes p, p is true, and S's belief that p is justified. So, for example, in order for me to know that most snow is white, I must believe that most snow is white, most snow must in fact be white, and I must have adequate evidence for my belief. The first condition is what renders knowledge a kind of propositional attitude. Since belief is a propositional attitude—that of taking the proposition toward which it is directed to be true or to accurately characterize the world—any state that includes belief will itself be a propositional attitude. The second condition renders knowledge a mixed state rather than a pure psychological state. In order to know something, a subject not only has to believe it but what she believes also has to be true or accurate. One's belief that the temperature of the planet is rising cannot count as knowledge unless what one believes is true, that is, unless the temperature of the planet is in fact rising. Finally, the third condition requires that in order to have knowledge we need to have an adequate basis for our beliefs. Suppose, for example, that someone based his or her opinions about climate change on the outcome of a coin toss. If the coin toss came out right, one might end up with a true belief about climate change. Nevertheless, one could

Knowledge vs. True Belief

One might wonder what the advantage is of knowledge over mere true belief, or, equivalently (at least according to the traditional account) of justified true belief over unjustified true belief. After all, in either case, acting on your beliefs is likely to enable you to achieve your goals. Suppose, for example, that while both Fred and Mary correctly believe that there is a six-pack of Molson Canadian hidden at the bottom of the boot box in the mudroom of their home, Mary has evidence for her belief—the direct (and surreptitious) observation of someone hiding it there, perhaps—but Fred does not. Fred's belief is instead the product of a hunch, or a lucky guess, or the like, rather than evidence. But despite his lack of evidence, Fred is just as likely as Mary to be able to successfully procure a bottle of Molson Canadian should he desire one. After all, like Mary, his belief about the location of the beer in question is correct. Nevertheless, knowledge does seem to have at least two advantages over true belief. First, knowledge is more stable. A competitor for the beer in question might be able to persuade Fred that it is located elsewhere, thereby lowering his odds of acquiring it. But given that Mary has evidence for the location of the beer, she is less likely to be susceptible to such persuasion. And second, evidence systematically leads to true beliefs, whereas hunches and lucky guesses do not. As a result, even though Fred might do as well as Mary in the specific case at hand, insofar as Mary systematically bases her beliefs about the locations of the things she wants on evidence and Fred systematically bases his beliefs on hunches and lucky guesses, Mary will likely do much better than Fred at getting what she wants in the long term.

not acquire knowledge about climate change on this basis. After all, the accuracy of one's belief would just be a matter of luck. What is required in addition is that the subject have evidence that justifies her belief and thus makes it reasonable for her to confidently hold it.

There are, however, a number of reasons to object to the traditional account of propositional knowledge. First, one might worry whether knowledge of a proposition really requires that the subject believe it. An unconfident student, for example, might arguably know the right answer to a test question despite not believing his answer to be correct. Second, one might argue that knowledge does not require truth. What is characteristic of knowledge, on this view, is certainty or a commitment to the truth of the proposition in question on the part of the person who claims to know something. If I claim to know that the temperature of the planet is rising, then this entails that I am certain that the temperature of the planet is rising or am committed to the truth of this proposition. But I can be certain or so committed even if as a matter of fact the temperature of the planet is not rising. And third, the notion of justification raises many challenging questions: What kinds of evidence are required for knowledge? What degree of justification is required? Does a given subject have to have the evidence for her beliefs herself or can she rely upon the justification of others?

But in addition to the question of whether each of the conditions invoked in the traditional account is individually necessary for knowledge, one might also wonder whether all three of them are jointly sufficient or good enough for knowledge. Consider, for example, a business owner, Jane, who has two employees: Fred and Mary. Suppose that Jane notices that Fred is regularly disoriented at work and, upon further investigation discovers baggies in his waste basket with cocaine residue in them and Fred's fingerprints on them. And suppose that on this basis Jane comes to believe both that Fred is using cocaine and, hence, that one of her employees is using cocaine. Given the evidence she has, both of these beliefs appear to be justified. But suppose that unbeknownst to Jane it is in fact Mary who is using cocaine. To hide her tracks, Mary has been storing her cocaine in Fred's discarded lunch bags, which she places back in Fred's wastebasket when she is finished with them. And the reason Fred has been disoriented at work is that he has taken on a second job in order to pay off his gambling debts. Now Jane's belief that Fred is using cocaine is false and so does not count as knowledge on the traditional account. But her belief that one of her employees is using cocaine is true—after all, Mary is—and so does count as knowledge on this view. But given that this belief is based on her false belief in Fred's cocaine use, Jane arguably does not know that one of her employees is using cocaine despite having a justified true belief to this effect.

> ## Necessary vs. Sufficient Conditions
>
> It is important to distinguish between two central sorts of relationship in which properties or kinds of things can stand. One property is a necessary condition for another just in case the occurrence of an instance of the former is an absolute requirement for the occurrence of an instance of the latter. The property of being a mammal is a necessary condition for the property of being a dog because a requirement for some entity counting as a dog is being a mammal. Anything that is not a mammal simply cannot be a dog. In contrast, one property is a sufficient condition for another just in case the occurrence of an instance of the former guarantees the occurrence of an instance of the latter. The property of being a mammal is a sufficient condition for the property of being an animal because any entity that is a mammal automatically counts as an animal. There are simply no mammals that are not at the same time animals.

3.3 Alternative Accounts of Knowledge

Numerous alternatives to the traditional account of knowledge have been developed in response to such counterexamples to it. We will consider two here: causal theories and reliability theories. Nearly all versions of these theories retain the first two conditions of the traditional account of knowledge—the requirements that a knowing subject believes the known proposition and that this proposition be true—and offer an additional condition that they take to be required for knowledge. Where they differ is over whether this additional condition is a requirement over and above the third condition of the traditional account—that the subject's belief is justified—or a replacement for it. That is, these alternatives can be understood to take knowledge to require justified true belief plus some further condition, or they can be understood to require merely true belief plus this further condition. For simplicity here, we will just assume the latter.

caused by True Beliefs.

According to **causal theories**, what is required for propositional knowledge in addition to true belief is that the subject's belief be caused by the facts that make her belief true. Many of our beliefs, at least, are learned or acquired rather than being innate, that is, psychological states that we are in some sense born with. Such beliefs can be the product of experience, or testimony, or reasoning, or some combination of these processes. Now in some cases, the beliefs one acquires are just false. So, for example, I might come to falsely believe that the Toronto Maple Leafs have won the Stanley Cup more times than the Montreal Canadiens on the basis of the testimony of my father, a lifelong Leafs fan. But in other cases, the acquired beliefs are true: had my father's testimony been different, I would have correctly believed that the Habs had more Stanley Cup victories than the Leafs. According to the causal theory, however, in addition to having a true belief, what is required for knowledge is that the fact that makes one's belief true be what caused one to acquire it. So, for example, in order for someone to know that there is a fallen tree in the road one would have to believe that there is a fallen tree in the road, there would in fact have to be a fallen tree in the road, and one's belief that there is a fallen tree in the road would have to be caused by the fact that there is. Hence, if one's belief in the presence of the fallen tree were the product of observations of the tree, then one would know that there is a fallen tree in the road. But if one's beliefs were caused instead by a dream or hallucination, then one would lack this knowledge despite having true beliefs. Moreover, the causal theory avoids the counterexample to the traditional account of knowledge considered above because it does not entail that Jane knows that one of her employees is using cocaine. And the reason it does not entail this is because the fact that makes it true that one of her employees is using cocaine true—Mary's cocaine use—is not what causes Jane to believe this proposition.

There are, however, a couple of reasons to worry about the causal theory. First, according to the causal theory, in order to know something, the fact that is known has to cause your belief about it. But, the objection goes, certain sorts of facts are simply incapable of causing beliefs about themselves. For example, I can have beliefs now about what is going to happen in the future. But since the facts that might make those beliefs true will not come into existence until the future (if they ever occur at all), they cannot cause my current beliefs. As a result, the causal theory seems to rule out the possibility of knowledge about the future. But at least some modest knowledge of the future does seem possible: for example, I might know that most of the students in my class will be turning in an essay assignment tomorrow, because, let us suppose, I gave them an assignment due tomorrow and most of them turned in their previous assignments on time. Second, there are lots of different ways in which facts can cause a subject to believe something, some of which do not result in knowledge. Suppose, for example, a live video feed of a tree in front of me is used to create a holographic image of a tree in the very same location in front of me (perhaps the actual tree is obscured by the presence of a screen onto which the holographic image is projected). And suppose this causes me to believe that there is a real tree in front of me. According to the causal theory, because (i) I believe there is a tree in front of me, (ii) it is true that there is a tree in front of me, and (iii) my belief that there is a tree in front of me is caused by the fact that there is a tree in front of me, it follows that I know there is a tree in front of me. But as a matter of fact, because experiences of holographic images—however generated—are poor guides to the presence of what they are images of, I lack knowledge of the presence of a tree in such circumstances.

An alternative to causal theories of knowledge are **reliability theories**. According to reliability theories, what is required for propositional knowledge over and above true belief is that the subject's belief be formed by a reliable process, that is, a process that yields true beliefs most of the time. So in order to know that there is a tree in front of

> ## Case Study 3.1:
> ## Trees in a Fake Forest
>
> Suppose that Fred inadvertently wanders into a movie set filled almost entirely with fake trees being used to film a forest scene. And suppose that while stopping to get his bearings, he happens to look at the only real tree on the set. And suppose that his experience of the tree causes him to believe he is looking at a tree.
>
> **QUESTION**: According to the causal theory, does Fred know that the object he is looking at is a tree? Does the predominance of fake trees in the vicinity undermine his knowledge in this case?

me I would have to believe there is a tree in front of me, it would have to be true that there is a tree in front of me, and that belief would have to be generated by a reliable process, rather than merely being caused by the fact. Suppose, for example, that someone forms the belief that the temperature of the planet is rising because she discovers that there is a wide consensus among the experts—climate scientists—that this is true. Since basing one's beliefs on the consensus of the relevant experts yields true beliefs most of the time, the subject would, according to the reliability theory, know that the temperature of the planet is rising. But if she formed her belief instead on the basis of an astrological forecast or a reading of tea leaves, then, because such processes are not very reliable, she would not know this proposition.

Although much of the critical discussion of reliability theories is too complex for our purposes, one worry is worth mentioning here. In particular, the worry is that reliability theories entail that people with propositional knowledge will often be unaware of the basis of this knowledge, or even whether they know at all. On the traditional account discussed above, subjects are aware of the reasons and evidence that justify their beliefs. As a result, they are well placed to be aware of—and perhaps even know—whether they have knowledge. But according to reliability theories, the basis of knowledge is not the evidence one has for one's beliefs but rather the processes by which they are formed. And not only are knowers often unaware of how their beliefs were formed but they are also regularly unaware of exactly how reliable these processes are.

3.4 Justification

Whether or not justified true belief is by itself sufficient for knowledge, as the traditional account would have it, the question of what is required for a belief to be justified is an interesting one in its own right. As a first pass, we might say that someone's belief in some proposition is justified just in case they have good enough reasons for holding it. A reason for believing a proposition is another proposition that the subject also believes and which, if true, makes the truth of the former proposition more likely. Mary might, for example, believe the proposition that Fred is wearing brown shoes, which, given Fred's past foot-attire practices, has a certain degree of likelihood. But if on the basis of a visual experience of Fred, Mary comes to believe that Fred's shoes appear to be brown, this increases the likelihood of the proposition that Fred is wearing brown shoes. It is worth noting that there is no uniform consensus about how likely a reason has to make a proposition in order for it to be good enough: **infallibilists** argue that a reason has to make a proposition certain in order for it to suffice for the justification of it; **fallibilists** argue, in contrast, that a reason can suffice for justification even if it makes the truth of the proposition at issue highly likely but not certain.

As it stands, however, this simple picture of justification runs into serious difficulties. In particular, it runs into an infinite regress. In order for one belief to provide justification for another, the former must itself be justified. If, for example, I offered my belief that cats contain the reincarnated souls of dead philosophers as a justification for my belief that cats are smarter than dogs but offered absolutely no evidence for the proposition that cats contain the reincarnated souls of dead philosophers, I would have ultimately offered no evidence or justification for my belief regarding the intellectual superiority of cats. But, based on the picture on offer here, this requires that there be a third belief that justifies this justifying belief. And by parity of reasoning, this third belief must itself be justified by a fourth belief, and so on *ad infinitum*. Suppose, for example, that Mary believes that Fred is wearing brown shoes. In order for her belief to be justified there must be some other proposition that Mary believes which makes the proposition that Fred is wearing brown shoes sufficiently likely. Mary's belief that Fred owns only brown shoes might serve this role. But in order for it to do so this latter belief must itself be justified, which requires that there be even another proposition that Mary believes which renders the proposition that Fred owns only brown shoes sufficiently likely. Mary's belief that Fred gets all his footwear from his brown-loving mother might serve this role, but again, in order for it to do so, Mary must believe another proposition that renders the proposition that Fred gets all of his footwear from his brown-loving mother sufficiently likely. Mary's belief that Fred has claimed that this is how he gets all his footwear might serve this role, but again, in order for it to do so, there must be some further belief of Mary's that renders it sufficiently likely. And so on. Unless this regress can be avoided, the upshot seems to be that for even one proposition to be justified, a subject needs to believe an infinite (or unlimited) number of propositions, which is impossible for finite (or limited) beings such as ourselves.

There are a number of different strategies for avoiding the regress problem, the most prominent of which are foundationalism and coherentism. We will consider each in turn. According to **foundationalism**, although most beliefs are justified in the way that the simple picture would have it—by other beliefs that render them sufficiently likely—certain beliefs are **self-evident** or **self-justifying** and, as such, stand in need of no justification by other beliefs. Moreover, these self-evident beliefs provide the ultimate justification for the remainder of a subject's beliefs, in effect providing the justificatory foundations for all that he or she believes (see Figure 3.2). Suppose, for example, that Mary's beliefs about the apparent colours of things are self-evident or self-justifying. If this is right, then her belief that Fred's shoes appear brown is automatically justified and does not require that any of her other beliefs render it sufficiently likely in order to be so. Moreover, insofar as such propositions about the apparent colours of things render propositions about the actual colours of things sufficiently likely, Mary's beliefs about the apparent colours of things can provide the ultimate justification for her beliefs about the actual colours of things, such as her belief that Fred is wearing brown shoes. Finally, as long as the justification for one's beliefs bottoms out in self-evident or self-justifying beliefs, one can have justified beliefs without possessing an infinite number of beliefs.

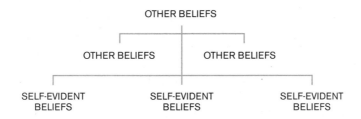

FIGURE 3.2 • *Foundationalist Pyramid*

There are a number of reasons to worry about the foundationalist account of justification. The worry we will focus on here is whether any beliefs both can serve as the ultimate justification for our beliefs and stand in no need of justification themselves. Although many different sorts of beliefs have been offered as the self-evident foundations of our beliefs, we will focus here on beliefs based on our experiences. Suppose, for example, that Mary has a visual tree-experience, that is, the kind of experience someone with properly functioning eyes normally has when looking at a tree on a clear, sunny day. There are two beliefs of interest here that Mary might form on the basis of this experience: the belief that she sees a tree and the belief that she seems to see a tree. Now the former belief—that she sees a tree—can serve as the ultimate justification of many of Mary's tree-beliefs, including, for example, that there is a tree in front of her. After all, if she sees a tree in front of her, it follows that there is a tree in front of her. The trouble, however, is that the belief that she sees a tree is itself in need of justification. This is because, rather than being caused by the interaction between sense organs and a tree, her tree-experience could for all she knows be the product of a vivid dream, a hallucination, or even seeing a realistic imitation of a tree. And unless these alternatives can be ruled out or established to be sufficiently unlikely, Mary's belief that she sees a tree will be unjustified. More to the point, because Mary's belief that she sees a tree needs to be justified in this way, it cannot be self-justifying. The latter belief—that she seems to see a tree—does not run into this difficulty, however. After all, whether her experience is caused by seeing a real tree, seeing a fake tree, a vivid dream, or a hallucination, it is still true that she seems to see a tree. The trouble, however, is that this belief cannot by itself serve as the justification for Mary's other tree-beliefs. After all, it simply does not follow from the fact that she seems to see a tree that there is, in fact, a tree in front of her.

The main alternative to the foundationalist account of justification is the coherence theory. According to **coherentism**, collections of beliefs or believed propositions can vary in terms of their degree of coherence. The coherence of a collection of beliefs is a measure of how well they hang together: the extent to which they support one another and yield a simple unified picture of reality (see Figure 3.3). Suppose, for example, that Mary believes that there is a tree in front of her, that if there is a tree in front of her she will see it, and that she sees a tree. Since these beliefs support one another, together they constitute a highly coherent collection of beliefs. But suppose instead that Mary believes that there is no tree in front of her, that if there is a tree in front of her she will see it, and that she sees a tree. Since these beliefs do not yield a simple unified picture of reality, together they constitute a less coherent collection of beliefs. An individual belief is justified, on the coherentist picture, to the extent that it contributes to the coherence of the collection of beliefs of which it is a part—or more minimally is supported by the beliefs that make up the collection—and it is unjustified to the extent to which it detracts from this coherence. Since the belief that there is a tree in front of her increases the coherence of the collection of beliefs that includes Mary's beliefs that if there is a tree in front of her she will see it and that she sees a tree, it is justified on this view. But since the belief that there is no tree in front of her detracts from the coherence of this collection of beliefs, it is unjustified. Finally, the coherence account of justification avoids the regress problem because it simply does not require that in order for a belief to be justified there needs to be another belief that by itself makes the former sufficiently likely. It is the overall coherence of the collection of which it is a part that renders a belief justified rather than any particular belief that might count in isolation as evidence for it.

FIGURE 3.3 • *Coherentist Raft*

As with foundationalism, there are a number of difficulties that arise for coherentism. The difficulty we will focus on here is that the coherence of a collection of beliefs does not by itself require that the beliefs that make up the collection are likely or probably true, but what it is for a belief to be justified is for there to be grounds to suppose it is likely true. Suppose, for example, that as a result of a delusional condition, Fred believes that his life is a reality television show, that crises in his life are staged events designed to get better ratings, and that he has little control over or responsibility for the difficulties he finds himself in. This collection of beliefs is fairly coherent—the beliefs that constitute it support one another and yield a simple, unified picture of Fred's reality. But each of these beliefs considered separately has little likelihood, and the coherence they have considered collectively does not increase this likelihood. The trouble seems to be that coherence is a matter of how beliefs relate to one another, but truth is a matter of the relation between beliefs and the world; and it is unclear why relations between or among beliefs should by themselves affect relations between beliefs and the world and, in particular, make it more or less likely that they accurately represent the world.

Finally, there are two broad traditions in theorizing about justification: empiricism and rationalism. According to **empiricism**, the justification for all of our beliefs comes ultimately from experience—what we see, hear, feel, taste, and smell. According to **rationalism**, in contrast, although many of our beliefs are justified by experience, at least some of our beliefs are justified by reason alone. This distinction is easiest to see from a foundationalist perspective. As above, according to foundationalism, all of our beliefs are ultimately justified by our self-evident beliefs. An empiricist foundationalist would add that all of our self-evident beliefs are beliefs about experience and, hence, that all of our beliefs are justified by experience. A rationalist foundationalist, in contrast, would argue that at least some of our self-evident beliefs are truths of reason rather than experiential truths. As a result, to the extent that any of our other beliefs are justified by these self-evident truths of reason alone, they are themselves ultimately justified by reason rather than experience.

3.5 Skepticism

We turn now to the problem of skepticism. **Skepticism** is the view that knowledge is impossible. For simplicity, in this discussion we will assume the traditional account of knowledge as justified true belief. Given this assumption, the issue becomes whether it is possible to have justified true beliefs. Since there seem to be few impediments to having beliefs of various kinds, the question becomes whether our beliefs can be both justified and true. And the skeptic claims that this is not possible. There is a variety of different kinds of skepticism that are distinguished primarily by the subject matter regarding which knowledge is claimed to be impossible. Our focus here is going to be on skepticism about the **external world**, that is, a world consisting of things whose existence does not depend on our minds. One way of motivating this kind of skepticism is by appeal to the movie *The Matrix*. In the movie, people hooked up to the matrix have experiences very similar to ours, but the beliefs they form on the basis of these experiences are systematically false. If, for example, one forms the belief that there is a car—an external object—in the vicinity on the basis of one's car experiences, this belief will be false. And this is because these experiences are caused by the matrix rather than by cars. But since our car experiences are very similar to those of people hooked up to the matrix, it is difficult to rule out the possibility that we too are hooked up to the matrix. As a result, our beliefs about the presence of cars—and other external things—are unjustified.

Our beliefs about the existence and nature of external objects are based on our experiences of them. As a result, skeptical arguments against the possibility of knowledge of external things are typically designed to establish the unreliability of our experiences. We will consider three separate skeptical arguments: the argument from error, the dream argument, and the brain in a vat argument. First, the **argument from error** can be reconstructed as follows:

PREMISE 1: Our perceptual beliefs have sometimes been mistaken.
PREMISE 2: The experiences that gave rise to our mistaken perceptual beliefs are indistinguishable from our current experiences.
PREMISE 3: If we cannot distinguish the experiences that yielded mistaken perceptual beliefs from our current experiences, then our current perceptual beliefs are unjustified.
CONCLUSION: Our current perceptual beliefs are unjustified.

The argument relies on the fact that most of us from time to time have had mistaken perceptual beliefs, that is, we have believed that we were seeing, or hearing, etc., something when as a matter of fact we were not. Mary, for example, might believe that she sees a tree when, as a matter of fact, due to an optical illusion or her poor vision or the fact that she is inebriated or what have you, she actually sees a mossy rock or perhaps even nothing at all. Now according to the argument from error, given that we have had mistaken perceptual beliefs in the past, we cannot be certain that our current perceptual beliefs are not mistaken as well. After all, the experiences that gave rise to our mistaken beliefs are just like the experiences that ground our current beliefs. And if we cannot be certain that our current perceptual beliefs are not mistaken, then they cannot be justified even if, as a matter of fact, they are true.

Second, the **dream argument** can be reconstructed as follows:

PREMISE 1: Any perceptual beliefs formed on the basis of our dream experiences are false.
PREMISE 2: Our dream experiences are sometimes indistinguishable from the experiences we have while awake.
PREMISE 3: If we cannot distinguish dreaming from awake experiences, then our perceptual beliefs are unjustified.
CONCLUSION: Our perceptual beliefs are unjustified.

At the core of the dream argument is the fact that if we are dreaming then we do not see, or hear, etc., anything. After all, perceiving things consists in having experiences that are caused by the (immediately prior) impact of those things on the sense organs. But, for example, given that one's eyes are closed, one's visual dream experiences cannot be caused in that way. As a result, any beliefs to the effect that one sees, or hears, etc., something resulting from dream experiences are false. But, the argument continues, the experiences we have while dreaming are, or at least can be, indistinguishable from those we have while awake. Fred might, for example, have a visual tree experience while dreaming that is indistinguishable from the experiences he has when seeing a tree while awake. And if we cannot distinguish dream from awake experience, then any perceptual beliefs formed on the basis of the latter are unjustified. Hence, our current perceptual beliefs are not justified even if they are not the product of dream experiences (and, hence, are true).

Finally, the **brain in a vat argument** can be reconstructed as follows:

PREMISE 1: If we were brains in vats, then any perceptual beliefs formed on the basis of our experiences would be false.

PREMISE 2: If we were brains in vats, then our experiences would be exactly like they in fact are.

PREMISE 3: If we cannot rule out the brain in a vat hypothesis, then our perceptual beliefs are unjustified.

CONCLUSION: Our perceptual beliefs are unjustified.

According to the brain in a vat hypothesis, rather than being embodied human persons whose experiences are (normally) caused by the impact of external things on our sense organs, we are instead disembodied brains in vats of fluid attached to supercomputers whose experiences are caused by programs running in those supercomputers. Moreover, these computers are programmed to give us exactly the same experiences we would have if we were embodied humans. As a matter of fact, I am currently having visual experiences of a computer screen that are caused by the impact of that screen on my eyes. If the brain in a vat hypothesis were true, I would be having qualitatively indistinguishable computer-screen experiences, but they would be caused instead by the program running in the supercomputer, thus rendering my perceptual belief that I see a computer screen false. As a result, nothing in our experience gives us any basis to rule out the brain in a vat hypothesis. But according to the argument, if we cannot rule out the brain in a vat hypothesis, then our perceptual beliefs are not justified, even if we are in fact not brains in vats.

One might have a number of different responses to these various skeptical arguments. First, one might argue that we can in fact distinguish between experiences that yield accurate perceptual beliefs and those that do not. After all, our past mistaken perceptual beliefs have occurred under very specific conditions—inebriation, poor lighting, being insufficiently close to the objects of experience, the lack of appropriate perceptual aids, etc.—that interfered with our perception of the objects under scrutiny. And we are, at least in principle, capable of determining whether these conditions obtain in the current case: we can tell if we are inebriated, or the lighting is poor, etc. Moreover, we can tell when we are dreaming because in dreams there are various spatio-temporal discontinuities and causal anomalies. We often jump from place to place and time to time in our dreams, and the laws of physics are frequently violated. And when these discontinuities and anomalies are absent, we can be confident that our experience occurred while awake and not while dreaming. There are, however, a couple of reasons for caution here. First, this strategy offers no help with the brain in a vat argument. After all, it is part of the brain in a vat hypothesis that the experiences we would have were we brains in vats are exactly like the experiences we in fact have. And second, even if the tests by which we distinguish experiences that produce accurate perceptual beliefs from those that do not are highly reliable, they do not yield perfect certainty. After all, one can certainly be highly confident that, for example, one is not inebriated if one did not knowingly take any drugs and if the sensations that have in the past accompanied drug use are absent; nevertheless, one cannot rule out the possibility that one has unknowingly ingested an inebriant with unfamiliar effects. As a result, insofar as knowledge requires certainty, this strategy is ultimately unsuccessful.

Second, one might argue that the skeptical arguments set the standards of knowledge and justification too high and, in particular, that the requirement of certainty is more than is required in order for one's belief to count as knowledge. To say of one's belief that is it certain is to say that its truth is not just highly likely given the evidence for it but rather is guaranteed by it. But not only does this standard render knowledge extremely rare, if possible at all, but it does not seem to be well motivated either. In particular, our ordinary attributions of knowledge to one another do not seem to require meeting such a stringent standard. For example, most of us would be willing to attribute knowledge of the temperature to someone who bases his or her temperature beliefs on observations of a suitably placed thermometer, even though the use of such a device does not render his or her beliefs certain in this sense. There are, however, a few problems here too. First, this strategy again offers no help with the brain in a vat argument. After all, given that our experiences are exactly as they would be were the brain in a vat hypothesis true, it is not clear that we have any evidence that renders this hypothesis less likely than the fact that our experiences are caused by the impact of external objects on our sense organs. And second, if certainty is not required, we are left with an open question as to how likely the evidence has to make our perceptual beliefs in order to have sufficient justification for knowledge.

And third, one might argue that as long as one's experiences are in fact caused by external things, then they provide sufficient justification for perceptual beliefs formed on their basis. So if, for example, Fred has a visual tree experience that is caused by seeing a tree, then his belief that he sees a tree is justified by this experience. But if his tree experience is a dream or is caused

Reasonable vs. Possible Doubt

During a criminal trial, the members of a jury are asked to judge whether the defendant is guilty of the crime with which he or she has been charged. But in order to render a verdict of guilty, it is not enough that they collectively believe that the defendant committed the crime; in addition, they must judge that the evidence they have been presented provides adequate justification for this belief. But it is worth emphasizing that the evidence need not make their belief in the defendant's guilt certain in the sense of ruling out all possible grounds for doubt. After all, a jury does not need to rule out the possibility that the defendant was framed by invisible aliens in order to find him or her guilty. Instead, the jury need only determine that there is no reasonable doubt that the defendant committed the crime. And although being framed by intelligent aliens may count as possible grounds for doubt, it is hardly reasonable and, as a result, need not be ruled out by a jury before it renders a verdict of guilty.

Case Study 3.2:
Virtual Vacations

You are the head of security for Virtual Vacations Inc., a company that uses highly realistic automated virtual-reality machines to provide its clients with experiences of exotic vacations which, for various reasons, they are unable to actually go on. Although the virtual vacations themselves differ, every client's experience ends the same way: they are automatically disconnected from the virtual reality machine in a private recovery room; for about a minute, although unable to move, they are able to see and otherwise experience the recovery room; and then they fall into a deep sleep after which they get up and go home, with memories to cherish for a lifetime. Recently, however, a number of clients reported experiencing someone manipulating the computers in their recovery rooms before they fell asleep, although their descriptions of this person differed rather significantly. An analysis of computer records revealed three things. First, a large sum of company money was diverted to an unknown location using a recovery-room computer during at least one of the sessions in question, although neither the computer nor the session(s) during which this occurred could be pinpointed. Second, a sub-program had been added to all of the virtual-reality machines which, when activated, caused clients to have virtual experiences of being disconnected from the machine and observing someone manipulating the recovery-room computer prior to falling asleep. Again, it could not be determined during which session(s) this sub-program had been activated. And third, for various reasons, the program the perpetrator used to divert the company funds could not run at the same time as the virtual-reality sub-program. As a result, the client (or clients) in the room when the theft occurred had actual rather than virtual experiences. Only one of the clients in question, Larissa Frederickson, has agreed to come in for an interview to provide a detailed account of her experiences (the remaining clients refused to do so as a result of embarrassment, fear of scandal, etc.).

QUESTION: Is this interview likely to be of use in tracking down the perpetrator, or is it pointless because Ms. Frederickson doesn't know anything?

by a computer program or by seeing a mossy rock rather than a tree, then it does not provide justification for his belief that he sees a tree. Unlike the other two responses to skeptical arguments, this approach can handle the brain in a vat argument as well as the argument from error and the dream argument. After all, if we are not brains in vats, then our experiences are in fact (normally) caused by the impact of external things on our sense organs, whether or not we are ourselves able to rule out the hypothesis. One worry, however, is that like the reliability theory considered above, it entails externalism, that is, the possibility that people can know they see, hear, taste, etc., various things while being unaware of the basis of this knowledge.

In this chapter, we considered the nature of knowledge, the requirements of justified belief, and skepticism about the external world. Although relatively few philosophers take such skepticism to be warranted, attempting to rebut it remains a fruitful exercise. In particular, trying to figure how—not whether—we have knowledge of an external world can yield insight into both knowledge and justification.

Reading Questions

1. What is the difference between knowing who someone is and being acquainted with him or her?

2. Suppose that I believe that the shape of the planet is roughly flat and that I have very strong evidence for my belief. Why can't I know that the planet is roughly flat, according to the traditional account?

3. What is the difference between a necessary and a sufficient condition for something? What is one reason for thinking that belief is not a necessary condition for propositional knowledge?

4. Why is the causal theory incompatible with knowledge of the future?

5. What does it mean to say that a process of forming beliefs is reliable?

6. What is the difference between fallibilist and infallibilist accounts of justification?

7. What has to be true for a belief to be justified on the coherentist picture?

8. What is the external world? What does it mean to be skeptical about it?

9. What is the brain in a vat hypothesis? What is it supposed to establish?

10. How might we distinguish between dream and awake experience?

Reflection Questions

1. Think of a number of different kinds of propositions that you judge yourself to know. What is the basis of your judgement that you know these things? How would you respond if someone challenged your knowledge of these things?

2. Is there some topic or subject matter regarding which you think knowledge is impossible? Sketch your reasons for thinking that knowledge of this kind is impossible. How might you respond to someone's claim to having such knowledge?

Further Reading

A good general introduction to the issues discussed here:
Jack Crumley II, *An Introduction to Epistemology*, 2nd ed. (Peterborough, ON: Broadview P, 2009).

The traditional account of knowledge, as well as objections to it:
Edmund Gettier, "Is Justified True Belief Knowledge?," *Analysis* 23 (1963): 121–23.
Plato, *Meno*, trans. G.M.A. Grube (Indianapolis: Hackett Classics, 1980).

Causal theory of knowledge:
Alvin Goldman, "A Causal Theory of Knowing," *The Journal of Philosophy* 64.12 (1967): 357–72.

Reliability theory of knowledge:
Fred Dretske, "Précis of *Knowledge and the Flow of Information*," *Naturalizing Epistemology*, ed. Hilary Kornblith (Cambridge, MA: MIT P, 1985), pp. 217–38.

Foundationalism:
René Descartes, *Meditations on First Philosophy*, ed. Andrew Bailey, trans. Ian Johnston (Peterborough, ON: Broadview P, 2013).

Coherentism:
Laurence Bonjour, "The Dialectic of Foundationalism and Coherentism," *The Blackwell Guide to Epistemology*, ed. John Greco and Ernest Sosa (Oxford: Blackwell, 1999), pp. 117–42.

Epistemological skepticism:
René Descartes, *Meditations on First Philosophy* (see above), and Barry Stroud, *The Significance of Philosophical Scepticism* (Oxford: Clarendon P, 1984).

4

PERSONAL IDENTITY AND SURVIVAL

On its face, the issue of personal identity is rather straightforward: what has to be true for someone to be you? Since what you are is a person, this amounts to the question of what it is for someone to be the same person as you. Answering this question requires coming to grips with three central concepts: *personhood*, *sameness* or *identity*, and *you* or, perhaps better, *who or what you are*. It is worth emphasizing that the same sort of question arises for a whole range of objects and not just for people. We might, for example, wonder what has to be true for something to be the same river as a stretch of water you frequently swim in, or for something to be the same car as the vehicle you currently drive.

Now one might think that issues of car or river identity are relatively trivial matters. There can, however, be certain practical issues at stake. If, for example, hazardous waste has been dumped into a river, it could be quite important to know whether this occurred in the same river as the one you swim in. And if your car has been stolen, whether or not a vehicle

CHAPTER CONTENTS:

- a taxonomy of various senses of identity is presented;
- the notion of a person is discussed;
- the problem of survival is introduced;
- the relationship between identity and souls is explored;
- theories of identity that invoke only the body are investigated; and
- appeals to psychological continuity are evaluated.

recovered by the police is the same as yours can affect your legal entitlement to drive it. But even so, the question of personal identity is a far more serious matter. This is because of its connection to survival. In order to survive some process—brain surgery, or even bodily death—not only does a person need to exist after its completion but that person also needs to be you rather than someone else.

4.1 Identity

In order to address the question of **personal identity,** we need to identify the relevant sense of identity. This can be a difficult task because a number of different senses of identity are easy to confuse with the notion at issue here. Moreover, not only are the alternatives perfectly good senses of identity but they are also often more familiar than the sense at issue. One central distinction is between predicational and relational senses of identity. To use the term in a **predicational** sense is to think of a person's identity as a possession that can be retained or lost, or as a property or feature that can undergo change. One familiar predicational notion is that your identity is your deeply felt sense of who you are, of what properties define you as a person. So, for example, my identity in this sense might consist in being a Nova Scotian, being a philosophy professor, and being a father. In this sense, just as one's self-definition can undergo change over time, so too can one's identity. When I was younger I was not a father, nor was I planning to become one; as a result, being a father was not part of my self-definition. It is worth emphasizing, however, that since a person can survive a change in his or her self-definition, this sense of identity is not tied to survival in the way in which we are concerned here. Although being forced to give up my career as a philosophy professor might cause me substantial psychological harm and lead me to conceive of myself differently, it would not cause me to cease to exist in any non-trivial sense.

To use the notion of identity in a **relational** sense is to use it to make a judgement regarding the relations or connections between objects rather than a judgement about the properties of a single object. Consider by way of analogy the notion of tallness. To use this notion in a predicational sense is to judge of an individual person that she is or is not tall. If, for example, you judge that Mary is tall, then you are using tallness in a predicational sense. To use this notion in a relational sense is to judge someone as taller than someone else, for example, that Mary is taller than Fred. One relational sense of identity is **qualitative identity.** If a pair of objects stands in a relation of qualitative identity, then they are exactly similar and, hence, share all properties. You might, for example, be qualitatively identical to your twin or clone. It is again worth emphasizing, however, that distinct people can (at least in principle) be qualitatively identical to one another. As a result, qualitative identity does not suffice for being the same person as you. After all, you are a different person from your twin or clone even if they are exactly similar to you.

Another relational sense of identity, and the one at issue here, is **numerical identity.** Numerical identity concerns the number of entities—people or rivers or cars—that are under discussion. Suppose, for example, we are having a conversation about rivers using two river names: "Goldenrod River" and "Alward's Brook." In this conversation we might be talking about one river or two rivers; that is, the names "Goldenrod River" and "Alward's Brook" might both refer to a single river, or they might refer to two distinct rivers. In the former case, Goldenrod River is numerically identical to Alward's Brook, or equivalently, Goldenrod River is one and the same river as Alward's Brook. In the latter case, Goldenrod River is numerically distinct from Alward's Brook, or equivalently, Goldenrod River and Alward's Brook are two distinct rivers. Similarly, since the names "George Eliot" and "Mary Anne Evans" refer to the same person, George Eliot is numerically identical to Mary Anne Evans. But since "George Eliot" and "Thomas Hardy" refer to different people, George Eliot is numerically distinct from Thomas Hardy.

Numerical identity is a reflexive, symmetrical, and transitive relation. To say a relation is **reflexive** is to say that everything it applies to stands in that relation to itself. In mathematics, the relation of being equal to is reflexive because every number is equal to itself: 3=3, 4=4, and so on. But the relation of being greater than is non-reflexive; after all, the number five, for example, is not greater than itself. Since everything is numerically identical to itself, numerical identity is reflexive.

To say a relation is **symmetrical** is to say that if something, x, stands in that relation to something, y, then y stands in that same relation to x. Being married to is a symmetrical relation; after all, if Jane is married to Mary, then Mary is married to Jane. But the relation of being the plural of is non-symmetrical: even though it is true that "cats" is the plural of "cat," it is false that "cat" is the plural of "cats." And since, for example, if George Eliot is one and the same person as Mary Anne Evans it follows that Mary Anne Evans is the same person as George Eliot, numerical identity is symmetrical.

Finally, to say a relation is **transitive** is to say that if x stands in that relation to y and y stands in it to z, it follows that x stands in the same relation to z. In mathematics, being greater than is transitive: for example, since 10 > 8 and 15 > 10, it follows that 15 > 8. But in the game rock, paper, scissors, defeats is a non-transitive relation: although rock defeats scissors, and paper defeats rock, it does not follow that paper defeats scissors. And since, for example, if George Eliot is one and the same person as the author of *Middlemarch*, and Mary Anne Evans is one and the

Case Study 4.1:
The Cadillac of Theseus

After years of scrimping and saving, Theseus was finally able to purchase his dream car: a pink Cadillac DeVille. Because he was so attached to his purchase, he took it in to be serviced once a week at his local shop: Unscrupulous Auto Repair. Every time he took his car in for service, the mechanics at UAR found a problem that required at least one part to be replaced. Eventually, over the course of several years, every original part of Theseus's Cadillac was replaced. But rather than discard these original parts, the UAR mechanics kept them and, when they had a complete set, put them together to create a car exactly similar to the car Theseus purchased. As a result, whereas originally there was only one pink Cadillac DeVille, now there are two.

QUESTION: Which car is Theseus's Cadillac?

same person as George Eliot, it follows that Mary Anne Evans is one and the same person as the author of *Middlemarch*, numerical identity is a transitive relation. The transitivity of numerical identity will prove to be important in what follows.

4.2 Persons

Since our concern is with personal identity—and not ship identity, river identity, or the like—it is worth saying a few things about the notion of a **person**. This is particularly important given our concern with the connection between identity and survival. After all, to survive some event or procedure in the sense that most of us care about is to survive as a person. Suppose, for example, that someone argued that you could survive an accident that left you in a permanent vegetative state because your living body continued to exist, or that you could survive bodily death because the atoms and molecules that make up your body continue to exist (despite being dispersed in various ways). You might respond that you would not survive in these situations because in neither case do you continue to exist as a person.

It is one thing to deny that a dispersed collection of molecules could be a person, but it is another thing to say what is positively required for something to have this status. The paradigmatic case of a person is a normal adult human like you or me. The first thing to note, however, is that being human—a biological status—is not by itself sufficient (or good enough) for being a person. Cancerous tumours, for example, are biologically human but not, for that reason, persons. More controversial cases include humans in permanent vegetative states and conceived but as-yet-unborn humans. Especially insofar as personhood is a moral status conferring upon its bearers a right to life among other things, your views about abortion, euthanasia, and the like will influence which human beings you take to be persons, and which persons you take to be human beings.

What distinguishes those humans that are uncontroversially persons from those that uncontroversially or arguably are not is **higher-order psychological states**. These include such things as consciousness, reason, the ability to use language, the ability to adopt and pursue goals, and the like. These are capacities that all normal adult humans possess and all cancer cells, humans in permanent vegetative states, and newly conceived humans lack. As a result, we might take personhood to consist in the possession of such higher-order psychological states. If this is right, however, it opens the door to at least the possibility of non-human persons. These could include certain non-human animals—such as dolphins or chimpanzees—as well as extraterrestrial life forms and intelligent computers or robots.

4.3 Survival

It is important to distinguish questions of identity at a time from questions of identity or persistence through time. The concern of the former is with how many people or rivers or cars there are at a given time. Consider, for example, a couple of friends on either side of a mountain range, each of whom is looking at a particular mountain, talking on the phone, and discussing whether it is the same mountain they are looking at. Since they are concerned with how many mountains exist at a single point in time—in this case the time of their conversation—what is at issue is identity at a time. It is the latter question, however—persistence through time—that is at issue when we are concerned with the possibility of **survival**. In order for you to survive some event or process, there must exist a person after this event has occurred who is numerically identical to you. And the question of persistence through time is exactly what conditions have to be satisfied in order for a person existing at one time and a person existing at another to be one and the same person rather than two distinct people.

There are a number of different sorts of cases in which the question of survival arises. The first includes events and processes that involve altering the human brain: traumatic events involving brain damage and various kinds of brain surgery, for example. Events of this kind can produce significant changes in the psychological states of a person who undergoes them. Given the connection between personhood and higher-order psychological states, even if someone having the status of a person is the product of some such process, this kind of change might count as the replacement of the original by a new person rather than a process that the original person survives. Suppose, for example, that Fred undergoes brain surgery and that the result of this process is a human being with sufficiently complex psychological states to count as a person but whose psychological states are entirely distinct from those Fred had prior to the operation. There might be a substantial question as to whether this resulting person is Fred or an entirely new person who came into existence as a result of the surgery.

A second kind of case involves bodily death. To avoid the issue of near-death experience and related concepts, I am simply going to stipulate here that by bodily death is meant the death and destruction of the body, and the dispersion of the atoms and molecules that constitute it. Now in order for you to survive bodily death there must exist a person some time after the fact who is you. Of course, this person cannot possess your physical body since by stipulation it no longer exists. She could, however, possess a distinct human body (having undergone some kind of reincarnation), a physical non-human body (having been "downloaded" into a computer), a body made out of some non-physical spiritual stuff (ectoplasm, or the like), or could simply exist as a disembodied soul. And the question is whether—and if so how—a person of some such kind could be you.

> ## Case Study 4.2:
> ## Culinary Loan Sharks
>
> Vito "Eggs" Benedict was released from Dorchester Penitentiary in January after serving a five-year term for running a protection racket. He promptly jumped bail and the authorities lost track of him. Tony "Noodles" Romanoff showed up in Lethbridge in July and began a loan-sharking operation. The Lethbridge police do not have enough evidence to bring charges against Noodles for his local criminal activity. But if they can prove that Noodles is actually Eggs, they can arrest him for violating his parole.
>
> **QUESTION**: What would have to be true for Eggs to be numerically identical to Noodles?

Finally, there are what me might call science-fiction cases. A well-known example of this kind involves the transporter from the *Star Trek* movies and television shows. This is nominally a transportation device that is used to "beam" people travelling on spaceships to and from the surfaces of various planets. People who utilize this device slowly disappear from one location and reappear in another location. And the question is whether they are really transported to a new location or whether they are killed and replaced by duplicates. Other science-fiction examples include fusion and fission cases—cases in which two people merge into one or one person splits into two. Suppose, for example, that for whatever reason two people get "fused" together in a single body. And the question is whether either or both original people are identical to this new fused person, or whether both of them were killed and replaced by someone entirely new. Ultimately, however, in order to assess whether you could survive any of these kinds of processes, we are going to need a defensible theory of personal identity—a theory that answers the question of what has to be true for a person existing at one time and a person existing at another to be numerically one and the same.

4.4 Identity and Souls

One common theory of personal identity appeals to the notion of a **soul**. Although there are numerous conceptions of the soul, a few recurring themes are worth delineating here. First, souls are normally thought to be immaterial or non-physical. On this view, in addition to the material or physical entities in the world—things constituted by physical matter and governed by physical laws, such as rocks, chairs, trees, and human bodies—there are immaterial or non-physical entities, like the soul, that are not constituted by physical matter or governed by the laws of physics. Human persons are, on this view, composite entities consisting of a physical body and an immaterial soul. Second, to say the soul is immaterial or non-physical is to define it negatively—to say what it is not rather than what it is. One commonly endorsed positive feature of the soul is that it is the subject of consciousness and other mental states. Human persons have properties of various kinds. Some of these properties are physical properties of their physical bodies, such as height, weight, chemical constitution, and the like. Other properties are broadly speaking psychological and include things as having various thoughts, feelings, and experiences. And soul advocates normally take these to be non-physical properties of non-physical souls. Third, despite being distinct entities, it is commonly held that there are causal relationships between the physical bodies and non-physical souls that constitute human persons. In particular, it is held that bodily changes of various kinds can cause changes in the psychological states of the soul, and changes in the states of the soul can cause bodily changes. Tissue damage, for example, might cause a sensation of pain; a desire to drink some beer—together with the belief that a certain glass contains beer—might cause one's arm to move toward and then clasp the glass in question. Finally, commitment to the existence of an immaterial soul is often associated with belief in immortality or, more modestly, survival of bodily death. If the soul is a distinct entity from the body, then the death and destruction of the latter is compatible with the continued existence of the former. Of course, despite being distinct from the body, a soul could cease to exist at bodily death and could also exist prior to the body's existence. Nevertheless, the existence of an immaterial or non-physical soul renders the survival of bodily death a possibility, at least insofar as a person is identified with his or her soul.

Our central question, however, concerns the correct theory of personal identity and not the nature and existence of souls. In particular, the question concerns what has to be true for a person existing at one time and a person existing at another time to be numerically one and the same person as opposed to two distinct people. According to the **soul theory**, what is required is that they share the same soul, that is, that the soul of the former person is numerically identical to the soul of the latter. So, for example, Professor Peter Alward, the author of this recently written manuscript is, according to the soul theory, the same person as Peter All-weird, a 15-year-old victim of surname-centred teasing many years ago, just in case the soul currently inhabiting Professor Alward's body is numerically the same as the one that inhabited the body of Peter All-weird all those years ago. If the soul currently inhabiting Professor Alward's body is the soul that once inhabited Peter All-weird's body—whether or not their bodies are numerically the same—then Professor Alward is (numerically identical to) Peter All-weird. But if the soul currently inhabiting Professor Alward's body is distinct from the soul that once inhabited Peter All-weird's body, then Professor Alward and Peter All-weird are two distinct people—even if their bodies are numerically the same.

There are, however, a number of reasons to take issue with the soul theory of personal identity. First, one might reasonably doubt the existence of souls. After all, insofar as they are non-physical, it is not clear how they can be experienced. After all, when we observe one another, all we experience are physical bodies and their behaviours. And if souls cannot be experienced, then one might argue that there are no good grounds to believe that they exist at all. One might, of course, argue that we are directly aware of our own souls in introspection. That is, when we look

A Terminological Note

The formulation of a theory of identity is a delicate matter. This is because if we have an instance of personal identity, we are talking only about one person. but if we fail to have an instance of personal identity. we are talking about two people. As a result, terminology that is neutral between talking about one or two people is required. One way to do this, and the way that will be used here, is to formulate the theory in terms of the conditions that have to hold in order for "a person existing at one time" and "a person existing at another time" to stand in a relation or personal identity. One common mistake is to talk of the conditions under which "two people"—or "a person existing at one time" and "a different person existing at another time"—are numerically identical. After all, if there are two people at issue, then they cannot be numerically one and the same. Another common mistake is to talk about what has to be true for "a person existing at one time" to be the same person "she or he was at another time." But this presupposes that we have the same person on both occasions and, hence, that we have an instance of personal identity.

inward at our own minds we observe our souls, even if we cannot directly observe the souls of other people. But a soul skeptic might rejoin that all we are introspectively aware of is a constant flux of thoughts, feelings, and experiences and not anything that plausibly counts as your enduring soul. As I look inward as I write this paragraph, all I am aware of is my experience of the computer screen, my coffee buzz, and my doubt that I'll ever finish this book. But I am never aware of my soul.

Second, even if you are aware of your own soul via introspection or in some other way, you have no way of knowing whether other human persons have souls as well. You might, of course, argue

> **Who's who?**
>
> After six weeks away studying philosophy (and other things), you finally return home for reading week. Two people greet you at your family home who look like and behave as your parents have always looked and behaved. Due to suspicions raised in your introductory philosophy class, you subject them to DNA tests and confirm that they possess the same bodies your parents did when you left home six weeks earlier. If the soul theory is true, do you have any grounds to suppose they are your parents? Or do you have simply no idea who these people are?

that since you consist of both a physical human body and an immaterial soul, and there is nothing unusual about you, it follows that all (or most) other possessors of human bodies have souls as well. A soul skeptic might rejoin, however, that one case is too small a sample size to draw a conclusion regarding a population of billions and, in addition, might question the basis for supposing that the sample in question—you—is representative.

Third, even if the existence of souls is conceded, it might be argued that, because they are non-physical, their natures are mysterious—that is, we cannot know what they are like. If this is right, then we are unlikely to have an adequate account of soul identity—what has to be true for a soul existing at one time and a soul existing at another to be numerically identical. But since the soul theory defines personal identity in terms of soul identity, these would leave us without an adequate account of personal identity as well.

And fourth, even if the existence of souls is conceded and an adequate account of soul identity is available, one might deny the relevance of the soul to personal identity. Even if human persons are composites of physical bodies and immaterial souls, the soul theory presupposes that what is essential is the soul—that the person is essentially a soul. But one might deny this and claim instead that what is essential is the body, and that the possession of an immaterial soul is a mere accidental feature of a person.

4.5 Identity and Bodies

The central difficulty with the soul theory concerns the uncertainty over the existence and nature of the immaterial soul. But what is uncontroversial is that human persons have physical bodies. In fact, one might argue that human persons just are their bodies. Of course, the bodies in question have to be living: a dead body is not a person, even if it is a human being. And in order to count as persons, they presumably have to have functioning brains as well. After all, insofar as the possession of higher-order cognitive abilities is required for personhood—and the possession of these abilities by human beings is a product of brain function—human persons need brains that function in the right way. So, the suggestion goes, a human person just is a living human body with a mature, functioning brain. Since, on the view at issue, there is no immaterial mind, states of consciousness and other psychological states are states of the body—and, in particular, the brain—rather than states of the soul. And insofar as bodily death involves the death and destruction of the body, a person could not survive any such event on this picture.

On its face, the **body theory** of personal identity—of what it takes for a person existing at one time and a person existing at another to be numerically the same person—is quite straightforward: they need to have numerically one and the same body. To revisit our earlier example, what is required for Professor Peter Alward and Peter All-weird to be the same person is for them to share the same body, something that, in principle, could easily be tested by fingerprint or DNA evidence. Of course, the body of 15-year-old Peter All-weird and that of the somewhat more aged Professor Alward are qualitatively different in many respects. But it is numerical sameness and not qualitative sameness that the body theory requires; and the former is, in principle, compatible with even radical qualitative bodily difference.

Unlike souls, there is little reason to question the existence of bodies. Unless one is in the grip of some kind of philosophical skepticism, one's experience of bodies—both one's own and those of others—will normally count as adequate grounds for belief in them. One might, however, worry about the nature of bodies. In particular, since the body theory defines personal identity in terms of bodily identity, in lieu of an adequate account of the latter it will ultimately prove to be empty. And providing an account of bodily identity is not a trivial matter: an enduring body can survive radical qualitative change, including both sudden changes due to accidents—such as severe burns—and gradual changes associated with aging; and it can undergo a more or less complete change in its constituent matter as a result of cellular replacement over time. Moreover, a human body can survive the replacement of its parts, not only with new living tissue but also with artificial parts: if I undergo knee-replacement surgery—which I fear may in fact be in my future—my body will not thereby be destroyed and replaced by a numerically distinct body.

A promising account of bodily identity may be found by appeal to some notion of bodily continuity. The basic idea is that for a body existing at one time and a body existing at another to be numerically one and the same, they have to be linked by an intervening series of "temporal stages" of bodies such that between any two successive pairs there are only gradual changes in spatial location, constituent matter, and qualitative properties. So, for example, Peter All-weird and Professor Alward can have numerically the same body despite rather radical differences in qualitative properties, constituent matter, and spatial location, as long as the differences are the product of a gradual continuous process. This is, of course, only the barest of sketches, and a worked-out theory of bodily identity may prove to be fraught with difficulties.

Case Study 4.3:
Transporters

Mr. Sulu is orbiting a planet on the USS Enterprise when Captain Kirk orders him immediately down to the planet surface. Since there is no time to take a space shuttle, Mr. Sulu is forced to use the transporter. This device works by breaking the body down to its basic elements, transmitting these elements to another location at extremely high speeds, and reconstructing a body out of these elements at this new location.

QUESTION: Assuming a continuity account of bodily identity, could the body that is reconstructed on the planet be Mr. Sulu's?

Case Study 4.4:
Radical Bodily Change

One can imagine waking one morning with a radically different body than one had when one fell asleep the previous evening—perhaps a robot body, or that of a giant insect. If this involves imagining that one has a numerically distinct body, rather than a qualitatively very different one, and what you can imagine is possible, then bodily identity is not necessary for personal identity. After all, if it is necessary, then it is not possible for a person existing at one time and a person existing at another time with numerically distinct bodies to nevertheless be numerically one and the same person.

QUESTION: Does this sort of case establish that bodily identity is not even necessary for personal identity?

As with the soul, one might deny the relevance of the body to personal identity, resisting the identification of a human person with a living and functioning human body. One might argue instead that what is essential to a human person is her psychology and, perhaps, that the enduring human body in which her psychological states are housed is inessential. Suppose that someone undergoes an event that produces a radical psychological break: the resulting person existing has different beliefs and values than the person existing beforehand, has a completely different personality, and does not have any recollection whatsoever of the experiences of this earlier person. According to the body theory, as long as the body existing before the event is numerically identical to the body existing afterwards, it is the same person on both occasions. But given the radical and permanent nature of the psychological break that has taken place, it is plausible to suppose that the original person has ceased to exist and a new person now inhabits the enduring (albeit qualitatively changed) body. Moreover, to the extent that we are disinclined to hold the person existing after the event responsible for the actions of the person existing beforehand—perhaps prior to the event in question, the person committed various crimes—this counts as evidence that there are numerically distinct persons before and afterwards.

4.6 Psychological Continuity

Psychological states play a central role in the notion of a person. Moreover, it is in some ways more natural to identify a person with her psychological states—her beliefs, values, personality, experiences, memories, etc.—than it is to identify her with an immaterial subject of psychological states or her physical body. As a result, a promising approach to personal identity might directly invoke such states. One way to do so might be to take exact psychological similarity as the requirement for a person existing at one time and a person existing at another to be numerically identical. However, not only is it in principle possible for distinct people to be psychologically identical but human persons also normally undergo psychological change over time. As a result, psychological identity is neither necessary nor sufficient for numerical identity. A better approach would be to require some kind of **psychological continuity** rather than psychological identity. This approach is most easily formulated by thinking of human persons as consisting of temporal parts. Just as we can divide a week into temporal parts—days—we can divide a person into those parts that exist during different periods of time. We might, for example, think of Peter All-weird as a temporal part of me that existed when I was 15 years old or thereabouts, and Professor Alward as a temporal part of me that has existed more recently. And once persons are thought of in this way, a theory of personal identity can be formulated in terms of a psychological continuity relation between temporal parts of persons. More precisely, on the picture at issue, what is required for a person existing at one time and a person existing at another time to be numerically identical is for the temporal part of the former person which exists at the former time and the temporal part of the latter person which exists at the latter time to be psychologically continuous. In order to cash this out, however, we need to know what psychological continuity consists in.

The simplest version of this view takes psychological continuity to be a memory relation. It is important to note that this does not involve the requirement that different person-parts have the same memories. After all, over time we have new experiences that generate new memories. As a result, a person-part existing at a later time will normally have memories that earlier parts of the same person lack. Rather, according to the **memory theory,** what is required for a person existing at one time and person existing at another to be numerically identical is for the person-stage existing at the later time to remember the experiences of the person-stage existing at the earlier time. So, for example, in order for Professor Alward to be numerically identical to Peter All-weird, the temporal part of Professor Alward that exists now must contain memories of the experiences of the part of Peter All-weird that existed when the latter was 15 years old.

There are, of course, some obvious counter-examples to the memory theory that need to be addressed before it can be taken seriously. First, we are constantly bombarded with experiences, and it is nearly impossible for someone to remember them all. Hence, the memory theory will minimally have to be adjusted to require only that a later person-stage remember some of the experiences of an earlier stage. Second, sometimes persons are unable to remember what are uncontroversially their own prior experiences. When you are very drunk, for example, you sometimes do not remember the embarrassing things you have done. But we would not say, for that reason, that it was not you who did them. And when one is asleep one arguably does not remember anything at all. As a result, the memory theory may have to be reformulated in terms of the possession of the basic capacity to remember previous experiences rather than requiring actual acts of remembering. The idea here is that although you might not actually remember what you had for dinner while you are sleeping, you nevertheless remain capable of remembering it in the sense that the information remains stored in your brain and it is accessible to you should you attempt to recall it. And third, many of us no longer have even the capacity to remember any of the experiences we had when we were very young. But we would be disinclined to say that we are numerically distinct from our younger selves for that reason. The solution to this worry is to not require memory relations between temporally discontinuous person-stages—stages with large gaps of time between them—but rather to require that they be linked by a series of continuous memory-linked person-stages. Professor Alward is not numerically identical to Peter All-weird because he remembers the latter's experiences but rather because he remembers the experiences of an immediately previous person-stage, who remembers the experiences of an immediately previous person stage, ... who remembers the experiences of Peter All-weird. The upshot of all this is the following more nuanced version of the memory theory: a person existing at one time and a person existing at another are numerically identical just in case either (a) the person-stage existing at the later time is capable of remembering the experiences of the person-stage existing at the earlier time or (b) the earlier and later person-stages are linked by a continuous series of intervening memory-linked person-stages.

Of course, in order to give an account of personal identity in terms of memory, we will have to provide an account of what memory consists in. Otherwise we will have no explanation of why someone who merely seems to remember the experiences of some long-dead historical figure is not numerically identical to that figure. The most plausible approach is some kind of **causal theory**. On this view, genuine memory—as opposed to false or merely apparent memory—requires the right kind of causal process from an original experience to a subsequent memory experience (or the subsequent capacity to have the latter). Ordinarily the process works roughly as follows: a person has an experience of some kind; information derived from this experience is stored in the brain; both the brain and the information recorded therein are retained for some period of time; this information is subsequently retrieved from the brain, resulting in a memory of the original experience. One might allow a broader range of causal processes that result in actual memory, perhaps including cases in which the information stored in a human brain is transferred at death into some kind of artificial computer brain. But it is important to note that not any causal process from original experience to memory will suffice. If, for example, information about an experience is irretrievably lost from your brain, or was never stored there in the first place, but is subsequently implanted there via some artificial means, such as hypnosis, even though you may have memories caused by your original experience they are arguably not genuine; that is, you do not really remember the experience.

One might argue, however, that memory by itself does not yield sufficient psychological continuity to ensure personal identity. If, for example, someone remembered the experiences of a previous person-stage but was otherwise entirely psychologically different, we might deny that that they are stages in the life of a single enduring person. In addition to memory, we might require continuity of beliefs and values, personality, and the like, as well as appropriate attitudes toward past and future person-stages, such as the anticipation of future experiences and the identification with past and future goals, projects, and activities, conceiving of them as one's own. As with memory, an account of some such more robust continuity relation will be required; that is, a specification is needed of what conditions must be met for two person-stages to be continuous in this sense. Of course, given the fact of psychological change over time, psychological identity cannot be required. But we might allow only gradual psychological change over time, ruling out radical psychological breaks. And, as in the case of memory, we might insist on some kind of appropriate causal link between psychologically continuous person-stages: a person-stage existing at an earlier time is continuous with a person-stage existing at a later time only if the psychological features of the latter

> ## Case Study 4.5: Hypothetical Futures
>
> Suppose that Mary has two possible futures:
>
> *Future 1*: Mary undergoes a series of gradual psychological changes. The upshot is a person with entirely different beliefs and values and an entirely different personality than Mary started out with.
>
> *Future 2*: Mary undergoes a severe brain trauma. The upshot is a person with entirely different beliefs and values and an entirely different personality than Mary started out with.
>
> **QUESTION**: Suppose the resultant person from each future is psychologically identical to the other. Does either have a better claim to being the same person as the original Mary?

were caused in the right way by the psychological features of the former.

One potential pitfall for the whole psychological continuity approach to personal identity is the **problem of multiple duplicates,** that is, the possibility that multiple persons might be psychologically continuous with a single original. There might be two (or more) people who actually remember the experiences of one original person or whose psychological states were caused in the right way, through a series of gradual steps, by the psychological states of the original. But if the memory theory—or the broader psychological continuity approach—is correct, then both subsequent people would be numerically identical to the original. But this runs afoul of the transitivity of identity discussed above: if x is one and the same person as y, and y is one and the same person as z, it follows that x is one and the same person as z. This principle implies that if both of the subsequent people are numerically the same as the original, then they are numerically identical to one another. But this is a contradiction: two distinct people cannot be numerically one and the same person.

One solution to this problem is to defend an account of psychological continuity that rules out the possibility of multiple psychological continuants. If, for example, you require numerical sameness of body as a condition of psychological continuity, then only the unique person having numerically the same body as an original can be numerically identical with her or him. However, not only would this rule out the possibility of surviving bodily death but one might also take exception on the grounds that sameness of body is not a psychological matter. An interesting alternative solution is to delink the issues of survival and personal identity. One might insist that psychological continuity is required to survive some event or process but deny that it is sufficient for personal identity. As long as there exists a person who is psychologically continuous with you after bodily death, for example, you have survived; but this does not entail that the survivor is numerically identical to you. Although the survival-without-identity approach may avoid the problem of multiple continuants—after all, if neither survivor is numerically identical to the original, transitivity does not apply—one might reasonably be suspicious of the suggestion that you can survive even if there does not exist a person who is numerically identical to you.

Reading Questions

1. What is the difference between qualitative and numerical identity? What does it mean to say that they are relational senses of identity?

2. What does it mean to say that numerical identity is a symmetrical relation?

3. What is the difference between being a person and being a human being?

4. What is the difference between synchronic and diachronic identity?

5. What, according to the soul theory, do human persons consist of?

6. Why is the fact that souls cannot be experienced a problem for the soul theory of personal identity?

7. Why is the survival of bodily death impossible, according to the body theory of personal identity?

8. What is the bodily continuity account of bodily identity?

9. How does the causal theory distinguish between genuine and artificial memory?

10. What is the problem of multiple duplicates?

Reflection Questions

1. Think of a number of ways in which you might continue to exist after your physical body is destroyed. In your view, would any of these suffice for genuine survival of bodily death?

2. Do you believe you have a soul? What evidence do you have either for or against the existence of your own soul?

Further Reading

A good general introduction to the issues discussed here:
John Perry, *A Dialogue on Personal Identity and Immortality* (Indianapolis: Hackett Philosophical Dialogues, 1978).

Identity in general:
Peter Geach, "Ontological Relativity and Relative Identity," *Logic and Ontology*, ed. M.K. Munitz (New York: New York UP, 1973), pp. 287–302.

Personhood:
Lynne Rudder Baker, *Persons and Bodies: A Constitution View* (Cambridge: Cambridge UP, 2000).

A contemporary version of the soul theory:
Richard Swinburne, "Personal Identity: The Dualist Theory," *Personal Identity*, ed. S. Shoemaker and R. Swinburne (Oxford: Blackwell, 1984), pp. 1–66.

Body theory of personal identity:
John Mackie, "Personal Identity and Dead People," *Philosophical Studies* 95 (1999): 219–42.

Memory theory:
H.P. Grice, "Personal Identity," *Personal Identity*, ed. John Perry (Berkeley: U of California P, 1975), pp. 73–98.

Psychological continuity:
Derek Parfit, "Personal Identity," *Philosophical Review* 80 (1971): 3–27.

5

FREE WILL AND DETERMINISM

Most of us believe that human persons have at least some degree of free will. Much of the time, what we do and what choices we make is largely up to us. Certain choices may, of course, have negative consequences, but if we are willing to face these consequences, there is no impediment to acting on these choices.

However, at the same time, there is good reason to believe that we live in a deterministic universe in which everything that happens—including everything we do—is governed by the laws of physics. But if this is right, it is far from clear how any of our actions can be free.

The central question of this chapter is whether and how free will can be reconciled with determinism. In order to address this question we will need to get clear about what freedom consists in and why the determinist picture of the universe might pose a problem for it. In addition, we will need to consider the relation between freedom and moral

CHAPTER CONTENTS:

- a taxonomy of various senses of freedom is presented;
- the thesis of determinism is introduced;
- the problem of free will is laid out;
- the incompatibilist approach to free will is presented;
- the hard determinist and libertarian variants of incompatibilism are investigated;
- compatibilist approaches to free will are explored; and
- the relationship between free will and responsibility is explored.

responsibility and whether people can be reasonably blamed or punished for acts that are not free.

5.1 Freedom

In order to determine whether we have free will, we need to get clear about the sense of freedom at issue. One important sense of freedom is **political freedom**. To be politically free is to be able to do what you want without interference from the state, that is, without being forcibly prevented from acting on your desires or threatened with some form of punishment if you do. Political freedom comes in degrees rather than being all or nothing: in all political systems, there is a range of activities in which individuals are able to engage without state interference and a range of activities with which the state will interfere; and differences in political freedom are determined by how broad the range of activities is in each case. Most states will attempt to both prevent and punish behaviour designed to harm other individuals, such as assault and murder. Less politically free states will additionally attempt to prevent or punish activities that harm only the perpetrator—such as drug use—or that harm no one but violate community moral standards—such as various forms of sexual activity. And very politically unfree societies will attempt to prevent or punish unsanctioned speech or worship, among other things.

A second important sense of freedom is **freedom from coercion**. To be subjected to coercion is to face a threat of undesirable treatment if you do not do what the person coercing you wants you to do. Coercion interferes with your freedom by interfering with your preferences. In the absence of coercion one might prefer to engage in a certain course of conduct, but if doing so were likely to result in undesirable consequences then one might no longer prefer, all things considered, to engage in this conduct. As a result, the threat of such consequences can alter one's preferences. A familiar case of coercion involves being threatened with physical violence by a mugger—normally by means of some weapon he is brandishing—if you fail to give over your purse or wallet to him. Ordinarily most of us would prefer to keep our purses and wallets rather than relinquish them to strangers. But by threatening violence if we do so, the mugger at least attempts to make us prefer the alternative. After all, although in ordinary circumstances I prefer to retain my wallet, if doing so would likely result in serious physical harm I would no longer prefer to retain it. As a result, coercion undermines our freedom to do as we otherwise would want.

A third sense of freedom is **freedom from limits**. Human persons typically have a number of preferences or goals. Which of these goals we can achieve, however, is constrained by the various limits we face: certain athletic goals we might hope to achieve—such as going to the Olympics—are constrained by our physical limitations; certain academic goals—such as getting a graduate degree—are constrained by our intellectual limitations; certain material goals we might have—such as going on exotic vacations, or even getting enough to eat—are constrained by our economic limitations. Like political freedom, freedom from limitations comes in degrees: some people simply face more or fewer limits than others, as well as different kinds of limits. But unlike political freedom or freedom from coercion, normally the limits to our freedom cannot be directly attributed to the actions of other individuals or the state. My inability to run fast enough to compete in an Olympic 100-metre sprint competition is not due to any kind of coercion but rather is the product of my basic physical endowments (with which no amount of training could yield Olympic-class speed over any distance). It is worth noting, however, that some limitations are due to social arrangements even if individual acts of coercion are not involved. The economic limitations people face, for example, are largely determined by the economic system in which they find themselves.

While political freedom and freedom from coercion or limits are important and interesting senses of freedom, they are not at issue here. Instead, what is at issue is a more fundamental sense of freedom—**metaphysical freedom**—that is presupposed by and required for freedom in any of these other senses. The question is whether any of our actions can be free even if they are not subject to coercion, political interference, or personal limitations of any sort. And what is required for metaphysical freedoms is that our actions—what we do—be under our control. If what we do is not under our control, then even if we are not subject to coercion or political interference and do not face physical, intellectual, or economic limits, our actions are not free. If, for example, the utterances I make are not under my control, then in a fundamental way those utterances are not free, even if the state does not punish me for making them.

5.2 Determinism

The main concern of this chapter is whether or not determinism undermines our metaphysical freedom by preventing us from having control over what we do. To this end, we will need to get clearer about exactly what determinism consists in. At its core, **determinism** is the view that everything that happens is caused by an event or events that occurred previously. To say that an event was caused by a previous event is to say that the previous event made it happen. Minimally, this requires that it be true that if the previous event had not occurred, the subsequent event would not have happened. Consider, for example, an avalanche preceded by a loud noise. In order for the noise to have caused the avalanche, it must be true that had the noise not occurred, the avalanche would not have happened (even though were the conditions still ripe, a subsequent noise might have caused a different avalanche). But if the avalanche would have occurred anyhow even without the noise, then the noise is not what caused it.

One of the central reasons one might have for accepting determinism is an adherence to physicalism. **Physicalism** is the view that everything that exists—including human persons—is a physical thing, wholly constituted by physical matter, whose behaviour is governed by the laws of nature. In particular, what happens to a physical thing is a function of the forces acting upon it, its internal constitution, and the natural laws governing the behaviour of things of that kind. As a result, any change in a physical thing—in either its internal constitution or external behaviour—is caused by a change in the external forces acting upon it. And since human beings are just complex physical objects, our behaviour too is governed in this sense by the laws of physics. Of course, given both the complex perceptual relations we stand in to the world and the myriad of internal states we are capable of finding ourselves in, our behaviour is far more difficult to predict than that of simpler entities. But even so, on the physicalist picture, everything we do is caused to occur by a prior event.

It is worth emphasizing here the difference between determinism and **fate**. To say that something is a person's fate is to say that it will inevitably happen to her or him. In particular, what is fated to happen to you will happen no matter what you do or what choices

> ## Dualist Determinism
>
> One might think that the rejection of physicalism in favour of a dualist picture according to which a human person consists of a physical body and a non-physical mind would undermine determinism and the threat to free will that it poses. But it is worth noting that dualism is compatible with determinism. As long as every mental event—as well as every physical event—is caused by a prior mental event, a prior physical event, or some combination of the two, the addition of non-physical minds to a physicalist picture of reality does nothing to undercut the determinism inherent therein. And insofar as indeterminism is thought to be required for free will, it can be just as easily imported into a physicalist picture as it can into a dualist picture.

you make. If, for example, Fred's fate is to be a successful entrepreneur when he is 50 years old, then this is what will happen whether he now decides to finish his management degree, transfer to a philosophy program, or drop out of university altogether. According to determinism, in contrast, what will happen to you in the future is determined because what you do and how you choose now are themselves determined by prior events. But if those prior events had been different and, as a result, you chose and acted differently now, what would happen to you in the future would be different as well. Prior events might, for example, determine that Fred will decide to finish his management degree and, as a result, eventually become a successful 50-year-old entrepreneur. But if these prior events had been different, Fred might instead have been determined to transfer to a philosophy program or drop out of university altogether, and that, in all likelihood, would have yielded a very different future for him.

5.3 The Problem of Free Will

The problem of free will stems from the fact there seem to be compelling reasons to endorse both determinism and the claim that at least some of our choices and actions are metaphysically free. The trouble is that there seems to be an incompatibility between these two theses, that is, that they cannot both be true. After all, if determinism is true, then everything that happens is caused by that something else that occurred previously, including our choices and actions. If, for example, I choose to have a ham sandwich for lunch, some event that occurred caused me to make it. But if how we choose and what we do are caused by prior events, it is far from clear how we can have control over our choices and actions. The upshot is that it is unclear how any of our actions and choices can be metaphysically free.

There are two broad approaches to the problem of free will: incompatibilism and compatibilism (see Figure 5.1). According to **incompatibilism**, determinism and free will are, in fact, incompatible, and as a result, at least one of these theses has to be abandoned. Different variants of incompatibilism are distinguished by which of these theses they reject. The hard determinist abandons free will, claiming that every event is caused and, hence, none of our actions are free. For example, because my so-called choice to have a ham sandwich for lunch was caused by a prior event, it was not free. The libertarian, in contrast, abandons determinism, claiming that because some of our actions are free, some events must be uncaused. So, for example, insofar as my choice to have a ham sandwich was free, it must have been uncaused. According to **compatibilism**, free will and determinism are compatible, so both theses can be retained. The soft determinist argues that some of our choices and actions are in our control despite the fact that they are caused by previous happenings. So, for example, even though my choice of a ham sandwich was caused by something that happened earlier, it nevertheless still might have been a free choice. We will consider each of these solutions to the free will problem below.

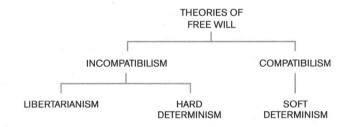

FIGURE 5.1 • *Theories of Free Will*

5.4 Incompatibilism

It is widely believed that not everything we do and not every choice we make is free. One kind of case often thought not to involve freedom consists of choices and actions made or performed unreflectively and out of habit. Consider, for example, habitually brushing one's teeth in the morning while thinking about other things. The paradigmatic examples of free choices are those that are the product of a process of **deliberation**, wherein a person considers his or her options, contemplates reasons for and against each option, and on that basis chooses to act on one of them. And the paradigmatic examples of free actions are those that are the products of free choices of this kind. If, for example, I consider whether I ought to brush my teeth before going to bed or waiting until the morning, weigh various reasons for and against each option, on the basis of these deliberations choose to brush my teeth before going to bed, and then, as a result, subsequently do so, both my choice to brush my teeth before going to bed and my action of so doing are free in this sense.

According to incompatibilism, even choices and actions that are the product of deliberation cannot be free if determinism is true. Although there are a number of ways in which one might try to establish the incompatibility of freedom and determinism, we will focus on one here: the **before birth argument**. This argument is designed to show that determinism is incompatible with freedom because it prevents you

> ## Case Study 5.1: Habitual Freedom?
>
> As a result of a process of careful deliberation, Mary decides to acquire the habit of taking the longer but more scenic drive to work. To this end, she makes a point of consciously choosing this route every morning until eventually she does so automatically without thinking about it.
>
> **QUESTION**: Given that she freely chose to acquire this habit, when Mary takes the long scenic route out of habit, are her actions free?

from having control over what you do. If determinism is true, everything you do and every choice you make is caused by some event that occurred prior to it. But these prior events were themselves caused by other events which occurred prior to them, which were caused by earlier events, and so on. Since this chain of causation can be traced backwards to events that occurred prior to your birth, determinism entails that every choice you make and everything you do is ultimately caused by events that occurred prior to your birth. But since you do not have any control over events that occurred prior to your birth, it follows, according to this argument, that you lack any control over the choices and actions you make now. Hence, if determinism is true, none of your choices or actions is free, including those that are the products of deliberation.

There are a number of responses one might have to the before birth argument. First, one might accept that free will and determinism are incompatible and conclude that, because determinism is true, we must lack free will. Second, one might accept the incompatibility of free will and determinism and conclude that, because some of our actions are free, determinism must be false. And third, one might resist the argument by rejecting the assumption that in order to have control over our behaviour we need to have control over the causes of our behaviour. We will consider each of these responses in turn.

5.5 Hard Determinism

Hard determinism is a position that combines determinism—the thesis that every event has a cause—with the rejection of human free will. Since we have already considered the case for incompatibilism, the focus of this section is on whether there is any good reason to believe that determinism is true. There are two approaches one might adopt toward establishing this thesis: by arguing that it is *a priori*—or knowable by means of reason alone—and by appeal to empirical evidence. We will consider each in turn.

As outlined above, determinism is the thesis that every event has a cause; hence, to establish that determinism is *a priori* is just to establish that the proposition that every event has a cause is *a priori*. One approach might involve attempting to argue that it is a truth of meaning. Consider, for example, the sentence "all sisters are female siblings." Because the word "sister" means the same thing as does the expression "female sibling," we can that know the proposition expressed by this sentence is true without having to engage in any kind of empirical study. Similarly, it might be argued that we can know that determinism is true simply by attending to the meanings of the words in the sentence "every event has a cause." The reason this might be tempting is because a closely related sentence—"every effect has a cause"—is a truth of meaning. After all, since what it means to be an effect

> ### A Priori vs. A Posteriori Truths
>
> One can distinguish between different sorts of truths or true propositions in terms of how we can come to know them. *A posteriori* or empirical truths are those that can be known only on the basis of empirical observations. So, for example, the proposition that there is currently a jar of glue on my dining table is *a posteriori* because the only way that you can come to know it is on the basis of empirical evidence. *A priori* truths are those that can be known on the basis of reason alone. Traditional examples include truths of meaning—such as the proposition that all bachelors are unmarried men—and truths of mathematics—that $2 + 2 = 4$, for example.

is to be something that is caused, anything that is an effect is by definition caused. But since "event" and "effect" differ in meaning, it does not follow from the fact that every effect has a cause is a truth of meaning that every event has a cause is as well. Considerations of meaning, after all, do not establish that every event is an effect.

Another approach to establishing that determinism is *a priori* might involve attempting to argue that the proposition that every event has a cause is in some sense innate. The idea is that rather than being something we acquire or learn, the concept of causation—and the belief that every event has a cause—is something we are "hard-wired" to have: given our human natures, we inevitably come to have the concept, and the corresponding belief, regardless of what experiences we have. As a result, the belief in determinism is *a priori* in the sense that in order to acquire it, we do not need to have the kind of pattern of experiences that would justify it. The trouble with this approach is that even if the proposition that every event has a cause is in this sense *a priori*, we have no basis for thinking this proposition is true. Our beliefs about things often diverge from how things in fact are. Many people used to believe, for example, that the Earth was flat when, as a matter of fact, it has always been roughly spherical. As a result, unless one wants to argue that reality depends in a strong sense on beliefs about it, establishing that the proposition that every event has a cause is *a priori* in the sense of being innate does not establish the objective truth of determinism.

Let us turn now to the question of whether the truth of determinism can be established empirically. Since determinism makes a universal claim to the effect that every event has a cause, the most obvious strategy would be to develop an inductive generalization. This argumentative strategy involves attempting to draw a conclusion about a group or population of things by appeal to the features of a representative sub-group or sample of the larger population. So, for example, if one could establish that every member of a randomly selected sample of American philosophy professors voted for Obama in the 2008 presidential election, then one might conclude on that basis that all American philosophy professors voted for Obama in the 2008 election. In an inductive argument, the evidence is not designed to establish that the conclusion must be true but only to render it highly likely; and the larger and more representative the sample size, the more likely the evidence makes the conclusion. In the case at hand, the population in question is the class of events or happenings and the feature in question is that of having a cause. The sample of the larger population of events would have to be those events we have observed or, perhaps more narrowly, those we have investigated. Now the positive case for determinism is that we have observed or found causes for the vast majority of the events we have observed or investigated. Moreover, given the advances in scientific knowledge that have occurred and continue to occur, there are very good grounds to be optimistic that we will eventually discover causes of those observed or investigated events whose causes have yet to be found. Finally, we have yet to establish the occurrence of even a single event that is uncaused. The upshot of this is that the evidence shows that determinism is very likely true.

There are a number of reasons to question the empirical case for determinism. One common reason for rejecting this argument is the view that quantum mechanics has shown that events involving microscopic entities are uncaused. According to quantum mechanics, we cannot predict the behaviour of microscopic entities but rather can only calculate the likelihoods that they will behave in a range of possible ways. If this is right, then events involving microscopic entities are not determined to occur in a certain way by prior events and so are uncaused. There are two responses the defender of the empirical argument for determinism might give here. First, she might point out that there are two ways of understanding quantum indeterminacies: metaphysically and epistemologically. On the metaphysical understanding, microscopic events really are uncaused, and how microscopic entities behave really is a probabilistic matter. On the epistemological understanding, in contrast, microscopic events are caused; hence, how microscopic entities behave is determined by prior events. What quantum indeterminacy amounts to is the fact that we human observers are in principle unable to know how these entities will behave and instead can only know the likelihood of various behaviours open to them. And if the latter understanding is correct, quantum mechanics poses no problems for determinism. And second, the advocate of the empirical case for determinism might concede that there are uncaused events at the micro-physical level but argue that this indeterminacy does not carry over to the macroscopic level of tables, chairs, plants, animals, and human beings. That is, although events involving microscopic entities are uncaused, all events involving macro entities nevertheless have determining causes. There is a lot more to be said regarding both of these responses to the quantum mechanical challenge to determinism, but this will have to do for our present purposes.

5.6 Libertarianism

Libertarianism is the view that at least some human choices and actions are free in the sense that they are uncaused by prior events. Since determinism is the view that all events are caused, libertarianism entails the falsity of determinism. It is worth emphasizing that libertarianism in the sense at issue is a metaphysical thesis in contrast to the political thesis of the same name, according to which individuals ought to be free from interference or coercion on the part of a centralized government. Libertarianism is normally motivated by the phenomenology of freedom—the introspected feeling of control over our choices and actions—together with the conviction that in order for a choice or action to be free, it must be uncaused. The reliability of introspection is, however, controversial; for example, one might believe on the basis of introspection that one is not jealous of the success of a friend when in fact one really is jealous of him or her. As a result, it is unclear exactly what if any support our introspected feelings of control provide for libertarianism. The main concern here, however, is with whether uncaused choices can be free.

The central difficulty for libertarianism is the **paradox of indeterminism**. The paradox stems from the libertarian claim that caused actions and choices cannot be free. The trouble is that there are good grounds to suppose that uncaused actions cannot be free either. And if neither caused actions nor uncaused actions can be free, then the libertarian is stuck with the conclusion that freedom is impossible. Suppose that a choice or action—for example, my choice to work on this manuscript rather than go to the beach—is uncaused by prior events. It follows that nothing prior to my choice determined that I would choose in the way that I did: everything prior to my choice could have been exactly the same, but I might have chosen to go to the beach instead. But if nothing made me choose the way that that I did, then it was just a matter of random chance that I chose to work on this manuscript rather than to go to the beach. And if my choice was simply the product of random chance, then I did not not have control over it, and hence it was unfree. After all, I would have had no more control over my choice than I would over the outcome of a fair coin toss.

There are three main strategies the libertarian might deploy in the attempt to show how uncaused choices and actions can be free. First, one might note that uncaused events need not be the product of random chance. Even if prior conditions do not determine that an event will occur, they can make it highly likely that it will. So, for example, rather than there being a 50-per-cent chance that I would choose to work on this manuscript and a 50-per-cent chance that I would choose to go to the beach, given the prior conditions there might have been an 80-per-cent chance that I would choose to work on the manuscript rather than the alternative. As a result, if prior conditions make a choice or decision likely to occur without causing it, then it is uncaused without being the product of random chance; and, the argument continues, this suffices for its being a choice or action that is free. The trouble with the probability strategy is twofold. First, if prior circumstances make one choice or action highly likely, the occurrence of any alternative choice or action is a matter of random chance. But if the alternatives could only be the product of random chance, they are not within the agent's control, and therefore he or she is not free to perform them.

Second, according to the before birth argument discussed above, the fact that an agent's choices or actions were caused by prior conditions places them outside his or her control and hence makes them unfree. But if this is true, it is not clear why the fact that these choices or actions were made likely—rather than caused—by previous conditions does not place them outside his or her control as well. After all, the agent would have no more control over the events and circumstances that make choices and actions likely than he or she does over events and circumstances that cause them.

Second, one might argue that uncaused choices or actions can be free if they are made or done for reasons. When choices or actions are made on the basis of deliberation, they are done for reasons. And if they are done for reasons, they are not the product of random chance even if they are uncaused. After all, an agent can appeal to his or her reasons as an explanation for why she or he chose or acted as he or she did. So, for example, I might offer as a reason for my choice to work on this manuscript my impending contractual deadline. The trouble with the reason strategy is that when a subject engages in a process of deliberation, she considers reasons for and against all of the options she is deciding among. For example, while deliberating over my choice I might have considered the pleasantness of frolicking on the beach as a reason for choosing to go there instead of working on this manuscript. As a result, had the subject chosen or acted differently, she would still have had reasons for what she did, just different ones. But even though she has reasons for what she does no matter what she does, which reasons she acts on remains a matter of random chance and are hence out of her control.

And third, one might argue that free actions are products of the metaphysical will. By means of the will, a person has the capacity to choose and to act on the basis of these choices. However, not only are willed choices and actions not caused by prior circumstances, but acts of will are also under the control of the subject rather than being the product of random chance. As a result, acts of will meet the conditions for being free on the libertarian picture: they are uncaused and under control. The trouble with the metaphysical will strategy is that it renders the will and its actions ultimately mysterious. What the libertarian needs in order to solve the paradox of indeterminism is, of course, for there to be uncaused choices and actions that are nevertheless in our control. The question is whether and how this is possible. To simply stipulate that there is an entity—the will—that has these powers without explaining how it could have them simply forestalls the question without answering it. Ultimately, it remains unclear how anyone or anything could be free in a libertarian sense. And simply stipulating the existence of a will that is free in this sense is of no help.

5.7 Compatibilism

Compatibilism is the view that freedom and determinism are compatible; that is, the fact that a choice or action is caused does not prevent it from being free. Despite believing that these two theses could both be true, one might, of course, reject one or the other thesis on independent grounds. After all, to say that a pair of theses could both be true does not entail that they both in fact are true. The soft determinist, however, not only acknowledges the compatibility of freedom and determinism but also accepts both theses: all events are caused, but some of our actions and choices are nevertheless free. Two central questions need to be addressed in a developed version of **soft determinism**: exactly which of our actions and choices count as free; and in what sense they are free given that they are caused. We will address each question in turn.

At first glance, the libertarian has a relatively easy test for distinguishing free from unfree actions: an act is free if it is uncaused and unfree if it is caused. But since the soft determinist believes that all actions are caused, this test is unavailable. A closer look, however, reveals that the libertarian may not have any such advantage over the soft determinist. The reason is that, even setting aside the paradox of determinism, there are reasons to believe that not all uncaused choices and actions are free. Consider, for example, actions based on snap judgements or unreflective choices. If such judgements are uncaused—and there is no reason to believe they could not be, on the libertarian view—then the libertarian may have to concede that they at least are the product of random chance and hence are unfree.

According to soft determinists, free choices and actions are not those that are uncaused but rather those that are caused in the right way. There are a number of varieties of soft determinism, but most variants take choices and actions that are caused by a process of deliberation to be free. So, for example, if I am caused to consider the options of working on my manuscript and going to the beach, and this causes me to consider reasons for and against working on my manuscript and reasons for and against going to the beach, and this causes me to choose to work on my manuscript, which causes me to go ahead and in fact work on it, then my decision and action were caused in the right way and thus count as free on the compatibilist picture. It is worth noting, however, that relatively few of our actions are produced in this way. After all, we make decisions and perform actions all the time and rarely go through some such painstaking process before we do so. As a result, if only such choices and actions were free, the range of free actions would be quite restricted; and insofar as freedom is required for responsibility, the range of actions for which we are responsible would be quite limited as well.

One way to increase the range of free actions would be to include certain actions that are products of snap judgements or unreflective choices as free. In particular, one might take those actions that are the products of habits of mind or character traits that the subject freely and consciously inculcated in herself to be free. Suppose, for example, that as a result of a process of deliberation, Fred decides to become the kind of person who says "hello" to strangers he passes in the street and makes a conscious point of doing so until it becomes a habit. If he succeeds in this project, he will eventually start to greet strangers in this way without thinking about it. But even though each instance of his current behaviour is caused by his habit and not by a process of deliberation, the soft determinist might still claim that Fred's actions are free because the habit that caused them was itself caused by a process of deliberation.

A soft determinist might also want to include as free certain actions that are the products of non-voluntary beliefs and values, and perhaps even traits of character— that is, beliefs and values that the subject did not freely choose. These include mental states that are the product of the subject's upbringing as well as those derived from her genetic makeup, if there are any. The motivation for taking such actions to be free is that, for most of us, very little of our behaviour is the product of mental states we have chosen rather than found ourselves with. Nevertheless, this is something of a delicate issue because actions produced by at least some non-voluntary mental states are arguably unfree. In particular, psychological states that are the products of indoctrination or abuse yield actions for which the subject has diminished responsibility exactly because those actions are to that extent unfree. If, for example, someone engages in acts of racism as a result of racist beliefs that are themselves the product of racist indoctrination as a child, his or her acts arguably have a diminished degree of freedom, if they are free at all. One way of distinguishing between those non-voluntary mental states that yield free actions and those that do not is in terms of evidence-sensitivity. To say that a subject's beliefs and values are evidence-sensitive is to say that were she presented with adequate evidence against them, she would revise them. Beliefs and values that are the products of indoctrination or abuse typically are not evidence-sensitive in this sense: because of the nature of their upbringing, such people will hold onto their beliefs and values regardless of the strength of the evidence they are presented against their attitudes. In effect, they are stuck with psychological states they did not choose. But if a subject's non-voluntary psychological states are sensitive to the evidence, then she is not stuck with them, and as a result, actions produced by them might reasonably be thought to be free.

The question that remains is the sense in which actions and choices of the kind delineated above count as free on the soft determinist picture. At its core, the idea is that it is the agent herself who causes her free choices and actions rather than something or someone external to her. Moreover, they are the products of beliefs and values that she chose herself or, at least, are under her control rather than psychological states imposed on her by others by means of indoctrination, abuse, and the like. Finally, if her choices or actions are free, the subject could have chosen or acted differently in the following sense: there are possible circumstances identical in all respects external to her in which she does act differently; but given that her actions are caused, these must be circumstances in which some of her internal states are different. Suppose, for example, that Fred, when faced by a mugger brandishing a gun, relinquishes his wallet to the mugger. If Fred's action is free, then there must be possible circumstances in which Fred is threatened by the very same mugger in the same way at the same time and place but in which he refuses to turn over his wallet. But again, in any such circumstances, due presumably to differences in his history, Fred must be internally different from how he in fact is, having different psychological or neurophysiological states. After all, given that his actions are caused, any difference in his behaviour must be explained by a difference in prior conditions.

The central objection to soft determinism is that the sense of freedom that the view attributes to human agents is not genuine. Although they could act differently in the very same external circumstances as long as their internal states were different, given the internal states they in fact have, they are determined to choose or act as they in fact do. To nevertheless describe these acts and choices as free, the objection goes, is to engage in semantics rather than serious metaphysics. More to the point, the sense in which choices and actions are free on the soft determinist picture does not suffice for responsibility; after all, if I am determined by prior conditions to choose and act as I do, I am not responsible for what I do. And if I am not responsible, then arguably my act was not free either. To adequately assess this argument, we will have to look at the notion of responsibility in more detail, which is the focus of the next section.

5.8 Responsibility

The question of human freedom is not merely a metaphysical issue. It is also tightly bound up with morality and, in particular, with **moral responsibility**. In order for a subject to deserve praise or blame, or punishment or reward, for something she has done, she has to be responsible for her actions. If, for example, my actions harm others but if, due to mental infirmity, non-voluntary inebriation, or what have you, I am not responsible for what I did, then I do not deserve to be blamed or punished. And in order to be responsible for my choices and actions, they must be metaphysically free. In this section we will address two questions: whether responsibility is compatible with determinism; and whether it is appropriate to blame or praise someone for acts for which she is not responsible.

First, although there are a number of arguments one might give for or against the compatibility of responsibility and determinism, we will focus on one that appeals to the compatibility of determinism with our shared concept of responsibility. Our shared concept of responsibility is implicit in the set of acts for which we collectively take people to be responsible. And although there are some controversial cases, there is broad agreement that people are responsible when they are not forced by external circumstances to act as they do. Suppose, for example, that I engage in behaviour that harms others. If I have been physically forced or coerced by a credible threat to act as I do, it would be generally agreed that I am not responsible. But if I am the source of this behaviour, and have not been forced or coerced to so behave, then it would be widely agreed that I am responsible. Moreover, the fact that the internal causes of my actions were themselves caused would be unlikely to significantly weaken this agreement. The upshot here is that actions caused by internal factors fall under our shared concept of moral responsibility, and, so the argument goes, it follows that responsibility and determinism are compatible.

The trouble with this argument is that it presupposes that a concept could not be widely misapplied, that is, that most people could not erroneously apply it to things to which it in fact does not apply. The correct application of certain concepts is determined by a group of experts who form a small minority of the population who use the concept. Many people use the terms "elm" and "beech," for example, but relatively few of us can correctly apply them to particular trees. As a result, it could turn out that although most people apply the concept of responsibility to actions that have internal but not external causes, the relevant experts—in this case metaphysicians—would not apply the concept to such actions.

Second, a soft determinist might concede that compatibilist freedom does not suffice for moral responsibility and, moreover, even grant that responsibility is not

compatible with determinism. Nevertheless she might argue that compatibilist freedom is nevertheless sufficient for the appropriateness of punishment and reward,
and praise and blame, and hence that the abandonment of responsibility comes at
no great cost to the view. The idea is that the appropriateness of praise and blame
stems from the positive consequences they produce. Praising and rewarding beneficial actions will encourage both the subject and others to engage in acts of that
kind in the future. And blaming and punishing harmful acts will deter the subject
and others from similarly harmful acts as well. And, it is important to note, having
such effects is compatible with determinism; after all, praise and blame might work
by causing changes in people's mental states which in turn cause them to engage in
desirable behaviour or refrain from engaging in undesirable behaviour.

The problem with this approach, however, is that it severs the link between the
appropriateness of praise and blame, punishment and reward, on the one hand, and
desert on the other. Ordinarily, the reason we think it is appropriate to praise or
blame someone for something they have done is because they deserve it. And the
reason they deserve it is because they were responsible for what they did. But on the
view at issue, praise and blame are appropriate whether or not the subject deserves it.

In this chapter, we have considered both compatibilist and incompatibilist
accounts of free will, as well as the relationship between freedom and responsibility. Recently some theorists have investigated the neurophysiology of the human
brain during choice situations in order to adjudicate the issue of free will and determinism. But this issue, as well as many others discussed here, remains a matter of
continuing controversy.

Reading Questions

1.   What is coercion? How does coercion interfere with freedom?

2.   What has to be true for one event to cause another?

3.   What is the difference between fatalism and determinism?

4.   What is the difference between hard and soft determinism?

5.   What is the difference between the two ways of understanding quantum
      indeterminacies?

6.   What does it mean to say that introspection is unreliable?

7.   What is the probability response to the paradox of indeterminism?

8.   What does it mean to say that one's beliefs are evidence-sensitive?

9.   What difference does it make to future conduct whether we praise or blame
      someone's actions?

Reflection Questions

1. Think of some things you have done in your life that you consider to be free. What kinds of influence did previous events in your life have on these actions? To what extent were these actions determined by these previous events?

2. Think of a number of things you have done that other people have praised or blamed you for. Have you always deserved the praise or blame you have received? Why or why not?

Further Reading

Good introductions to the issues discussed here:
Robert Kane, *A Contemporary Introduction to Free Will* (Oxford: Oxford UP, 2005).
Clifford Williams, *Free Will and Determinism* (Indianapolis: Hackett Philosophical Dialogues, 1980).

Freedom:
John Martin Fischer, *The Metaphysics of Free Will* (Oxford: Blackwell, 1994).

Determinism:
John Earman, *A Primer on Determinism* (Dordrecht, Netherlands: Reidel, 1986).

Incompatibilism:
Peter van Inwagen, "The Incompatibility of Free Will and Determinism," *Philosophical Studies* 25 (1975): 185–99.

Hard determinism:
Derk Pereboom, *Living without Free Will* (Cambridge: Cambridge UP, 2001).

Libertarianism:
Peter van Inwagen, *An Essay on Free Will* (Oxford: Clarendon, 1983).

Soft determinism:
Daniel Dennett, *Elbow Room: The Varieties of Free Will Worth Wanting* (Cambridge, MA: MIT P, 1984).

Freedom and responsibility:
Dana Nelkin, *Making Sense of Freedom and Responsibility* (Oxford: Oxford UP, 2011).

6

MODALITY AND CAUSATION

[handwritten annotations: "Notes Book off 4.00", "• Might OR must be!!!", "2+2 = Necessarily 4", "Two plus two nec", "Might OR must be"]

In addition to claims about how things in fact are (or were or will be), people often make claims about how things might or must be. One might, for example, claim not only that two plus two in fact equals four but more strongly that two plus two necessarily equals four, or that cats might be more loyal than dogs whether or not they are in fact so. Such claims are puzzling, however, not only because it is not entirely clear what it means to claim that something might or must be the case but also because it is unclear exactly what sorts of facts could make such claims true or false. Causal claims—claims about what causes what—run into similar difficulties because they are a species of claim about what must happen. To say something causes a certain effect is to say that the cause produces the effect or makes it happen. And this is to say that given that the cause has occurred, the effect must occur.

CHAPTER CONTENTS:

- modal claims, about how things might or must be, are introduced;
- the question of the truth conditions of modal claims is investigated; *[handwritten: Possible]*
- the possible worlds approach to modality is explored;
- the basic problem of events and causation is laid out;
- skepticism about causation is considered;
- the relation between causation and laws of nature is investigated; and
- analyses of causation in terms of counterfactual conditionals are explored.

[handwritten: Given]

The central concern of this chapter is the nature of modality—necessity and possibility—and its relation to causation. To this end, we will determine whether modal claims are even intelligible and, if so, whether they are capable of truth or falsity. Moreover, we will have to ascertain exactly what sorts of modal claims underlie our talk of causation, and whether they are tenable.

6.1 Modal Claims

Extensional claims are claims about how things in fact are, were, or will be. These include claims such as

> Margaret Atwood is the author of *The Handmaid's Tale*

and

> Sisters are female siblings.

Extensional claims can be either true or false. The above examples are both true, whereas extensional claims such as

> Margaret Atwood is the current Canadian prime minister

and

> Bachelors are married men

are both false. **Modal claims**, in contrast, are claims about how things might or must be. Examples include such claims as

> It is possible that Danielle Steel won the 2012 US presidential election

and

> It is necessary that sisters are female siblings.

As with extensional claims, modal claims seem capable of truth or falsity. The claim

> It is necessary that sisters are female siblings,

for example, is arguably true, whereas the claim

> It is possible that two plus two equals five

seems clearly false.

(handwritten annotations at top: ● Extensial Claims can Be Either True or False ● How Things turned out)

There are two basic ways of understanding modal claims: metaphysically and epistemologically. The epistemological understanding concerns how things could in fact be, given what we know. In this sense, the claim

It is possible that Danielle Steel won the 2012 US presidential election

is false. After all, given that we know that Barack Obama won that election, it is not possible that Steel in fact did so. The metaphysical understanding, in contrast, concerns not how things in fact are but rather how they could have been. Although our knowledge that Obama won the 2012 election—together with our knowledge that there can be only be one winner—rules out the possibility that Steel in fact won, it does nothing to undermine the fact that she could have won had she run for the office, and had the US political landscape been somewhat different prior to the 2012 election. In this chapter, the focus will be on the metaphysical understanding of modal claims.

Finally, it is worth highlighting one important kind of modal claim that will prove to be important in our discussion of causation—counterfactual conditionals. A conditional claim is an "if-then" claim. An example is

(handwritten: ● How could have Been)

If it is snowing then it is cold.

The **antecedent** of the conditional is the claim that follows the word "if," namely

(handwritten: ● Antecedent)

It is snowing, *then*

and the **consequent** is the claim that follows the word "then":

(handwritten: ● Consequent)

It is cold.

In an ordinary **material conditional,** both the antecedent and the consequent are extensional claims. In a **subjunctive conditional**, in contrast, the "if" and "then" clauses have a subjunctive or "were-would" form. Consider, for example, the claim

If it were snowing, then it would be cold.

(handwritten: Material Conditional, Both the Antecedent and Consequent are extensional Claims.)

Because the "if"-clause is

If it were snowing

rather than

If it is snowing,

and the "then"-clause is

then it would be cold

rather than

then it is cold

it counts as a subjunctive conditional rather than a material conditional. A counterfactual conditional is a subjunctive conditional whose antecedent is false, rendering it "counter to fact." Consider, for example, the conditional claim

> If Margaret Atwood were the current Canadian prime minister, then funding the arts would be a budget priority.

The fact that it has a "were-would" form makes it a subjunctive conditional, and the fact that the antecedent is false—Justin Trudeau, not Margaret Atwood, is after all the current prime minister—makes it a counterfactual.

6.2 Modal Truth Conditions

Let us turn now to the question of modal truth conditions. In particular, the question is whether modal claims are capable of truth and, if so, how things have to be for them in fact to be true. Consider, by way of illustration, the claim

> Alward is a professor.

The **truth conditions** of this claim—how things have to be in order for it to be true—require that a certain person, namely myself, occupy a faculty position at a university. And since I do occupy some such position, the claim at issue is true. The concern here, however, is with the truth conditions of a claim such as

> It is possible that Alward is a professor,

which could (arguably) be true even if I did not in fact occupy a faculty position at a university. Suppose that as a matter of fact I were a professional basketball player rather than a professor. In such circumstances it would nevertheless be true that I could have been a professor. There are three basic approaches to this question: modal skepticism, modal reductionism, and modal realism. We will consider each in turn.

MODAL SKEPTICISM

According to the **modal skeptic**, modal claims lack truth conditions and are therefore incapable of truth or falsity. Although there are a number of different reasons one might have for holding this view, one motivation is that suggesting the truth and falsity of modal claims requires the existence of modal facts—facts about necessities, possibilities, and the like—but the existence of facts of these kinds are problematic. On this view, it is conceded that there are facts about how things are, were, and, perhaps, will be, and that we can have knowledge of such facts on the basis of our experiences. For example, the claim

> Alward has ten fingers

is true because it is a fact that I have ten fingers and, moreover, one that can be ascertained by observations of my hands. The trouble with modal facts is that experience yields no knowledge of them, offering instead evidence only for what is, was, or will be and not for what must or may be. Moreover, leaving aside questions about whether we could have knowledge of them, modal facts are problematic in their own right. Consider, for example, the claim

> It is possible that Alward has five genius children.

In order for this claim to be true it seems as though there would have to be facts about non-existent children; but, the objection goes, there can be facts only about existing things.

There are, however, a number of problems with modal skepticism. First, knowledge of certain claims—mathematical claims, for example—is based on reasoning rather than empirical observation. As a result, the fact that modal claims cannot be known on the basis of observation does not establish that they cannot be known at all. Moreover, claims that can be known on the basis of reasoning—logical and mathematical theorems, for example—are exactly the sorts of claims that are candidates for being necessary truths. And second, the rejection of modal truth conditions runs into serious difficulties in its own right. Not only are many modal claims clearly true—consider again the claim that it is possible that Margaret Atwood is the current Canadian prime minister—but insofar as causal claims presuppose the truth of modal claims of various kinds, modal skepticism seems to require the rejection of causation as well.

MODAL REDUCTIONISM

According to **modal reductionism**, modal claims have truth conditions—and so are capable of truth or falsity—but these truth conditions do not involve irreducible modal facts. Instead, they involve only non-modal facts about how things are, were, or will be. Although there are numerous non-modal facts in terms of which one might attempt to analyze the truth conditions of modal claims, the most common approach is to do so in terms of the notions of logical truth and analyticity. To say a claim is a logical truth is to say that it is true in virtue of its form alone—that its truth depends neither on the meanings of non-logical words nor on the facts. Consider, for example, the claim

> If snow is white then snow is white.

This statement is true whether or not snow is white and, hence, its truth does not depend on the facts. But moreover its truth does not depend on the meaning of "snow is white" either. If one were to replace each occurrence of this sentence with any other sentence—"grass is green" or "snow is black," for example—the resulting claim would still be true. As a result,

> If snow is white then snow is white

is a logical truth, as is

> If grass is green then grass is green

and

> If snow is black then snow is black.

To say a claim is analytic is to say that it is true in virtue of its meaning alone, and again its truth is independent of the facts. Given that "sister" means "female sibling," the claim

> All sisters are female siblings

is true in virtue of its meaning alone and, hence, counts as analytic.

In order to give an account of the truth conditions of modal claims in terms of logical truth and analyticity, we will need to distinguish within such claims between the "modal operator" and the "embedded sentence." The modal operators of interest here are the phrases "it is necessary that" and "it is possible that," and the embedded sentence in a modal claim is the sentence that follows the modal operator. So, for example, in the claim

> It is possible that Alward is a professor,

the modal operator is "it is possible that" and the embedded sentence is "Alward is a professor." The truth conditions for necessity claims—claims in which the modal operator is "it is necessary that"—are quite straightforward, on the modal reductionist view: a necessity claim is true just in case the embedded sentence is either analytic or a logical truth. Since, for example, the sentence

> All sisters are female siblings

is analytic, the necessity claim

> It is necessary that all sisters are female siblings

is true. And since the sentence

Alward is a professor

is neither a logical truth nor analytic, the modal claim

It is necessary that Alward is a professor

is false. The truth conditions of possibility claims—claims in which the modal operator is "it is possible that"—are a little more complicated. To develop them we need to introduce the notion of the negation of a sentence. The **negation** of a sentence can be formed by placing the word "not" in it or removing the word "not" from it. So, for example, the negation of

Alward is a professor

is

Alward is not a professor.

The truth conditions of possibility claims are as follows: a possibility claim is true just in case the negation of the embedded sentence is neither analytic nor a logical truth. Consider, for example, the possibility claim

It is possible that Alward is not a professor.

Since the negation of the embedded sentence—"Alward is a professor"—is neither a logical truth nor analytic, this claim is true. But consider now

It is possible that not all sisters are female siblings.

Since the negation of the embedded sentence—"all sisters are female siblings"—is analytic, then this possibility claim is false.

The reductionist approach to modal truth conditions is a tempting one because it allows modal claims to be true or false without having to invoke suspect modal facts. Nevertheless, it does run into certain difficulties. In particular, there are reasons for thinking that being analytic or a logical truth is neither necessary nor sufficient for being necessary and, hence, that an analysis of the truth conditions of modal claims in terms of such features will not do. First, consider, for example, the sentence

I am here now.

Although not strictly analytic or logically true, like sentences of those kinds its truth does not depend on the facts. After all, regardless of who says it—or where or when it is said—it is automatically true. Now suppose, for example, Mary utters this sentence in her apartment at noon. Since in her mouth "I" refers to Mary, "here" refers to Mary's apartment, and "now" refers to noon, what she says is true. But suppose that Mary makes the following claim as well:

> It is necessary that I am here now.

Since the truth of the embedded sentence is independent of the facts, modal reductionism seems to entail that Mary's claim is true. But as a matter of fact, this claim is false. After all, Mary could have been in the park and not her apartment at noon, and could have been in her apartment at 2 p.m. and not noon. Second, consider the sentence

> Water is H_2O.

This sentence is neither analytic nor a logical truth. As a result, modal reductionism entails that

> It is necessary that water is H_2O

is false. But although a substance superficially similar to water might have a different chemical composition, water itself—a liquid in fact composed of H_2O molecules—arguably could not have a different composition. After all, any liquid made up of different types of molecules simply would not be water. As a result, the claim

> It is necessary that water is H_2O

is true despite the fact that the embedded sentence is neither analytic nor a logical truth, contra modal reductionism. Finally, it is worth noting that some critics of modal reductionism have argued that the notion of analyticity is itself suspect and so cannot be used in an account of modal truth conditions. A discussion of this issue is, however, too technical for an introductory course in philosophy and so will not be addressed here.

6.3 Modal Realism and Possible Worlds

Modal realism is the view that modal claims have truth conditions and, moreover, these truth conditions involve irreducible modal facts—facts about necessities and possibilities. Although there are a number of accounts one might give of modal facts, the most prominent approach invokes the notion of **possible worlds**. The actual world is the shared universe we inhabit, including all past, present, and future objects and events. Non-actual possible worlds correspond to ways in which the actual world could have been. Some possible worlds differ only slightly from the actual world. Consider, for example, a world exactly like ours but in which I have one more hair on my head or am a millimetre taller. Other worlds involve more substantial deviations from actuality. Consider, for example, worlds in which Margaret Atwood is the current Canadian prime minister or in which the Toronto Maple Leafs are Stanley Cup champions. And, finally, there are worlds that are radically different from the world we in fact inhabit. These include worlds without gravity as well as worlds consisting entirely of a single object. It is worth emphasizing that insofar as one is a modal realist rather than a modal reductionist, one needs to take non-actual possible worlds to be just as real as the actual world, inhabited by concrete objects that are involved in genuine events. Nevertheless, objects in distinct possible worlds are causally and spatio-temporally isolated from one another. They do not exist in the same space or time and exert no causal influence over one another: what happens in one possible world has no impact on what happens in another.

The possible worlds approach to truth conditions for modal claims is quite straightforward. Consider, first, necessity claims. According to the possible worlds approach, a necessity claim is true if the embedded sentence is true in all possible worlds, and false otherwise. Since, for example, the sentence

> All sisters are female siblings

is true in all possible worlds—"sister" just means "female sibling," after all—the modal claim

> It is necessary that all sisters are female siblings

is true on this view. But the sentence

> Alward is a professor

is false in some possible worlds; since I could have been a plumber or a professional basketball player, there are possible worlds in which I have one of these occupations rather than being a professor. As a result, the necessity claim

> It is necessary that Alward is a professor

is false. Consider now possibility claims. According to the possible worlds approach, a possibility claim is true just in case the embedded sentence is true in at least one possible world. Since, for example, the sentence

> Alward is a plumber

is true in at least one possible world, the modal claim

> It is possible that Alward is a professor

is true. But since there is no possible world in which

>Two plus two equals five

is true, the possibility claim

>It is possible that two plus two equals five

is false.

The possible worlds approach also offers a simple and compelling account of the truth conditions of counterfactual conditionals. A presupposition of this account is that non-actual possible worlds can be ranked in terms of their degree of overall similarity to the actual world. So, for example, a world differing from actuality only in my having one more hair on my head is more similar to the actual world than any world in which the Toronto Maple Leafs are the current Stanley Cup champions, but a world in which the Leafs won the most recent Stanley Cup is more similar to the actual world than a world without gravity. Now as noted above, the antecedent of a counterfactual claim is actually false. And possible worlds in which the antecedent is true can differ in their degree of overall similarity to the actual world. According to the possible worlds approach, a counterfactual claim is true if a world in which the antecedent and the consequent are true is more similar to the actual world than any world in which the antecedent is true and the consequent is false. Consider, for example, the counterfactual claim

>If Margaret Atwood were the current Canadian prime minister, then funding the arts would be a budget priority.

Now we need to compare two sorts of possible worlds: worlds in which Atwood is prime minister and arts funding is a budget priority on the one hand, and worlds in which Atwood is prime minister and arts funding is not a budget priority. If the former worlds are more similar to how things actually are than the latter, then the counterfactual claim is true. But if the latter are more or equally similar to actuality than the former, then it is false. And insofar as a world in which Margaret Atwood has both different political ambitions and different attitudes toward the arts is less similar to actuality than a world in which she has different political ambitions but retains her actual attitudes toward the arts, the counterfactual is true, according to the possible worlds analysis.

There have been numerous objections raised against the modal realist account of the truth conditions of modal claims, a few of which will be considered here. First, one might object to the idea that non-actual possible worlds of the kind that modal realists invoke really exist. Not only is this idea just bizarre but one might also argue that it violates the methodological principle that simpler theories—theories that invoke fewer fundamental kinds of entities—are to be preferred. And second, insofar as non-actual possible worlds are spatio-temporally and causally isolated from the actual world, it is not clear how we could have any knowledge of them. If they stand in no spatial or temporal relations to our world and have no impact or influence upon it, then we are simply in no position to know whether such worlds exist or what they are like. Moreover, one might argue that since we do have knowledge of the truth or falsity of at least certain modal claims but lack knowledge of other possible worlds, non-actual possible worlds are not involved in the truth conditions of modal claims.

A third objection goes as follows: if non-actual possible worlds are real in exactly the same sense that the actual world is, then it is not clear how actual objects can exist in non-actual possible worlds. Insofar as my computer, for example, is a concrete object existing in the actual world, it is far from clear how it can literally be a concrete object existing in a distinct, non-actual possible world. But if actual objects do not exist in other worlds, it is not clear how the goings on in such worlds can be relevant to the truth conditions of modal claims about actual objects. If, for example, Danielle Steel exists only in the actual world, then there is no possible world in which she exists and won the 2012 US presidential election. As a result, even if there is a possible world in which someone similar to Steel won the 2012 US presidential election—or a presidential election in a country similar to the United States—it is not clear how this can establish the truth of the modal claim

It is possible that Danielle Steel won the 2012 US presidential election.

6.4 Events and Causation

Let us turn now to our discussion of causation. The question we want to address here is what it is for one thing to cause another, that is, why we say that turning on my coffeemaker causes coffee to appear in the pot, but not that the arrival of the recycling truck causes my alarm to go off, even though in both cases one event reliably precedes the other. This topic includes both particular causal claims, such as

The depression of the "t" button on my computer keyboard causes the appearance of the character "t" on my computer screen,

as well as general causal claims, such as

Smoking cigarettes causes cancer.

The first thing to note is that causation is a relation. Just as being greater than is a relation that holds between two numbers, causation is a relation between such things as the depression of keyboard buttons and the appearance of characters on computer screens, as well as smoking cigarettes and getting cancer. As a result, in order to understand causation, we need to determine what sorts of things stand in the causal relation and what has to be true of such things in order for them to be related causally to one another as opposed to standing in some other relation. We will consider each question in turn.

First, in order to understand a relation, one important thing to know is what the **causal relata** are: exactly what sorts of things are capable of standing in that relation to one another. So, for example, to understand the relation of being greater than, one needs to know that numbers are what stand in this relation and hence are the sorts of things capable of being greater than one another. The relata of the causal relation are not numbers but events. **Events** are things that happen, such as weddings and the depression of keyboard buttons. One way of viewing events is as consisting in changes in the properties of objects. So, for example, a depression of a computer button might consist in a change in its location. We can distinguish between particular events and event types or kinds. A particular event is something that happens at a specific time and place. An event type, in contrast, is something that can happen on multiple occasions, at different places and times. Weddings, for example, are a type or kind of event; the wedding of Prince William and Kate Middleton is a particular event. Although both particular events and event types or kinds can be the relata of the causal relation, causal relations between event types are arguably in some sense derivative. The general causal claim

> Smoking causes cancer,

for example, is true only in virtue of the cumulative causal impact of particular acts of smoking.

Second, although the nature of the causal relation will be the topic of the remainder of this chapter, there are a few general comments about it worth making at this juncture. The first thing to note is that the causal relation is not symmetric: if, for example, the depression of a button causes the appearance of a character, it is not true that the appearance of the character causes the depression of the button. More to the point, the relata of the causal relation fall into two categories: events that are causes and events that are effects. And when two events stand in a causal relation, the cause makes the effect occur, but not vice versa. The second thing to note is that events produce the effects that they do only in the right kinds of conditions. Striking a match, for example, will produce a flame only in the presence of oxygen. As a result, strictly speaking it is not a triggering event that produces a particular effect but rather the combination of the trigger and the circumstances in which it occurs. And the third thing to note is that the causal relation is a modal relation. In order for one event to cause another, it is not enough that the occurrence of one is succeeded by the occurrence of the other. What is required in addition is that the former makes the latter occur, that given the occurrence of the former, the latter in some sense must occur.

6.5 Skepticism and Regularities

The modal character of the causal relation has led some people to endorse a kind of **causal skepticism**: the view that no events ever cause or are caused by other events. After all, if one is a modal skeptic—denying there are any modal facts—then, insofar as causation requires modal facts, one must deny the existence of causation as well. Consider, for example, the following two events: a cue ball rolls across a pool table until it contacts the eight ball; the eight ball subsequently begins moving and rolls into the corner pocket. In order for the former event to have caused the latter, there must be some kind of modal connection between them: the fact that the cue ball made contact with it must have made it necessary that the eight ball began rolling toward the corner pocket. But, the skeptic argues, all we observe is the first event involving the cue ball and the second event involving the eight ball; we never observe any necessary connection between them. As a result, we have no empirical evidence that there is any kind of modal connection between them, including a causal connection. And in the absence of such evidence we ought not to believe that they are causally connected. All the evidence entitles us to believe is that the individual events occurred in the order and locations in which they were observed to occur.

The view that events never stand in causal relations to one another—that, for example, being contacted by the cue ball did not cause the eight ball to roll into the corner pocket—is quite counterintuitive. As a result, the causal skeptic owes us an explanation of our widespread erroneous tendency that various events cause one another. Although there are a number of ways in which the skeptic might do this, the most common approach is to appeal to regularities or patterns among types of events. Suppose, for example, that you have observed in the past that whenever a rolling cue ball makes contact with another pool ball, the latter ball itself begins to roll. As a result of these observations, you might come to expect any pool ball contacted in this way by a cue ball to begin moving. According to the causal skeptic, when you judge the cue ball to have caused the other ball to begin moving, what you have done is, in effect, confused this expectation of yours—a mere habit of the mind—with a genuine necessary connection between the observed events.

There are, of course, a number of reasons to be dissatisfied with causal skepticism. First, the claim that we cannot directly observe a modal connection between two events does not establish that there is no empirical evidence for such a connection. After all, we can have empirical evidence for fundamental particles of various kinds without directly observing them. Insofar as positing or hypothesizing the existence of such entities explains patterns of direct observations we in fact make, these observations count as empirical evidence of them. Similarly, if positing necessary connections between events explains patterns or correlations among them, then our observations of these patterns provides empirical evidence of such modal facts. Second, unless we suppose there are causal connections between events, then patterns among types of events have to be viewed as increasingly unlikely coincidences. If the pattern of contact by rolling cue balls being followed by movement on the part of the contacted ball is not explained by any kind of causal connection, then it is simply happenstance, akin to heads continually coming up in a series of fair coin tosses. And finally, not all of our causal judgements can be explained by past observations of regularities among types of events. After all, you might judge there to be a causal connection between events one has never encountered before. Suppose, for example, one encountered some alien technology for the first time and observed, first, an orange being zapped by it and, second, the orange subsequently changing into a tulip. One might naturally assume that the first event caused the second, despite never having encountered events of either kind before.

6.6 Causation and Laws

One prominent alternative to causal skepticism gives an account of the causal relation in terms of laws of nature. A **law of nature** describes a pattern or regularity among types of events. But laws differ from more commonplace regularities in at least two respects. First, they are supposed to be fundamental regularities as opposed to mere happenstance. They correspond to the basic principles governing the behaviour of things in our world or universe—everything that happens is the result of the laws of nature. And second, they are supposed to be necessary regularities. It is not simply a matter of fact that events do conform to the laws, but, more strongly, they in some sense must do so. If there were a law to the effect that all A-events are followed by B-events and an A-event occurs, it would not simply be true that a B-event will occur. It would rather be true that a B-event must occur, which of course ensures that it will.

Before providing an account of the causal relation in terms of laws, it is worth noting again that exactly what effects an event causes depends on the circumstances in which it occurs. For example, a match striking in the presence of oxygen will normally have very different consequences from one that occurs in the absence of oxygen. As a result, the laws at issue will have to be formulated in terms of regularities between event types under certain sorts of conditions, rather than simply in terms of event types alone. That is, they will have to take the following form:

> All A-events in conditions C are followed by B-events.

Now according to the law-based or **nomological** account of causation, in order for two events to stand in causal relation to one another, the statement that the cause occurred and statements describing the conditions under which it occurred and the laws of nature have to logically entail the statement that the effect occurred. Suppose, for example, that an event in which a match was struck was followed by an event in which a flame was produced. And suppose, moreover, that the event in which the match was struck occurred in the presence of oxygen and that the following is a law of nature:

> All match strikings in the presence of oxygen are followed by the production of flames.

Since this law, together with the statement that a match was struck and the statement that this event occurred in the presence of oxygen, jointly entails the statement that a flame-producing event occurred, the two events in question stand in causal relation.

One can be dissatisfied with the nomological account of causation for a number of reasons. First, this view seems to presuppose a deterministic picture of reality wherein everything that happens is wholly determined by what occurred previously. But quantum mechanics arguably shows that at least events involving microparticles are not determined. According to quantum mechanics, as we saw in the previous chapter, we cannot predict the behaviour of microscopic entities but rather can only calculate the likelihoods that they will behave in a range possible ways. Moreover, it seems that micro-events can stand in causal relation despite this lack of micro-determination. Suppose, for example, that the occurrence of one micro-event increased the likelihood that another micro-event of a certain type would occur. If a micro-event of this latter type then did occur, we might reasonably claim that it was caused by the prior micro-event. The nomological account of causation, however, requires deterministic causal laws in order for events to stand in causal relation, which in the case at issue are absent.

Second, even if the view is restricted to the causal relation between events involving macro-entities—tables and chairs and trees and rocks and the like—it is not clear that there are natural laws governing the event types into which causally related macro-events fall. Suppose, for example, that a loud noise causes a leaf to fall from a tree. According to the nomological account, this requires that there be a law to the effect that all noises of that kind, which occur under the right sorts of conditions, are followed by events in which leaves fall from trees. But it is far from clear that there is any regularity of this kind, let alone one that counts as a fundamental law of nature.

And third, the fact that the regularities that count as laws are necessary plays no role in the nomological account of causation. Whether or not a statement describing an effect is logically entailed by a statement describing a cause, a statement of conditions under which the cause occurred, and a regularity is independent of the necessity of the regularity. As a result, it is not entirely clear how fundamentally different the nomological account is from the causal skeptic's appeal to regularities.

6.7 Causation and Counterfactuals

A running theme of this chapter has been the necessity of the causal relation: in order for one event to cause another, the occurrence of the former must in some sense necessitate the occurrence of the latter. Although there is disagreement about the exact sense of necessity at issue here, there is broad agreement that minimally it requires that the causal relation entails the truth of certain counterfactual conditionals. In particular, in order for one event to cause another, it has to be true that had the cause not occurred, the effect would not have occurred. Consider again a case in which a rolling cue ball contacts an eight ball and the eight ball subsequently begins rolling itself. In order for the contact of the cue ball to have caused the subsequent rolling of the eight ball, the following counterfactual has to be true: if the cue ball had not contacted the eight ball, the eight ball would not have begun rolling.

Insofar as it is already granted that causation requires this kind of **counterfactual dependence** of the occurrence of the effect on the occurrence of the cause, a tempting approach is to identify the causal relation with counterfactual dependence. On this view, the counterfactual truth is not just an incidental fact about a given causal relationship; rather, the causal relationship just is the counterfactual truth. Suppose again that a rolling cue ball contacts an eight ball and the latter subsequently begins rolling itself. On the counterfactual analysis of causation, what it is for the former event to have caused the latter simply is for it to be true that, had the rolling cue ball not contacted the eight ball, the eight ball would not have begun rolling.

Now of course one might wonder about the truth conditions of such counterfactual conditionals, that is, how things have to be in order for them to be true. And although there are numerous accounts of counterfactuals, we will focus here on the possible worlds approach discussed above. Recall that on this view, a counterfactual claim is true if a world in which the antecedent and the consequent are true is more similar to the actual world than any world in which the antecedent is true and the consequent is false. As a result, the counterfactual account of causation and the possible worlds account of counterfactuals together yield the following: an event A caused an event B just in case a non-actual possible world in which neither A nor B occurs is more similar to the actual world than a world in which B occurs even though A does not. Consider one more time an event in which a rolling cue ball contacts an eight ball and the eight ball subsequently starts moving. On the view at issue, in order for the former event to cause the latter, a possible world in which the cue ball does not contact the eight ball and the eight ball does not begin to move has to be more similar to the actual world than a world in which the cue ball does not strike the eight ball but the eight ball begins to move anyhow. And since our world is not one in which unstruck pool balls spontaneously begin moving, the former world is in fact more similar. As a result, the counterfactual approach entails that these two events are causally related.

There are, however, a number of possible objections to the counterfactual account of causation. First, even if one concedes the existence of non-actual possible worlds, one might wonder what, if anything, the goings on in those worlds have to do with the relations between objects and events in this one. In particular, one might argue that the occurrence or non-occurrence of distinct events involving different objects in worlds that are spatio-temporally isolated from this one has nothing to do with whether or not events occurring here are causally related to one another, regardless of how similar they are to actual events and objects.

Second, the counterfactual account of causation runs afoul of the problem of causal overdetermination, which occurs when two distinct events independently produce the same effect. Suppose, for example, that someone is fed a lethal poison and at the moment the poison kills him he is simultaneously stabbed to death. According to the counterfactual account, however, neither the poisoning nor the stabbing causes the victim's death. This is because it is neither true that had the victim not been poisoned he would not have died nor true that had the victim not been stabbed he would not have died. After all, in the most similar world in which he is not stabbed, the poison kills him, and in the closest world in which he is not poisoned, the stabbing kills him.

And third, causation is an asymmetrical relation in the sense that if an event A causes another event B, then B does not itself cause A. But the counterfactual analysis seems to allow one event to both cause and be caused by another. All that is required is that a world in which neither event occurs is closer than any world in which just one or the other occurs. Consider one final time a case in which a rolling cue ball contacts an eight ball and the eight ball subsequently begins rolling. It is pretty clear that a world in which neither event occurs is more similar to actuality that either a world in which the cue ball does not contact the eight ball but the eight begins to move or a world in which the cue ball does contact the eight ball but it does not begin to move. As a result, it is true both that had the cue ball not contacted it, the eight ball would not have begun to roll, and that had the eight ball not begun to roll, the cue ball would not have struck it. As a result, on the counterfactual analysis both the contact by the cue ball caused the eight ball to roll and the rolling of the eight ball caused the contact by the cue ball.

In this chapter we have considered skeptical, reductionist, and realist accounts of both modality and causation. Talk of possible worlds has become increasingly common in discussions of both issues, but how possible worlds should be understood—and whether they exist at all—remain matters of ongoing discussion.

Reading Questions

1. What is the difference between extensional claims and modal claims?

2. What is a material conditional?

3. Explain one objection to modal skepticism.

4. What is the difference between modal realism and modal reductionism?

5. What is required for a possibility claim to be true on the possible worlds approach to modal truth conditions?

6. What is the difference between particular and general causal claims?

7. What is the significance of regularities among types of events, according to causal skepticism?

8. What is a law of nature?

9. What does it mean to say that one event is counterfactually dependent on another?

10. What is causal overdetermination?

Reflection Questions

1.   Think of a number of facts about yourself or things you have done that
     might have been different. Can you predict ways in which your life would
     have changed had they been different?

2.   Think of a number of events that you take yourself to have made happen.
     How do you think you made these things happen? What, if any, role do you
     attribute to laws of nature or people similar to you in other places?

Further Reading

Modal claims and modal truth conditions:
R. Bradley and N. Schwartz, *Possible Worlds: An Introduction to Logic and Its
     Philosophy* (Indianapolis: Hackett, 1979).

Possible worlds and modal realism:
David Lewis, *On the Plurality of Worlds* (Oxford: Blackwell, 1986).

The nature of events:
Jonathan Bennett, *Events and their Names* (Indianapolis: Hackett, 1988).

General introduction to causation:
Stephen Mumford and Rani Anjum, *Causation: A Very Short Introduction*
     (Oxford: Oxford UP, 2013).

Causal skepticism:
David Hume, *An Enquiry Concerning Human Understanding*, ed. Lorne
     Falkenstein (Peterborough, ON: Broadview P, 2011).

Nomological approaches to causation:
John Mackie, "Causes and Conditions," *American Philosophical Quarterly* 2.4
     (1965): 245–64.

Counterfactual analyses of causation:
David Lewis, "Causation," *Journal of Philosophy* 70 (1973): 556–67.

7

GOD AND RELIGION

Belief in the existence of a god or gods has historically been and remains very widespread. Moreover, such beings are often thought to play a significant role in both cosmology and morality—as creators of the universe and the source of moral rightness and wrongness. Nevertheless, both the existence of such entities and their ability to play such roles are controversial: not only are there grounds to doubt their existence but there is also reason to be skeptical that they can be responsible for either morality or the universe even if they do exist. Moreover, exactly what sorts of entities gods are supposed to be is itself a matter of controversy.

The central concern of this chapter is whether there is any good reason to believe that a god or gods exist. To that end, we will need to consider the nature of such beings and whether there are any good arguments for or against their existence. Moreover, we will have to consider whether, in the absence of evidence, the case can be made for belief.

CHAPTER CONTENTS:

- the nature of god or gods is discussed;
- the relation between gods and religion is considered;
- arguments for the existence of gods are evaluated;
- arguments against the existence of gods are evaluated; and
- the question of religious belief, in the absence of evidence, is addressed.

7.1 The Nature of God

Before attempting to establish whether or not a **god** exists, it is important to become clear on the nature of the being at issue. This is difficult, however, because many different conceptions of gods have been advocated. Moreover, these conceptions can differ not only over relatively superficial details—such as the particular features and activities attributed to a god—but also over the fundamental kind of entity a god is supposed to be. One basic question concerns whether a god needs to be in some sense intelligent or whether a non-intelligent force or principle could count as a god. Arguably, everything that exists is either intelligent or not, although there may be some borderline cases: included in the former category are human beings and at least certain non-human animals, such as chimpanzees and dolphins; included in the class of non-intelligent things are plants, most (if not all) human artifacts, planets, gravity, and so on. Many people would insist that a god has to fall in the former category, perhaps arguing that only an intelligent being is worthy of worship. But opponents of this view might rejoin that, for example, nature itself is worthy of worship despite lacking intelligence in any literal sense.

Even if we assume that a god must be intelligent, a number of distinctions can still be made among god-conceptions. First, according to **monotheistic** conceptions there is only a single god, whereas according to **polytheistic** conceptions there are multiple gods, often with distinct roles and falling within some kind of hierarchy. This distinction is sometimes difficult to draw in religious traditions with multiple god-names that can be understood either as names of distinct gods or as names of distinct incarnations of a single god.

Second, a distinction can be made between immanent and transcendent conceptions of gods. According to an **immanent** conception, gods share the physical world we inhabit and experience. In effect, on this view gods are physical beings just like us, only vastly superior in important respects, such as intelligence, power, virtue, and the like. According to a **transcendent** conception, gods transcend or stand outside the physical world we inhabit, rendering them not only non-physical but also fundamentally different sorts of beings from us, existing outside of space and time (or at least our space and our time). A god-conception might allow that some gods are immanent and others transcendent or even that a single god can have both immanent and transcendent incarnations.

Third, we can distinguish between god-conceptions that are **anthropomorphic** and those that are not. To say that a conception is anthropomorphic is to say that it takes gods to be similar to human beings in important respects. Although there are a number of respects in which a god might be similar to us, the view that will concern us here is that gods are psychologically like us, having minds that function as our minds do and being intelligent in the same sense we are, only more so. **Anti-anthropomorphic** conceptions deny that gods are similar to humans, psychologically or otherwise. One might, of course, wonder how a god could be both psychologically unlike us but nevertheless literally intelligent. To worries of this kind, advocates of this conception sometimes claim that the nature of gods is mysterious.

Case Study 7.1: Angels

Christianity is often viewed as a paradigmatic example of a monotheistic religion. But according to some versions of Christianity, in addition to God the creator there also literally exist a number of other superior intelligent beings. These include both angels—servants of God—and Satan—a fallen angel acting in opposition to God's will.

QUESTION: Does this version of Christianity count as a kind of monotheism or polytheism?

Case Study 7.2: Intelligent Aliens

Suppose that in our universe there is a species of highly intelligent aliens. And suppose that rather than being created by some kind of transcendent being, the human species was instead created by alien scientists.

QUESTION: Would such aliens count as gods? What difference would it make if they themselves were created by another even more intelligent species of aliens?

In addition to distinguishing between god-conceptions in terms of the features they take gods to have, we might also distinguish between them in terms of the activities they take gods to engage in and, in particular, the kinds of interventions they make in our immanent physical world. At one extreme, there might be an entirely **non-interventionist** god-conception—a conception of gods who neither created our world nor pay any attention to it whatsoever. At the other extreme would be a highly **interventionist** god-conception—a conception of gods who created the world, pay close attention to the goings on herein, listen to entreaties of various kinds from their devotees, and constantly act to cause physical happenings of various kinds. Intermediate cases include conceptions of gods who created the world but have subsequently ignored it, gods who watch and listen without acting, and gods who act only to cause people to have religious experiences of various kinds.

As a result of the wide variety of god-conceptions, it does not make sense to attempt to establish the existence or non-existence of a god or gods; rather, it only makes sense to attempt to prove or disprove the existence of entities corresponding to a certain god-conception. For present purposes, we are going to focus on a particular god-conception: **Omni-God**. According to this conception, there is a single god characterized by the presence of three central characteristics: omnipotence, omniscience, and omni-benevolence. To be **omnipotent** is to have as much power as it is possible to have: an omnipotent being can do anything that is possible. To be omniscient is to have as much knowledge as it is possible to have: an **omniscient** being knows everything that can be known. And to be omni-benevolent is to have as much moral goodness as it is possible to have: an **omni-benevolent** being is as morally good as it is possible to be. In addition to having these features, Omni-God is supposed to have intervened in the word in one central way: by creating the world. The central focus of the remainder of this chapter is whether there are good grounds for believing in the existence or non-existence of Omni-God. It is worth emphasizing, however, that at least some of the arguments considered below apply to other god-conceptions as well.

7.2 God and Religion

Before considering arguments for and against the existence of Omni-God, it is worth pausing for a moment to consider the general relation between gods and religion. The first thing we need to get clear on is exactly what we mean by religion. Although there are a wide variety of religions—and a corresponding variety of definitions of this phenomenon—they share a number of typical or characteristic features. At its core, a **religion** consists of a system of beliefs and practices shared by the members of a community. The beliefs in question together form a comprehensive worldview, often including an account of the origins of the universe, an account of the basis and requirements of morality, and guidelines for leading a meaningful life. At the core of the belief system is usually some divine or sacred element, which may but need not be some kind of god or gods. The practices in question—which can range from communal rituals to private meditation and prayer—are often designed to get practitioners to lead what count as moral and meaningful lives according to the corresponding belief system, as well as to develop a significant relationship to the divine element. Finally, although their may be evidence offered in favour of some aspects of the belief system, evidence is typically not the basis of belief for most practitioners.

Now there are three basic attitudes one can have toward a god or gods: theism, atheism, and agnosticism. A **theist** is someone who believes in the existence of the gods in question. An **atheist** is someone who disbelieves in the existence of these gods or, equivalently, believes that they do not exist. An **agnostic** is someone who neither believes nor disbelieves in their existence, someone who having considered the question of their existence remains in a state of uncertainty. It is worth emphasizing that almost everyone has an atheistical attitude toward some god-conceptions: only the most inclusive believer would endorse the existence of gods corresponding to every god-conception. For terminological convenience, however, we will take an atheist to be someone who disbelieves in the existence of gods however they are conceived, and a theist to be someone who believes in the existence of the gods of at least one god-conception. Since someone could believe in the existence of the gods of one god-conception and be uncertain about the existence of gods of another conception, we will reserve the term "agnostic" for those who are uncertain about the existence of Omni-God.

The question to be addressed in the remainder of this section is whether all and only theists must be religious practitioners, or whether there can be religious atheists and non-religious theists. Consider, first, the possibility of a religious atheist. There seem to be at least three different ways in which this could occur. One way is by being a member of a religious community in which the divine element is not a god. A religious group might, for example, worship nature without attributing any kind of intelligence to it. Another way of being a religious atheist would be through membership in a religious community in which the divine element is a kind of god, sharing the religious beliefs of the community, but understanding all references to gods metaphorically rather than literally. Finally, one might be religious atheist by means of engaging in the religious practices without sharing the religious beliefs of a community of which one is a member.

Consider, second, the possibility of a non-religious theist. There seem to be at least two ways in which this could occur. One way is by believing in the existence of a god that does not serve as the divine element in any existing religion. One might, for example, believe that our world was created by a god that no one worships, perhaps an incompetent god who is not only ashamed of its creation but is also derided by his fellow gods for it. Another way of being a religious atheist is by believing in the existence of a god that is the divine element of a particular religion without being a member of the religious community in question or engaging in their religious practices. The upshot of this discussion is that questions concerning gods and religions are distinct and independent, and inferences between them are tendentious. In particular, one could not conclude that a disproof of the existence of a god worshiped in a given religion would compel its practitioners to abandon it, nor that a proof of the existence of a god worshiped in a particular religion would compel others to adopt it.

7.3 Arguments for Omni-God

Numerous arguments have been proposed for the existence of Omni-God, three of which will be considered here: the cosmological argument, the ontological argument, and the design argument.

COSMOLOGICAL ARGUMENT

Although there are a number of variants of the **cosmological argument**, the basic version can be reconstructed as follows:

PREMISE 1: Every contingent being has a cause.
PREMISE 2: There cannot be—or there is something explanatorily unsatisfactory about—an infinite series of causes.
PREMISE 3: If every contingent being has a cause, then, unless there is a first cause that exists necessarily, there will be an infinite series of causes.
CONCLUSION: There must exist a first cause that exists necessarily, namely Omni-God.

A **contingent** being is an entity that exists but might not have existed: had things been appropriately different, it would not have existed. Most familiar objects—tables, trees, planets, humans, and so on—are contingent in this sense. Since it is true of such things that they might not have existed, the question arises concerning exactly why they do exist. And this question is answered by appeal to what caused them to exist. Now if the cause is itself a contingent entity and, hence, might not have existed, the question of why it in fact exists arises as well. Moreover, without an explanation of why its cause exists, the explanation of why the original being exists is rendered unsatisfactory: if my existence is explained by my being caused by my parents, but if there is no explanation of the existence of my parents, then the question of why I exist ultimately remains unanswered. Now one might argue that as long as the cause of an entity itself has a cause, and the cause of the cause has a cause, and so on—that is, as long as we have a chain of causes extending endlessly back in time—we have a satisfactory explanation of the entity with which we were originally concerned.

There are two reasons, however, that one might be dissatisfied at this point. First, one might think that there is something incoherent or unintelligible about a chain of causes stretching infinitely backwards in time. And second, even if the notion of an infinite causal chain is coherent, one might argue that it provides an unsatisfactory explanation of the existence of the entity under consideration. After all, since the causal chain itself is contingent—and a distinct chain of events might have occurred instead—it is also in need of explanation. And in lieu of such an explanation, there is no ultimate explanation of the existence of any given contingent entity. The only alternative appears to be a **necessarily existing entity**—whose existence is therefore not in need of explanation—who initiated the causal chains of events that culminated in the existence of the things that currently exist.

There are, however, a number of reasons to be dissatisfied with the cosmological argument. First, there are grounds for thinking that the argument for the conclusion that there is a necessary existing first cause is unsound. One might, for example, deny Premise 1 and claim instead that there can be uncaused contingent events. If this is right, then even if there is something suspect about an infinite series of causes, the first cause need not be necessary. One might instead deny Premise 2 and claim that the existence of a particular causal chain is simply a brute fact for which there can be no explanation. At a certain point in our explanations of things we inevitably hit bedrock—basic facts about how things are—and at that point no further elucidation is possible. And, the objection continues, the existence of one causal chain rather than another just is one kind of explanatory bedrock. Alternatively, one might concede that the occurrence of one causal chain rather than another is in need of explanation but might claim that as long as each event in the chain is explained by a prior event, the whole chain itself is explained. As a result, the occurrence of a chain of causes extending endlessly back in time is automatically explained by the fact that each event in the chain is explained by a prior event. And second, there are grounds for thinking that a necessary existing first cause need not be a god at all, let alone Omni-God. In order to count as a god, minimally a being needs to count as intelligent; but there is no reason that something needs to be intelligent to be a cause, even a necessarily existing first cause. Moreover, even granting that a necessary first cause is a god, there is no reason to identify it with Omni-God. After all, not only is Omni-God arguably contingent—even if such a being actually exists, it might not have—there seems to be no reason to think that it could not have been caused itself. And if it was caused, then it cannot be the first cause.

ONTOLOGICAL ARGUMENT

Let us turn now to the **ontological argument** for the existence of Omni-God. Although there are a number of variants of the ontological argument, a typical version is as follows:

PREMISE 1: The idea of Omni-God is the idea of the greatest conceivable being.

PREMISE 2: It is better to exist in reality than to exist merely as an idea.

PREMISE 3: If Omni-God exists merely as an idea, then a being greater than Omni-God can be conceived—an omnipotent, omniscient, omni-benevolent being that exists in reality.

PREMISE 4: It is contradictory to suppose that one can conceive of a being greater than the greatest conceivable being.

CONCLUSION: Omni-God exists in reality.

The overall strategy of the ontological argument is to argue from the nature of our idea of Omni-God to the existence of this being. Now of course it is true that we have lots of ideas of things that do not exist. Consider, for example, our widely shared ideas of Santa Claus and the Easter Bunny. What is unique about the idea of Omni-God, however, is that it is the idea of the greatest conceivable being. To conceive of this being is to conceive of something that is perfect. As a result, it is impossible to conceive of anything better. A key move in the argument is the thesis that existing in reality is better than existing merely as an idea. Consider, for example, a fancy sports car or other desirable item. Now compare circumstances in which one simply has the idea of the sports car with circumstances in which one has the car itself—or equivalently, circumstances in which the car exists merely as an idea and circumstances in which it exists in reality. The latter circumstances are pretty clearly preferable to the former. Finally, since the idea of Omni-God is the idea of the greatest conceivable being—and existence in reality is better than existence as a mere idea—the idea of Omni-God existing merely as an idea is incoherent. Hence, Omni-God must exist in reality.

A number of objections might be raised against the ontological argument. First, the whole strategy of arguing from the idea of Omni-God to the existence of Omni-God seems suspicious. In general, what we can conceive of does not determine what exists. And even given the unique nature of our idea of Omni-God, our ability to conceive of such a being does not seem to give any grounds to suppose it exists. Second, one might balk at the generality of Premise 2: that it is better to exist in reality than to exist merely as an idea. In at least some cases, existence merely as an idea is preferable to existence in reality. For example, it would be better if chemical or biological weapons existed merely as an idea than really existing, as they in fact do. And third, one might argue that the claim that the idea of a non-existent perfect being is incoherent is also suspect because existence is not a property. One way of casting this point is to argue that we cannot distinguish between the idea of an existent perfect being and the idea of a non-existent perfect being. Rather, there is just one idea or concept, and one might either believe or disbelieve in the existence of the entity that it is an idea of. Alternatively, one might argue that although it may be true that it would be better if Omni-God existed in reality than merely as an idea, it does not follow from this that there is a distinct idea of an existent Omni-God over and above the idea of an omnipotent, omniscient, omni-benevolent being. Either way, what we are left with is just a single coherent idea.

DESIGN ARGUMENT

The final argument for the existence of Omni-God we will consider here is the **design argument,** which can be reconstructed as follows:

> PREMISE 1: The universe and its natural contents are similar to human artifacts.
> PREMISE 2: Human artifacts are designed and created by intelligent beings, in particular, human beings.
> PREMISE 3: Similar effects have similar causes or origins.
> CONCLUSION: The universe and its natural contents were designed and created by an intelligent being, in particular Omni-God.

The design argument is, fundamentally, an argument by **analogy.** As such, it proceeds by noting similarities between the universe as a whole and human artifacts—objects designed and created by human beings—and on that basis concluding that certain features of artifacts are possessed by the universe as well. The relevant respect of similarity at issue are the features of artifacts that are the product of intelligent design—in particular, being made up of constituents that are put together in just the right way so as to enable them to fulfill certain functions or purposes. A computer, for example, consists of a number of parts that are put together in just the right way to serve the purpose of creating and editing academic essays, as well as surfing the Internet, for example. If the same parts were put together differently, or different parts were used instead, the resulting object would not serve these purposes. In addition, the universe and its natural contents consist of similarly ordered parts. If, for example, the parts of the human body were put together differently, we would not be able to do the things we do, or even survive at all.

In order to conclude that the universe is the product of intelligent design, the design argument relies on the **principle of sufficient reason:** that is, similar effects have similar causes. Suppose, for example, that I produce a soup with an unpleasant flavour and that last week I produced a stew with that same flavour, which could be traced to my use of old bouillon cubes. The principle of sufficient reason would allow me to conclude that the unpleasant flavour of my current soup is also due to my use of old bouillon cubes. The upshot is that the similarity between the universe and human artifacts—together with the fact that the latter are the products of intelligent design—allows us to conclude that the universe and its natural contents are also the product of an intelligent designer, in particular Omni-God. Finally, it is worth noting that unlike the other arguments for the existence of Omni-God that we have considered, the design argument is an inductive argument: the premises are intended not to guarantee the truth of the conclusion but rather only to establish its likelihood.

Someone might object to the design argument for several reasons. First, one might note that the strength of an argument by analogy—how likely it makes the conclusion—is a function of the degree of similarity between the objects under consideration. But given the minimal similarity and the vast dissimilarity between the universe and human artifacts, the design argument at best renders the intelligent origins of the former only marginally likely. Moreover, insofar as the universe is more similar to something other than human artifacts—animals or vegetables for example—with different sorts of origins, this style of argument renders other hypotheses about the origins of the universe—sexual reproduction, for example—more likely than intelligent design. Second, one might balk at the degree of generality of the principle of sufficient reason. Although it is certainly true that in some cases similar effects have similar causes, it is often the case that similar effects can have different causes. Consider, for example, the number of distinct underlying medical conditions that might produce the same symptoms. And the lower degree of generality of the principle of sufficient reason, the less likely the design argument renders the conclusion. Finally, one might argue that even if the design argument does establish that the universe has intelligent origins, it does not establish that it was created by Omni-God. Although some human artifacts are designed and created by a single person, in many cases not only are the creator and the designer different but it is also often a team of people, rather than a single person, that designs or creates a given artifact. As a result, the design argument gives at least as much support to the thesis that the universe was designed and created by a team of lesser gods, or designed by one god and created by another, as it does for the hypothesis that it was both designed and created by a single all-powerful deity. Moreover, given the flaws in our universe—famine, disease, earthquakes, meteor strikes, and so forth—the hypothesis that it was created by a flawed god of some kind seems more likely, given the evidence, than the hypothesis that it was created by a perfect being.

7.4 Arguments against Omni-God

In addition to arguments for the existence of Omni-God, there have been numerous arguments offered against the existence of some such being, two of which will be considered here: the argument from simplicity, and the argument from evil.

ARGUMENT FROM SIMPLICITY

The argument from simplicity can be formulated as follows:

PREMISE 1: If two theories have the same explanatory power, the simpler theory ought to be endorsed.

PREMISE 2: A theory that includes all of the physical things in the universe,
   but not Omni-God, is simpler than a theory that includes Omni-God in
   addition to all of the physical things in the universe.
PREMISE 3: A theory that includes Omni-God is no more explanatorily powerful than a theory that does not.
CONCLUSION: A theory that includes Omni-God ought not to be endorsed.

The basic idea is that we ought to believe in the existence of Omni-God only if this
entity plays an essential role in the theory that offers the best explanation of the
world of our experience. Although there are a number of bases on which one might
assess theories as better or worse than one another, one important basis is that of
simplicity. Of course, a simple theory that does not explain anything is worse than
a more complex theory that is capable of explaining a variety of phenomena. As a
result, the role of **simplicity** ought to be understood as a tie-breaker between otherwise equally good theories: only if two competing theories provide equally good
explanations of the phenomena they are designed to illuminate should simplicity
be invoked as a basis for preferring one over the other. And the reason the simpler
theory should be preferred is that the extra complexity in its competitor is not
doing any explanatory work; it is simply an unnecessary add-on.

Now a theory that includes all of the physical things in the universe and Omni-
God is more complex than a theory that includes all such physical things but omits
Omni-God. After all, not only does it include a higher total number of entities but
it also includes an entity of fundamentally different kind than the physical entities
that both theories share. The question is whether this extra complexity brings with
it any extra **explanatory power**, that is, whether the more complex theory explains
phenomena that the simpler theory cannot. And the advocate of the argument from
simplicity claims that it does not. As science progresses, we are increasingly confident—and rightly so—that every thing that happens in the experienced world can
be given a purely physical explanation. As a result, a theory that invokes Omni-
God is more complex but no more explanatorily powerful than one that does not,
so only the latter should be endorsed. Finally, it is worth noting that the argument
from simplicity is not designed to prove the non-existence of Omni-God; rather, it
is designed to show that there is no evidence for the existence of this being. Hence,
insofar as one ought to believe in the existence only of those things for which one
has adequate evidence, one ought not to believe in the existence of Omni-God.

There are, however, a couple of reasons to be dissatisfied with the argument
from simplicity. First, one might deny Premise 3 and argue that there are certain
phenomena that cannot be adequately explained by appeal to physical things alone
and that, moreover, can be explained by appeal to a non-physical entity like Omni-
God. One might, for example, argue that the occurrence of miracles and various
sorts of religious experiences resists explanation in physical terms alone but can be
explained by appeal to Omni-God. Second, one might argue that there are various
phenomena that scientific investigation has not yet provided an explanation for. As
it remains an open question whether a satisfactory explanation of such phenomena
in purely physical terms will ever be generated, it also remains an open question

whether appeal to Omni-God will be required to explain them. And third, one might argue against the very principle that simpler theories are preferable. After all, this principle seems to assume that reality is simple rather than complex, but it is not clear what the basis of this assumption might be. And the fact that we prefer simpler theories does not establish that they are more likely to accurately represent reality.

ARGUMENT FROM EVIL

The second argument against the existence of Omni-God we will consider here is the argument from evil:

> PREMISE 1: There is evil in the world.
> PREMISE 2: The only world that Omni-God would create is a world without evil.
> CONCLUSION: Omni-God did not create the world.

The argument takes as its starting point the existence of evils in the world. By evils are meant things that cause misery and suffering, such as famine, war, and disease. The central claim of the argument is that the existence of evil is incompatible with the creation of the world by Omni-God: any world that such a being would create would be a world without evil. This conclusion is supposed to follow from the characteristic features of Omni-God: omnipotence, omniscience, and omni-benevolence. In the background is the following principle governing the behaviour of intelligent beings: an intelligent being will try to do what she believes will achieve what she most wants. So, for example, if a soccer player desires to personally score the winning goal and believes the best way to do so is to dribble the ball through all the opposing defenders without passing, then that is exactly what he will try to do. However, not only might his desire be self-centered but he might also be wrong that the best way to achieve this goal is to do it all by himself, and he might simply be unable to dribble through all the opposing defenders. But consider now Omni-God. Since this being is omni-benevolent—as good as it is possible to be—it will desire a world without any evil in it. Moreover, since this being is omniscient—knowing everything it is possible to know—it will know how to create a world without evil. Finally, since this being is omnipotent—as powerful as it is possible to be—it will be able to create a world without any evil in it. The upshot is that since, like any intelligent being, Omni-God will try to do what it believes will achieve what it most wants, the only world it would produce is a world without evil. But since our world contains evil, Omi-God would not have created it. It is worth noting again that, strictly speaking, the argument from evil is not designed to establish that Omni-God does not exist but rather only that it did not create the world. Moreover, in order to reconcile creation of the world by some kind of god with the existence of evil, one only needs to suppose that this being lacks one of the omni-properties. For example, an omniscient, omni-benevolent, but not omnipotent god might create a world with evil in it; after all, the existence of evil is compatible with creation by a being that desires a world without evil, knows how to create some such world, but lacks the ability to do so.

There are a number of responses that one might give to the argument from evil. First, one might argue that ours is the best possible world despite the existence of evil within it. The idea is that there cannot be a world with goodness in it without the presence of a certain amount of evil as well. This could be because the appreciation of good things—things that cause pleasure and happiness—requires the experience of suffering and misery as a contrast, or because creating a world requires balancing competing factors, some of which are good and others evil. In any event, as long as our world consists of the best possible balance of good over evil, it could have been created by Omni-God despite the presence of some evil. And second, one might argue that the evil in the world was not placed there by Omni-God but rather is the product of human free will. Rather than creating only entities whose behaviour is governed by the laws of nature, Omni-God also created beings with free will, namely us. And although we could act in such a way so as to avoid causing evil—and Omni-God desires that we do so—sometimes we choose to act otherwise. As a result, we, rather than Omni-God, are responsible for the evil in the world.

> ### Case Study 7.3: Omni-Satan
>
> Omni-Satan is an entity that, like Omni-God, is both omnipotent and omniscient. But rather than being omni-benevolent, Omni-Satan is instead omni-malevolent—as morally bad as it is possible to be.
>
> **QUESTION**: Does the existence of goodness show that the world could not have been created by Omni-Satan?

7.5 Belief without Evidence

To this point, we have been considering whether there is good evidence for the existence of Omni-God. A common view is that one ought to believe in the existence of Omni-God—or more generally, to believe anything at all—only if you have sufficient evidence that what you believe is true. And if this is right, whether you believe in the existence of Omni-God should depend on your assessment of the adequacy of the arguments we have just considered and, perhaps, other arguments for or against this entity's existence. This common view can, however, be challenged. Someone might, for example, argue that one ought to believe in the existence of Omni-God because one finds it personally comforting even in the absence of adequate evidence for this belief. We might call this a **pragmatic basis of belief** in contrast to the **evidentiary basis** presupposed by the common view.

Now insofar as one insists that our beliefs ought to have an evidentiary basis, it is reasonable to have a belief only to the extent that one has evidence for it. As a result, on this view it is unreasonable to believe something for which one has no evidence; so whether one ought to believe in Omni-God is wholly a matter of the evidence for or against this being's existence. But if we allow that our beliefs may have a pragmatic basis, then it can be reasonable to believe in the existence of Omni-God in the absence of evidence. The measure of the reasonability of beliefs in the absence of evidence is the extent to which it makes the subject better off or enables her to further her goals. Belief in the sanctity of the rules of golf, for example, might further the interests of someone whose goal is to be on the golfing rules committee, whereas the belief that one is invulnerable to car accidents might frustrate the interests of someone who desires longevity. At first glance, this seems to suggest that whether belief in Omni-God is reasonable in this sense will vary from subject to subject, depending on what the consequences of this belief are for a given subject and what her goals are. If, for example, someone values maintaining her relationships with her atheist friends and believing in the existence of Omni-God would cause her to engage in behaviour that would undermine these relationships, then this belief would not be reasonable in her case. But if someone values a sense of meaningfulness, and belief in Omni-God provides this sense, then her belief would be reasonable.

There is, however, an argument—**Pascal's Wager**—that is designed to show that belief in the existence of Omni-God is reasonable for everyone and that disbelief is unreasonable. In order to understand this argument, one needs to introduce the notion of expected utility. The expected utility of something is a measure of the average value of its consequences. It is calculated by taking the sum of the value of each possible consequence of that thing multiplied by the likelihood of its occurrence. Suppose, for example, that if a coin toss comes up heads, I receive $10, and if it comes up tails, I receive $4. Assuming it is a fair coin—that is, there is a 50-per-cent chance it will come up heads and a 50-per-cent chance it will come up tails—then the expected utility of the coin toss can be calculated as follows:

$$(\$10 \times \tfrac{1}{2}) + (\$4 \times \tfrac{1}{2}) = \$7$$

If, however, it is a two-headed coin—and hence there is a 100-per-cent chance it will come up heads—then the expected utility of the coin toss is $10 rather than $7. A central presupposition of Pascal's Wager is that in any choice situation the reasonable thing to do is to act on whichever option has the highest expected utility. And the strategy of the argument is to show that belief in the existence of Omni-God has a higher expected utility than disbelief. In order to establish this, a central assumption of the argument needs to be that if Omni-God exists, a subject will be rewarded for believing in him and punished for disbelieving in him. Now the expected utility of belief in Omni-God is determined by adding together the value of this belief in circumstances in which Omni-God exists multiplied by the likelihood that it exists and the value of belief in circumstances in which Omni-God does not exist multiplied by the likelihood that it does not exist. Similarly, the expected utility of disbelief in Omni-God is the sum of the value of disbelief in circumstances in which Omni-God exists multiplied by the likelihood that it exists and the value of disbelief in circumstances in which Omni-God does not exist multiplied by the likelihood that it does not exist. We can represent this as follows:

Expected Utility of Belief:
[Value (Belief & existence) x likelihood (existence)] + [Value (Belief + non-existence) x Likelihood (non-existence)]

Expected Utility of Disbelief:
[Value (Disbelief & existence) x likelihood (existence)] + [Value (Disbelief + non-existence) x Likelihood (non-existence)]

Although we may not know the likelihood that Omni-God exists, as long as it is greater than 0 and the reward for belief in the existence of Omni-God is infinitely good, or the punishment for disbelief is infinitely bad, or both, then we can know that the expected utility of belief will always be higher than that of disbelief. After all, the product of infinity and any non-zero number will always be itself infinite. Suppose, for example, that the likelihood that Omni-God exists is 1 per cent and the likelihood of non-existence is 99 per cent. And suppose that the following chart reflects the amount of happiness one would have under various possible circumstances:

	Belief in Omni-God	Disbelief in Omni-God
Omni-God exists	∞ units of happiness	0 units of happiness
Omni-God doesn't exist	500 units of happiness	1000 units of happiness

In this case, the expected utility of belief in the existence of Omni-God would be

(∞ units of happiness x .01) + (500 units of happiness x .99) = ∞ units of happiness

and the expected utility of disbelief would be

(0 units of happiness x .01) + (1000 units of happiness x .99) = 990 units of happiness.

So even if the likelihood of the existence of Omni-God is extremely small, the expected utility of belief in its existence is infinite. Hence, we all have pragmatic reasons to believe in the existence of Omni-God.

There are many reasons to be dissatisfied with Pascal's Wager. First, one might reject the presupposition that the expected utility of a course of action always determines whether it is reasonable. In particular, it might be argued that a very unlikely possibility ought to be ignored in determining what course of action is reasonable, especially when the value of the consequences of that possibility is significantly out of line with the alternatives. As a result, if the existence of Omni-God is very unlikely, this possibility ought to play no role in determining whether belief in its existence is reasonable. Second, the presupposition that Omni-God rewards belief and punishes disbelief can be contested. After all, there is no more reason to suppose this than that Omni-God rewards disbelief and punishes belief. And if this is true, then disbelief in the existence of Omni-God has a higher expected utility than belief. And third, even if one accepts that belief in the existence of Omni-God is reasonable and that disbelief is unreasonable, attempting to acquire this belief may prove futile. Many people, especially those inclined toward atheism, may simply find it impossible to acquire this belief.

Finally, we might consider whether it is reasonable to believe in the existence of Omni-God, not because one has adequate evidence or because it furthers one's interest but rather on the basis of faith alone. In order to assess the reasonability of faith, we need to get clearer on exactly what it consists in. One might define faith purely negatively as belief whose basis is neither evidence nor self-interest or, perhaps more strongly, as belief without any basis whatsoever. But not only would this definition be too broad—including thoughts that just pop into your head—but there is also little reason to suppose that it would be generally reasonable to have such beliefs. If, for example, I believe in the existence of Bigfoot without having any evidence and despite the negative impact of this belief on my interests, then not only does my belief count as faith according to this definition but it is also unclear how it can be reasonable if it does not have any other basis. Alternatively, one might define faith positively in terms of hope, perhaps taking a belief to be based on faith if one believes it, not because of evidence or self-interest but rather because one hopes it is true. So, for example, if I believe that human beings are ultimately morally good because this is something I hope for, the basis of my belief is faith according to this definition. Moreover, one might take a faith-based belief to be reasonable, on this view, just in case what you believe is something worth hoping for. Hence, since human goodness is worth hoping for, faith in human goodness is reasonable. As it stands, however, even this positive account of faith-based belief runs into some difficulties. First, someone might simply reject the account of reasonability on offer here, claiming instead that there are plenty of things worth hoping for that are unreasonable to believe in. And second, even if one concedes that it is reasonable to have faith in what is worth hoping for, one might argue that the existence of Omni-God is not something worth hoping for.

In this chapter we have considered a variety of arguments for and against the existence of Omni-God, as well as whether belief in the existence of this entity needs to be based on evidence. Many of these arguments have been under discussion for hundreds of years, and disagreement remains as to whether they suffice to establish their conclusions.

Reading Questions

1. What is the difference between an immanent and a transcendent god-conception?

2. What does it mean for a god to be omniscient?

3. What is the difference between an atheist and an agnostic?

4.   What is the difference between a contingent and a necessary being or entity?

5.   What does it mean to exist as an idea? How does this differ from existing in reality?

6.   What is the principle of sufficient reason?

7.   What does it mean to say that one theory is simpler than another?

8.   What does it mean to say that ours is the best possible world?

9.   What is the difference between a pragmatic and an evidentiary basis of belief?

10.   What does it mean to define faith negatively?

Reflection Questions

1.   Think of a number of manufactured items that you think of as useful, nifty, or cool. What if any conclusions can you draw from such features of these items regarding the people who designed or built them?

2.   Think of a number of beliefs and opinions you hold. How did you come to have those opinions? Do you have good reasons for continuing to have them?

Further Reading

General introduction to issues in the philosophy of religion:
Andrew Bailey and Robert Martin, eds., *First Philosophy II: God, Mind, and Freedom*, 2nd ed. (Peterborough, ON: Broadview P, 2011).
M. Peterson, W. Hasker, B. Reichenbach, and David Basinger, *Reason and Religious Belief: An Introduction to the Philosophy of Religion*, 5th ed. (Oxford: Oxford UP, 2013).

The nature of God:
Edward Wierenga, *The Nature of God: An Inquiry into Divine Attributes* (Ithaca, NY: Cornell UP, 1989).

The cosmological argument:
William Lane Craig, *The Cosmological Argument from Plato to Leibniz* (Eugene, OR: Wipf and Stock, 2001).

The ontological argument:
Graham Oppy, *Ontological Arguments and Belief in God* (Cambridge: Cambridge UP, 1995).

The design argument and the problem of evil:
David Hume, *Dialogues Concerning Natural Religion*, 2nd ed. (Indianapolis: Hackett Classics, 1998).

Pascal's Wager:
Jeff Jordan, *Pascal's Wager: Pragmatic Arguments and Belief in God* (Oxford: Clarendon P, 2006).

8

TRUTH AND FICTION

Truth is one of our most familiar—and, at the same time, most puzzling—concepts. Even though our ordinary conversation is rife with truth talk, and truth is often held to be a fundamental goal of our shared intellectual endeavours, it remains unclear exactly what truth is or whether there even is such a thing. Fiction is often thought to be the opposite of truth, perhaps consisting of intentional falsehoods or even lies. However, not only do certain fictions consist largely of truths but also relatively few fictions are in any sense deceptive.

The central concern of this chapter is the nature of truth and its relation to fiction. Insofar as truth is a property, we will have to determine what the bearers of this property are, as well as determine what conditions have to be satisfied in order for something to bear this property. Moreover, we will have to delineate the differences between fictional talk and talk that consists of truth claims.

CHAPTER CONTENTS:

- the bearers of the property of truth are introduced;
- the correspondence theory of truth is developed;
- alternative theories of truth are considered;
- the nature of fictionality is explored;
- the puzzle of fictional names is investigated; and
- the question of fictional truth is addressed.

8.1 Truth Bearers

In order to determine the nature of truth, the first question that needs to be addressed is what kind of thing it is or, as philosophers like to put it, into what ontological category it falls. Sometimes people speak as if truth is some kind of object or entity that it is the goal of intellectual inquiries of various kinds to discover. So, for example, one might say,

> I want to find the truth,

and understand "the truth" to literally refer to an entity one hopes to (literally) find. The trouble with this suggestion is that rather than being one unique truth, there are multiple true statements. For example, included among the truths are both

$$2 + 2 = 4$$

and

> Justin Trudeau is the current Canadian prime minister.

As a result, it is preferable to treat truth as a property shared by truths rather than as some kind of object.

Although the central focus of this discussion is the nature of the property of truth, an important preliminary question is exactly what the bearers of this property are; that is, exactly what are the entities that are capable of being true (or false). Consider, for example, the property of redness. Certain objects are capable of being red, in particular, physical objects such as shirts and various fruits and vegetables; but other things, such as numbers or ideas, cannot be red. And in order to determine the nature of redness, one ought to figure out exactly what sorts of objects can be red. Now it is generally agreed that there are two basic sorts of truth bearers: statements and thoughts. First, someone makes a **statement** when she utters a

Ontological Categories

A system of ontological categories provides a taxonomy of the fundamental kinds of things there are (or could be). Although there are a number of distinct ontological systems, many of them include the following four categories: entities, properties and relations, events, and facts or states of affairs. **Entities** are particular things, such as Donald Trump or the Eiffel Tower, that bear properties and stand in relations to one another. **Properties** and **relations** are universals, such as redness or being taller than, that can be shared by distinct entities. **Events** are happenings, such as a wedding or a square dance, that normally involve a change in the properties or relations of one or more entities. And **facts** or **states of affairs** consist in the possession of properties or the instantiation of relations on the part of various entities, such as the fact that Trump is the current American president or that he is bigger than a breadbox. We will return to breadboxes below.

declarative sentence with the right kind of intentions—either to get her listeners to believe what she says or, more modestly, to commit herself to the truth of what she says. So, for example, if I utter the sentence

> I am a professor

with the intention of getting you to believe that I am a professor, then I thereby make a statement to that effect. And my statement is the kind of thing that is capable of being true. Second, some of our psychological states have meanings or contents. So, for example, my belief that I am a professor has a meaning or content to the effect that I am a professor. And such psychological states are capable of truth. After all, if I am in fact a professor, then my belief to that effect will be true.

It is perhaps unsatisfying to find that two very different kinds of things—linguistic entities and psychological entities—are truth bearers. After all, a simpler, more unified account is normally preferable if it is available. A first step in this direction would be to note that by means of making statements we (typically) thereby express our thoughts. If, for example, I am thinking that Donald Trump is bigger than a breadbox and wish to express this thought to you, I can do so by means of uttering the sentence

> Donald Trump is bigger than a breadbox

with the requisite intentions. One way of capturing this idea is to invoke the notion of a proposition. **Propositions** are theoretical entities that are supposed to serve as both the meanings of statements and the contents of thoughts. So, in the case at hand, the proposition that Donald Trump is bigger than a breadbox is the meaning of my statement and the content of my thought. Moreover, on this view, propositions are the primary truth bearers, and thoughts and statements are capable of truth only in a secondary or derivative sense: a thought or statement is true just in case the proposition that serves as its meaning or content is.

8.2 Correspondence

The most common account of the nature of truth is the correspondence theory. The basic idea underlying this view is that what it is for a thought or statement to be true is for it to accurately reflect how the world is. So, for example, the reason my statement

> Donald Trump is bigger than Queen Elizabeth's breadbox

is true, if it is, is because as a matter of fact Trump is of a larger size than the Queen's breadbox. Although there are many different versions of the correspondence theory, we will focus on two here: the simple theory and the complex, or representational, theory (see Figure 8.1). According to the **simple correspondence**

theory, reality is made up of or consists of a number of facts. These include such things as the fact that most snow is white and that I am currently typing on my computer. And what it is for a thought or statement to be true is for it to correspond to one of these facts. So, for example, my belief that most snow is white is true just in case there exists some fact to which it corresponds. As a result, insofar as there is a fact to the effect that most snow is white, then my belief has the property of truth.

According to the **representational theory,** in contrast, truth is a complex property defined in terms of a representation relation and the property of obtaining. Representation is a relation that holds between thoughts or statements and possible states of affairs when the latter corresponds to how a subject thinks or says things are. So, for example, if I say

> Donald Trump is smaller than Queen Elizabeth's breadbox,

my statement stands in the representation relation to the possible (not actual) circumstances in which Trump is of a smaller stature than the Queen's breadbox. Obtaining is a property possessed by possible states of affairs when they are actual. So, for example, while the possible circumstances in which Trump is larger than Queen Elizabeth's breadbox obtain, the possible circumstances in which he is smaller than this breadbox do not. Putting these two pieces together, we get that a thought or statement is true just in case it represents a possible state of affairs that obtains. So, since my thought that Donald Trump is bigger than Queen Elizabeth's breadbox represents possible circumstances in which Trump is of a larger size than the Queen's breadbox and these possible circumstances obtain, my thought is true according to the representational theory.

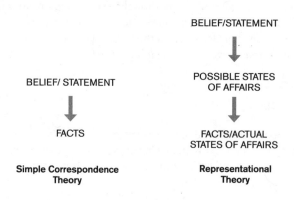

FIGURE 8.1 • *Correspondence Theories*

Despite its intuitive plausibility, there have been a number of serious objections raised against both versions of the correspondence theory. First, there are a number of objections to the role played by facts in the theory. One might, for instance, argue that the ontological category of facts is suspect, that all that exist are objects and their properties and relations and not, in addition, facts. Alternatively, one might concede that although certain facts exist, there are subject matters in which there are truths but no facts. One might argue, for example, that although the statement

> Killing innocent people except in self-defence is wrong

and the belief that the *Mona Lisa* is beautiful are both true, there exist neither moral nor aesthetic facts for these entities to correspond to. Finally, one might argue that even if there are facts for all subject matters in which there are truths, the correspondence theory is in addition committed to "funny" facts whose existence cannot be tolerated. For example, the truth of my belief that Hillary Clinton is not a flamingo seems to require the existence of the negative fact of Clinton not being a flamingo over and above all the positive facts independently involving Clinton and flamingos. One might suppose that the appeal to states of affairs instead of facts offers some advantage to the representational theory on this count. But even if states of affairs are, in general, both different from and less problematic than facts, the invocation of possible but non-actual states of affairs brings with it a whole host of problems in its own right. Many people find the suggestion that there are entities that do not actually exist but that nevertheless have some kind of being to be deeply troubling.

Second, there are a number of objections to the relations that putatively hold between truth bearers and the world. Although the representation relation between truth bearers and possible states of affairs may seem innocuous—after all, it is simply a product of the meanings or contents of the former—the correspondence relation and the property of obtaining are more worrisome. Not only are they obscure, since it is far from clear what it takes for a thought or statement to correspond to the facts, but they also have an air of triviality to them: to say that a statement corresponds to the facts, or of a possible state of affairs that it obtains, just seems to be another way of saying it is true rather than providing a substantive account of the nature of truth.

Third, some people object to the correspondence theory on the ground that it presupposes that reality has an objective nature. But metaphysical relativists argue that reality has a nature only relative to the interests of individuals or groups. And metaphysical nihilists argue that reality has no nature at all. Either way, if reality lacks an objective nature, then there are no facts for thoughts or statements to correspond to and there is no fact of the matter about which possible states of affairs obtain. A related objection, specifically directed toward the representational theory, concedes that reality may have an objective nature but argues that thoughts and statements lack any determinate meanings or contents. But since they do not stand in the representation relation to any particular possible state of affairs, there is no fact of the matter about which thoughts and statements are true, even if there is a fact of the matter about which possible states of affairs obtain. It is worth noting that metaphysical relativism and metaphysical nihilism are controversial in their own right, perhaps even more so than the correspondence theory and the metaphysical objectivity it presupposes.

Finally, it has been argued that, insofar as truth requires a correspondence between our thoughts and statements and reality in itself, in order to know whether our thoughts and statements are true we need to "step outside" our language and psychology and compare them to reality. But we cannot step outside our language and psychology to do so; after all, we are capable of making any kind of comparison only by means of our own thought and talk. As a result, we cannot know whether our thoughts and statements are true. This is a suggestive and puzzling argument, much of whose discussion falls beyond the scope of an introductory philosophy course. Nevertheless, a couple of comments are worth making here. First, if the traditional view that knowledge consists in having justified true beliefs is correct, then this argument does not entail that the correspondence theory is incompatible with knowledge. After all, one's beliefs can in fact be true even if one does not know that they are; and the former is all that is required for knowledge on the traditional account (even if it does not suffice for knowing that you know). And second, the argument presupposes that the correspondence theory requires a correspondence between thoughts and statements, and unconceptualized reality—that is, reality in itself, neither thought about nor spoken about by beings like us. But if the correspondence theory is understood to require a correspondence with conceptualized reality—reality as we think and talk about it—then the difficulty raised here does not arise.

8.3 Alternative Theories of Truth

COHERENCE THEORY

There are a number of alternative theories to the correspondence theory of truth, two of which we will consider here: the coherence theory and the redundancy theory. According to the **coherence theory**, truth is a relation between thoughts or statements and a set of beliefs (or believed propositions) rather than belief-independent facts or states of affairs. In particular, what is required in order for a thought or statement to be true is for it, or the proposition expressed by it, to cohere with the members of this set of beliefs. Suppose, for example, the set in question includes the beliefs that Donald Trump is over six feet tall and that all breadboxes are less than two feet high. According to the coherence theory, because the proposition expressed by the statement

Donald Trump is bigger than Queen Elizabeth's breadbox

coheres with the members of this set, whereas

Donald Trump is smaller than Queen Elizabeth's breadbox

does not, the former statement is true and the latter false.

There are a couple of central reasons one might have for endorsing the coherence theory. First, one might endorse an idealist or anti-realist metaphysical picture according to which reality depends on our beliefs and other psychological states. On this view, how things are depends on our beliefs about them. And so, since truth is concerned with how things are, whether or not a thought or statement is true depends on its relation to our (other) beliefs. Second, although we may not be able to ascertain whether our thoughts and statements correspond to mind-independent reality, we are able to know the relations between them and our other beliefs. As a result, unlike the correspondence theory, the coherence theory is does not rule out the possibility of knowledge of whether our thoughts and statements are true.

There are, however, a number of problems with the coherence theory. Some of these concern the formulation of the view. Insofar as truth is coherence with a set of beliefs, we need to know both what coherence is and with which set of beliefs a thought or statement needs to cohere in order to be true. But difficulties arise with attempts to address both issues. Consider, first, the coherence relation. Suppose that coherence is understood to be a relatively thin notion such as consistency. To say a thought or statement is consistent with a set of beliefs is to say that they do not jointly entail a contradiction. However, this account of coherence yields too many truths. More to the point, contradictory statements can each be consistent with a single set of beliefs and, as a result, the coherence theory entails that we have equal grounds for saying that each of statements is true, but clearly they cannot both be true. For example, both

Donald Trump is bigger than Queen Elizabeth's breadbox

and

Donald Trump is smaller than Queen Elizabeth's breadbox

might be consistent with a set of beliefs with very little information about the sizes of breadboxes. Suppose instead that coherence is a much more robust relation, perhaps the requirement that a thought or statement at issue be entailed by a set of beliefs. But this account of coherence yields too few truths, however. At least one of

Donald Trump is bigger than Queen Elizabeth's breadbox

and

Donald Trump is smaller than Queen Elizabeth's breadbox

is arguably true. But neither of them might be entailed by a given set of beliefs that, again, contains little information about breadboxes.

One might think that the problems that arise for the coherence relation can be resolved by focusing on the right set of beliefs, a set with which only one of a pair of contradictory statements will be consistent, or by which at least one of a pair of contradictory statements will be entailed. The trouble is that it is far from clear what the right set of beliefs is. One suggestion might be that the relevant set consists of the beliefs of the person whose thought or statement it is. So, for example, if it is Mary who makes the statement

Donald Trump is bigger than Queen Elizabeth's breadbox,

then it is true just in case it coheres with Mary's beliefs, whereas if Fred makes the same statement, its truth depends on whether it coheres with Fred's beliefs. The trouble with this suggestion is that it results in an unpalatable kind of relativism in which thoughts and statements are not objectively true but rather merely true for one or another person; moreover, unless the subject misspeaks and fails to say what she thinks (or misthinks and fails to think what she thinks), then what she says is automatically true. Another suggestion might be that the relevant set consists of the shared beliefs of a certain group, perhaps a given society or even the whole of humanity. The trouble with this suggestion is that the larger the group, the fewer beliefs will be shared, but unless the group consists of the whole of humanity, the threat of relativism will re-emerge. Moreover, widely shared beliefs of human communities have often proven to be unreliable—consider, for example, the once widely held belief that the Earth is flat. As a result, shared social beliefs seem a poor measure of the truth of thoughts and statements. Finally, one might take the relevant set to consist of the beliefs of some kind of idealized subject. The challenge for this approach is coming up with some kind of rationale as to why the beliefs of this subject are authoritative that does not presuppose that its beliefs are accurate or correspond to the facts. After all, the coherence theory of truth is supposed to be an alternative to the correspondence theory and so cannot be ultimately based upon it.

In addition to the formulation difficulties, there are a number of more general worries about the view. First, one might simply reject the kind of idealist metaphysical picture that the coherence theory seems to presuppose. Many think that the world has an objective nature and that truth is a function of that nature rather than our beliefs about it. Anyone who accepts this kind of metaphysical realism will simply consider the coherence theory to be a non-starter. And second, one might argue that the coherence theory confuses truth with evidence of truth: the fact that a thought or statement coheres with the relevant set of beliefs might well count as evidence that it is true rather than being in what its truth consists. One reason for adopting this argument stems from the fact that while evidence comes in degrees, thereby making the truth of a thought or statement more or less likely, truth itself is all or nothing: either

Donald Trump is bigger than Queen Elizabeth's breadbox

is true or it is not; there is no in between. Moreover, in an intuitive sense at least, coherence comes in degrees: rather than thinking of sets of beliefs as either coherent or not, it seems more natural to think of them as more or less coherent. As a result, insofar as coherence really does comes in degrees, it is better suited to play a role in an account of evidence for truth than to play a role in an account of the nature of truth itself.

REDUNDANCY THEORY

Another alternative to the correspondence theory of truth is the **redundancy theory**. The guiding idea of this view is that a statement such as

It is true that Donald Trump is bigger than Queen Elizabeth's breadbox

says nothing more than the simpler statement

Donald Trump is bigger than Queen Elizabeth's breadbox.

As a result, truth-talk is redundant and does not contribute to the meanings of statements in which it occurs. More generally, the idea is that there is no property that the various truths share in virtue of being true that explains why they are true. The statement

Donald Trump is bigger than Queen Elizabeth's breadbox

is true simply because as a matter of fact Trump is bigger than Queen Elizabeth's breadbox. And the statement

$2 + 2 = 4$

is true simply because, as a matter of fact, $2 + 2 = 4$. But according to the redundancy theory there is no general explanation as to why both statements are true in terms of correspondence, coherence, or the like.

There are a number of reasons one might have for endorsing the redundancy theory. First, one might attribute the difficulties in providing an account of the nature of truth to the fact that truth does not have a nature. Both the correspondence and coherence theories ran into problems in articulating respectively what correspondence and coherence are, and hence in explaining what truth is. But if truth lacks any kind of substantial nature, difficulties in the attempt to explain its nature should be expected. Second, one might argue that substantive theories of truth involve metaphysical commitments that possession of the concept of truth does not require. As we have seen, the correspondence theory presupposes a mind-independent world consisting of facts or states of affairs, whereas the coherence theory presupposes some kind of metaphysical idealism. But one can be fully competent with the use of the term "true" without having any views on this issue. And third, one might simply be impressed with the redundancy intuition that truth-talk contributes nothing to the meaning of statements in which it occurs and conclude that truth lacks any kind of substantial nature.

One question that naturally arises about the redundancy theory is the following: if truth-talk is redundant, why do we ever use it? The typical answer to this question is that although redundant, truth-talk is nevertheless quite useful for expressing certain sort of generalizations. Suppose you wish to assert all of the propositions of a certain kind—the axioms of set theory, the principles of quantum mechanics, or even things your dad says. But suppose that the number of propositions of the kind in question is really large, or that you do not know what all of them are. Truth-talk enables you to assert these propositions despite these difficulties. Suppose, for example, that your father only ever says three things:

> George Eliot is Mary Anne Evans,

> Hillary Clinton is not a flamingo,

and

> Donald Trump is bigger than Queen Elizabeth's breadbox.

Now given that, according to the redundancy theory,

> It is true that George Eliot is Mary Anne Evans

means the same as

> George Eliot is Mary Anne Evans

and the same holds for the other things your father says, if you were to say

> Everything my father says is true,

you would thereby assert

> George Eliot is Mary Anne Evans and Hillary Clinton is not a flamingo
> and Donald Trump is bigger than Queen Elizabeth's breadbox.

Your ability to assert the conjunction of the things your father says in this way is not limited by the number of statements he makes, nor does it require that you even know what he says.

Although there have been many objections raised against the redundancy theory, many of these are quite technical and beyond the scope of this book. There is, however, one important objection worth considering here. Insofar as there is nothing more to truth than the various instances of the equivalence schema, then there is nothing that truths have in common. The statement

> Donald Trump is bigger than Queen Elizabeth's breadbox

is true simply because Trump is bigger than the Queen's breadbox, whereas the statement

Hillary Clinton is not a flamingo

is true simply because Hillary Clinton is not a flamingo: there is nothing they have in common that makes these statements both true. In effect, the upshot is that truth is not a real or substantial property shared by its bearers, according to the redundancy theory. But, the objection goes, as a matter of fact truth is a substantive property shared by true thoughts and statements. One reason for thinking this is that truth makes a substantive causal difference in the world. In particular, people with true beliefs are more likely to be successful in their endeavours. Suppose, for example, that you and I both desire to drive to Toronto, but whereas you truly believe that Toronto is in southern Ontario, I falsely believe it to be in North Carolina. In such circumstances, you are objectively more likely to satisfy your desire to drive to Toronto than am I. More generally, people with true beliefs are systematically more successful in getting what they want than those without true beliefs. As a result, given the causal significance of truth, one might reasonably expect it to be a genuine property shared by its instances, contra the redundancy theory.

8.4 Fictional Talk and Fictionality

Let us turn now from truth to fiction. Fictional discourse falls into two broad categories: fictional talk and talk about fiction. **Fictional talk** consists of the sentences that make up fictional stories. More or less any sentence of more or less any novel counts as an example, but we will use the clichéd

It was a dark and stormy night

for illustrative purposes here. Talk about fiction, in contrast, consists of claims or statements made about the events or characters that occur or appear in fictional stories. Examples include statements such as

Hermione Granger was a muggle

and

Gandalf the Grey was a more powerful wizard than Albus Dumbledore.

In this section the focus will be on fictional talk. Talk about fiction will be the topic of the next section.

One basic account of the difference between non-fiction and fiction is that it is, essentially, the distinction between truth and falsity: non-fiction consists of true statements and fiction consists of falsehoods. This basic account is, however, subject

to obvious counter-examples. Statements of non-fiction are frequently false, sometimes due to errors of fact on the part of people who make them, just as fictional
sentences are regularly true—works of historical fiction, for example, contain many
true sentences. One might try to amend this basic account by taking non-fiction to
involve truth-telling—saying only what you believe to be true—and taking fiction
to involve lying—saying what you know to be false with the intent to deceive. But
again, not only can statements of non-fiction be lies—propaganda is pretty clearly
non-fiction but often contains intentional falsehoods—but it is also far from clear
that fictional talk consists of lies. We generally take those to be engaged in non-
fiction to be obligated to say only what they believe to be true, at least if they are
speaking literally, and rightly criticize them if they fail to do so. But we do not take
those who produce fictional talk to be similarly obligated. We do not criticize J.K.
Rowling or J.R.R. Tolkien for producing sentences they do not believe to be true
and, moreover, we hope and expect them to refrain from saying or writing only
what they believe.

A better approach is to suppose that those engaged in fictional talk are not making statements at all. Someone who makes a statement commits herself to the truth
of what she says, perhaps with the intention that her audience come to believe what
she says. Moreover, since one commits oneself to the truth of what one says, one
is obligated to say only what one believes. As a result, only someone who makes a
statement can strictly be charged with lying. And as should be clear, non-fictional
talk consists largely of statements. But as we have seen, those who produce fiction
neither typically do, nor are obligated to, believe what they say.

But if fictional talk does not consist of statements, the question is what exactly it
does consist in. One suggestion is that rather than actually making statements, what
those who produce fictional talk do is pretend to make statements. So, for example,
someone who, while engaged in fiction, says

> It was a dark and stormy night

pretends to state that a certain night was dark and stormy and, hence, pretends to
commit herself to the truth of this proposition without actually doing so. On this
view, the statement the speaker pretends to make may be either true or false and,
if it makes reference to entities that do not exist, may even be neither. Moreover,
since a speaker of fiction only pretends to commit himself to the truth of what he
says, the speaker is under no obligation to believe what he says and so is not guilty
of lying if he fails to do so.

Despite its virtues, the pretense account of fiction runs into serious difficulties.
In particular, pretending to make a statement is neither necessary nor sufficient
for producing fiction. It is not necessary because there are fictions that are not the
product of such pretense. A painting of an imaginary village, for example, can be
fictional, but its being so does not require that the painter pretended to state anything. And it is not sufficient because one can engage in pretense without generating
fiction. I might, for example, pretend to state that my friend, Paul, is not very smart
by saying

> Paul is an idiot,

not in order to produce fiction but rather to report something that his archrival, Kent, said about him.

An alternative to the pretense theory is the view that there is a uniquely fictional kind of talk whose guiding purpose is to get the audience to imagine what the speaker says rather than believe it. So, for example, on the fictional speech act view, someone who says

> It was a dark and stormy night,

while engaged in fiction, neither intends to get her audience to believe what she says nor pretends to do so. Rather, she intends to get her audience to imagine that a certain night was dark and stormy. There is a lot to be said for the fictional speech act theory. One virtue of the view is that it fits nicely with a plausible account of what it is to be "caught up" in a fictional story. When engaged with fiction in this way, we arguably imagine the occurrence of the events of the story rather than believing them to have occurred. And, on the view at issue, this is exactly what fiction makers hope to achieve.

Nevertheless, this view also runs into serious difficulties. First, it runs into some of the same difficulties that beset the pretense theory. For example, a painter can produce a fictional painting without either pretending to make a statement or engaging in speech designed to get her audience to imagine something. And second, fictional talk includes not only "fictional statements" such as

> It was a dark and stormy night

but also "fictional questions":

> Was it a dark and stormy night?

and "fictional requests":

> Walk with me, dear reader, on this dark and stormy night.

And while the fictional speech act theory gives a plausible account of the purpose underlying "fictional statements"—that the audience imagine what is said—it does not seem particularly well suited to the other cases.

8.5 Talk about Fiction: Fictional Names

Let us turn now to **talk about fiction**. The first thing to note is that, unlike fictional talk, talk about fiction is a kind of non-fiction. If I say

Gandalf the Grey was a more powerful wizard than Albus Dumbledore,

I make a statement: I thereby commit myself to the truth of what I say, and if I do not believe it myself, I am guilty of lying. Nevertheless such statements are puzzling for two distinct reasons. First, talk about fiction contains fictional names—such as "Gandalf" and "Albus Dumbledore"—that do not refer to anyone. As a result, it is not clear how such statements can be used to say anything at all. And second, although it is clear that we do distinguish between true and false statements about fiction—compare

Sherlock Holmes was a detective

with

Sherlock Holmes was an architect

for example—it is far from clear how they can be true. After all, in most cases, the events described in talk about fiction did not occur and, as a result, there are no facts for such statements to correspond to. We will consider each of these puzzles in turn.

There are three basic accounts of fictional names: fictional realism, the pretense theory, and conceptualism. According to **fictional realism**, fictional names in fact do have referents—fictional characters—but their referents are unlike the referents of ordinary non-fictional names. The referents of ordinary names are actually existing, concrete, flesh-and-blood things. According to one version of fictional realism, fictional characters are concrete entities that do not actually exist but rather have some other kind of being. And according to another version of the view, fictional characters actually exist but are abstract things, like numbers, rather than concrete entities, like tables, trees, and human beings.

There are, however, objections to both versions of the view. The concrete non-existent version runs into difficulty because, even if the idea of non-existent objects makes sense, it is not clear how we could refer to them. And the abstract existent version runs into trouble because abstract entities lack many of the features we take the fictional characters we talk about to have. For example, although most of us would take the statement

Sherlock Holmes is a human being

to be true, it is false if the referent of "Sherlock Holmes" is some kind of abstract entity.

According to the **pretense theory** of fictional names, talk about fiction does not consist of statements, but instead, those who engage in such talk merely pretend to make statements. In effect, talk about fiction is itself a kind of fiction, and those who use it are engaged in a kind of play-acting. Moreover, when the sentences they utter contain fictional names, they merely pretend to refer by means of their use of them rather than actually doing so. So, for example, someone who says

Sherlock Holmes was a detective

not only merely pretends to thereby make a statement but also only pretends to refer to something by means of her use of the name "Sherlock Holmes." As a result, the pretense theorist has no need to take fictional characters to be in any sense real in order to make sense of talk about fiction.

There are, however, a number of potential difficulties with this view. First, as noted above, talk about fiction seems capable of being true or false. But if fictional names lack referents, it is not clear how it can be. After all, what it takes for a sentence such as

Peter Alward is a professor

to be true is for the referent of the name "Peter Alward"—me—to have the property of being a professor. And second, it seems possible to have genuine disagreements about fiction. I might, for example, insist upon the statement

Gandalf the Grey was a more powerful wizard than Albus Dumbledore,

whereas you might disagree by saying

Albus Dumbledore was a more powerful wizard than Gandalf the Grey.

But if we are just play-acting, as the pretense theory would have it, we are not really disagreeing at all but only pretending to do so.

Finally, according to **conceptualism**, the meaning of a name is a concept or idea. In the case of non-fictional names, there are people or things that these concepts are concepts of—something that uniquely fits or satisfies the concept—that are their referents. So, for example, the meaning of the name "George Washington" might be the concept "the first American president," and since George Washington uniquely satisfies that concept, he is the referent of the name. In the case of fictional names, in contrast, there is nothing that the concepts in question are concepts of, and hence they lack referents. So, for example, the meaning of "Bilbo Baggins" might be the concept "the hobbit who avoiding being eaten by Gollum by defeating him in a riddle game." And since nothing uniquely fits this concept, the name does not refer to anything. Nevertheless, because fictional names have meanings—concepts or ideas derived from the stories in which they occur—speakers are able to say something by means of their use of them.

There are, again, many objections to this view. First, insofar as the meanings of fictional names are concepts or ideas that speakers associate with them, then although they can say something by means of them, different speakers will inevitably say different things. After all, different people frequently associate different ideas with fictional names. Second, it could turn out that some real thing actually satisfies a concept associated with a fictional name. If, for example, the meaning of "Harry Potter" is the concept "the talented orphan who attended Hogwarts" and Fred is a talented orphan who attended a school of that name, he would be the referent of the name—Harry Potter himself—on the conceptualist view. And third, if fictional names have meanings but lack referents, then, although speakers can say something by means of their use of them, it is unclear how what they say can be true. After all, whether a statement containing a name is true depends on whether the referent of the name has the property attributed to it by the statement.

8.6 Talk about Fiction: Fictional Truth

The final issue to be addressed in this chapter is that of **fictional truth**. As above, the concern is with how talk about fiction can be true or false. It is worth emphasizing from the start the distinction between two kinds of fictional truth: truth in fiction and truth through fiction. Truth in fiction concerns the goings on in particular fictional stories. For example, the statement

> Sherlock Holmes was a detective

is true in the Holmes stories, whereas the statement

> Sherlock Holmes was an architect

is false in this sense. Truth through fiction concerns claims made about the actual non-fictional world by means of fictional stories. Consider, for example, the well-known fable of the tortoise and the hare in which a tortoise defeats the much faster hare in a footrace, when the latter stops for a nap while the former trudges slowly on. The moral of the story—that proceeding carefully and methodically is more likely to yield success—is a claim not about the events of the story but rather about the actual world and, as such, is a candidate for truth *through* fiction. Truth *in* fiction is the primary concern of this section.

At least on the face of things, it is not clear how one could give a correspondence account of truth in fiction. Recall: according to the correspondence theory, a thought or statement is true just in case it corresponds to the facts. But since the events described in fictional stories are not factual, there are no facts for statements about fictional events to correspond to. Since, for example, Sherlock Holmes does not exist and there are therefore no Holmes facts, the truth of the statement

> Holmes was a detective

cannot consist in its corresponding to the facts. One might be tempted by the suggestion that in addition to the actual world, there also exist a multitude of fictional worlds: worlds in which fictional characters and places exist, and in which the events described in fictional stories occur. If such worlds exist, then fictional truth can be understood as correspondence to the facts in the relevant fictional world rather than correspondence to the actual facts. Since in the world of the Holmes stories it is a fact that Holmes was a detective, the statement

> Holmes was a detective

corresponds to the facts of that world, whereas the statement

> Holmes was an architect

does not.

But this appeal to fictional worlds is troubling in a number of respects. First, in order for a statement to correspond to the fictional facts, it has to refer to fictional characters and events. But insofar as these are non-existent things, it is unclear how we can refer to them. And second, insofar as fictional worlds exist independently of the fictional stories that describe them, this view seems to entail that authors discover rather than create fictional facts.

Rather than taking fictional truth to consist in correspondence to fictional facts, a more promising approach might be to understand it in terms of the sentences that make up fictional stories. One strategy might be to require that in order for a statement about fiction to be true, the sentence used in the statement must occur in the story with which it is concerned. So, for example, in order for the statement

> Holmes was a detective

to be true, the sentence "Holmes was a detective" must itself occur in the Holmes stories.

The trouble with this suggestion is twofold. First, it automatically rules out the truth of statements made about fictional stories in languages other those in which the stories are written. The statement

> Holmes était détective

is presumably true despite the fact that the Holmes stories were written in English. And second, contra this view, it seems possible to make a true statement about fiction without using the exact words that occur in the story. The statement

> Holmes is a detective

is true after all, despite the fact that this exact sentence occurs nowhere in the Holmes stories.

A better strategy might consist in the requirement that in order for a statement about fiction to be true, the sentence used in making it need not occur in the fictional story but rather only that some sentence or other that means the same as it needs to occur in the story. So, for example, both

> Holmes is a detective

and

> Holmes est détective

can be true despite not occurring in the Holmes stories, as long as some sentence that means the same occurs in them.

There are, however, two central difficulties with this approach. First, there are usually numerous fictional truths that are never explicitly stated in a given fictional story. The statement

> Holmes wears underpants

is presumably a fictional truth, despite the fact that neither this very sentence nor any sentence that means the same as it occurs anywhere in the Holmes stories. And second, some fictional stories contain unreliable narrators: narrators who say things that are not true in the story. As a result, there is no guarantee that a statement about a story that means the same as a sentence occurring in the story will be a fictional truth.

In this chapter we have considered a variety of theories regarding the nature of truth, as well as a number of issues regarding various kinds of fictional discourse. Questions about truth and fiction arise not only in philosophical discussions but in conversations that many of us have almost every day. As a result, acquiring an understanding of these concepts is important for a wide range of human activities.

Reading Questions

1.   What are the two basic kinds of truth bearers?

2.   According to the simple correspondence theory, what is required for a statement to be true?

3.   What is metaphysical nihilism? Why is this view incompatible with the correspondence theory?

4.   According to the coherence theory, what is required for a belief to be true?

5.   What does it mean to say that truth is redundant?

6.   What is the basic account of the difference between non-fiction and fiction? What is one problem with this account?

7. What is the difference between the pretense account and the fictional speech act account of fictional talk?

8. What do fictional names refer to, according to fictional realism?

9. How does the conceptualist account of fictional names differ from fictional realism?

10. What is the difficulty with giving a correspondence account of truth in fiction?

Reflection Questions

1. Think of a variety of beliefs or statements on different topics that you consider to be true. What do those various beliefs and statements have in common? Is there anything they have in common that explains why they are true?

2. Think of various things you might be willing to say using the names of fictional characters. What, if anything, do you take yourself to be referring to or talking about by means of these names? Which, if any, of the things you say using these names do you think are objectively true or false?

Further Reading

General introduction to the nature of truth:
Michael Devitt, *Realism and Truth* (Oxford: Blackwell, 1984).

Correspondence theory:
Marian David, *Correspondence and Disquotation* (Oxford: Oxford UP, 1994).

Coherence theory:
James Young, "A Defense of the Coherence Theory of Truth," *Journal of Philosophical Research* 26 (2001): 89–101.

Redundancy theory:
Paul Horwich, *Truth* (Oxford: Blackwell, 1990).

Fictional talk:
John Searle, "The Logical Status of Fictional Discourse," *New Literary History* 6.2 (1975): 319–32.

Pretense theories of fiction:
Kendall Walton, *Mimesis as Make-Believe* (Cambridge, MA: Harvard UP, 1990).

Fictional realism:
Amy Thomasson, *Fiction and Metaphysics* (Cambridge: Cambridge UP, 1999).

Fictional truth:
David Lewis, "Truth in Fiction," *American Philosophical Quarterly* 15 (1978):
    37–46.

PART II

Ethics and Political Philosophy

9

MORAL SKEPTICISM

A common reaction to talk of ethics and morality, and especially to the suggestion that one is, in some sense, bound by it, is to dismiss it as empty. Some people claim that moral judgements are, like judgements of taste, mere matters of opinion. Others claim instead that morality is relative—to culture, the individual, or what have you. But the suggestion that there are culturally independent universally applying moral principles is commonly eschewed. But given how widespread the phenomenon of morality is, and how objective moral talk on the surface appears to be, one might reasonably wonder whether there is any good reason to suppose that it is defective in the ways in which moral skeptics of various kinds take it to be.

Morality is an essentially normative phenomenon: it involves evaluating people, actions, and circumstances as good or bad, right or wrong, rather than merely describing those people, actions or circumstances. As a result, at the core of the skeptical challenge to morality is the idea that normative judgements cannot be objective or factual. In order to assess this skeptical challenge, we will need to distinguish between objectivism, relativism, and nihilism as they pertain to normativity in

CHAPTER CONTENTS:

- the question of morality is introduced;
- a taxonomy skeptical views is developed;
- nihilistic approaches to morality are explored;
- relativistic accounts of morality are evaluated; and
- individualistic approaches to morality are analyzed.

general and morality in particular, and to determine whether there is any good reason to reject moral objectivity.

9.1 Morality

Morality is an extremely widespread—and arguably universal—social phenomenon. At its core, it consists of certain patterns of behaviour among members of a social group as well as characteristic attitudes toward this behaviour and deviations from it. For example, there might be a pattern of promise keeping among the members of a social group—that is, they might generally do what they commit themselves to doing—and promise keeping might be looked upon favourably while promise breaking is looked upon unfavourably. It is sometimes thought that morality narrowly consists in prudish attitudes toward various kinds of sexual acts. Although moral attitudes are often directed toward sexual behaviour, it is worth emphasizing that the scope of morality is much broader than this. It is also concerned with, among other things, respectful interpersonal interchanges—promising, lying, and so on—as well as behaviour we often think of as criminal. Assault, murder, and the like are not just illegal but are also generally thought to be morally wrong. Manners are something of a borderline case: although most of us would probably agree that one should not be rude, it normally seems too strong to describe politeness as morally required and rudeness as morally wrong. It is worth emphasizing that not all questions concerning morality are sociological questions regarding patterns of thought and talk in social groups. In particular, philosophical questions regarding moral objectivity—which are the focus here—depend on a broader array of considerations.

Moral attitudes are typically expressed using a characteristic form of talk: behaviour toward which one has an attitude of approval is described as "right"; and

Case Study 9.1:
Reputation and Cheating

Suppose that Fred enters into an agreement with Mary to build her a deck in exchange for a certain amount of money up front. And suppose that Fred breaks this agreement by accepting the money but refraining from building the deck. In the short term, Fred will be better off: after all, he received payment without having to spend the time and energy and material costs of building a deck. But in the longer term, he may be worse off: if he acquires a reputation for breaking agreements, then people will be disinclined to enter into agreements with him, even in those cases in which he intends to keep his end of the deal. So Fred has a reason to keep his agreement with Mary, even though carrying through and doing so after she has already paid him makes him worse off in the short run. Of course, what will make Fred best off in both the short and long terms is breaking his agreement with Mary while retaining a reputation for keeping agreements. But this outcome may be difficult for Fred to secure.

QUESTION: What reasons does Fred have for keeping the agreement, and what kinds of reasons are they (social, moral, legal, practical)? If Fred could achieve these goals without keeping the agreement with Mary, are there any reasons for him not to do so?

behaviour of which one disapproves is called "wrong." Conformity to patterns of behaviour of which the members of a community approve is rarely uniform, even among those who approve of it. Community attitudes, of approval toward those who conform and disapproval toward those who fail to do so, are one mechanism that nevertheless helps keep the rate of conformity reasonably high. If I need to be well thought of in order to secure the cooperation of others in the pursuit of my own goals, or if I just value having a good reputation, then I have a reason to engage in behaviour of which the community approves. In some cases, however, community disapproval is insufficient, and the threat of sanction by the state is required to keep rates of conformity acceptably high. Still, it is important to note that legal and moral standards of behaviour are distinct: lying is wrong but except in special circumstances is not illegal; and although jaywalking is illegal, at least arguably, it is not morally wrong. Finally, it is worth noting that although the focus here is on the moral evaluation of behaviour, moral attitudes are often directed toward persons and circumstances as well. For example, Mahatma Gandhi is commonly thought of as virtuous, as a morally good person; and widespread hunger is thought of as deplorable, as an extremely bad state of affairs whose badness is morally significant (at least insofar as we are responsible for it or able to relieve it).

9.2 Taxonomy of Claims

The central concern of this chapter is the status of moral claims. **Moral claims** are used to morally evaluate actions—that is, things people do. Moral claims can assess both particular actions as well as more general kinds of actions. So, for example,

> Giving to charity is the right thing to do

and

> What Fred did was wrong

both count as moral claims, where the expression "what Fred did" picks out a particular action of Fred's. Moral claims are a species of normative claims. While **descriptive claims** are claims about how things in fact are, **normative claims** are claims about how things ought to be or whether how things are is good or bad. Moreover, whereas all moral claims are normative claims, it is worth noting that the reverse is not true. Consider, for example, a claim such as

> You should watch the Grey Cup at my house this year.

Although this is certainly a normative claim—concerned not with what one in fact will do but rather what one should do—the location where someone watches a sporting event hardly counts as a moral matter.

There are three separate categories into which a class of claims might fall: they might be objective, they might be empty, and they might be relative. We will consider each in turn. To say that a class of claims is **objective** is to say that the claims concern issues regarding which there is a fact of the matter. Consider, for example, claims about the current state of the weather in one's vicinity, such as

It is raining

or

It is sunny and warm.

There is a fact of the matter concerning the weather conditions at the time and place that some such claim is made, which the claim can characterize accurately or inaccurately. If, for example, I claim that it is raining on a warm and sunny day in my vicinity, then my claim is inaccurate. There may, of course, be borderline cases: the claim that it is raining made on a drizzly day may be neither determinately true nor false. But nevertheless, because there is a fact of the matter that such claims can, in principle, characterize accurately, the class of claims counts as objective.

To say a class of claims is **empty** is to say the claims concern issues regarding which there is no fact of the matter. Consider, for example, claims about ghosts, such as,

Ghosts are souls trapped between the material and spiritual realms

or

Ghosts, unlike poltergeists, haunt a specific location rather than a particular person.

Since there are no such things as ghosts, claims about the nature of ghosts can be neither accurate nor inaccurate. Claims about the existence of ghosts, however, are simply false. For example, if I claim that ghosts are transparent, what I say is neither accurate nor inaccurate; but if I claim that there is a ghost haunting my bathroom, what I say is just false. Moreover, since I am not talking about anything in either case, my claims are in that sense empty. It is worth noting, however, that even though claims about ghosts are empty, claims about ghost-beliefs or ghost-myths are not. Consider, for example, claims such as

Case Study 9.2: Ghost Stories

Suppose that while telling a ghost story around a campfire, Fred finishes by softly saying, "And the very same ghosts possess all who sleep in these woods to this day." And suppose that Mary repeats this line to Tom, who promptly packs up his gear and flees the campsite.

QUESTION: Are Fred and Mary both best understood as having made empty claims?

> According to mythology, ghosts are souls trapped between the material
> and spiritual realms

or

> Many people believe that ghosts, unlike poltergeists, haunt a specific
> location rather than a particular person.

After all, beliefs and myths are part of our psychological and social reality, so claims regarding them can be accurate or inaccurate.

To say that a class of claims is **relative** is to say that the claims concern issues regarding which there is a fact of the matter, but that the claims leave out, or omit explicit mention of, an essential aspect of these issues. Consider, for example, claims about things being to the right or left of one another, such as

> Mary is to the left of Fred

or

> Toronto is to the right of Calgary.

Now while there is certainly a fact of the matter about the relative locations of things, these locations can be characterized in terms of something's being to the right and left only relative to a perspective or point of view. After all, Toronto is to the right of Calgary from some perspectives and to the left of it from others. There is no sense in which Toronto is absolutely to the right or left of Calgary, which is independent of any perspective someone might occupy. Hence, claims about things being to the right or left of one another can only accurately or inaccurately characterize the locations of those things relative to some such perspective. It is worth emphasizing, however, that simply saying of a class of claims that it is relative is not very informative. Minimally what is required is an account of exactly what those claims are relative to and how they are relative to it. For example, simply saying that being to the left is relative to the perspective of an observer does not by itself yield a formula regarding which of a pair of objects is to the left of the other from that perspective. One needs in addition to say something along the following lines: one object is to the left of another object relative to a perspective just in case it is on the same side of the body as the heart of a person occupying that perspective when she or he is oriented toward those objects. In what follows, we will be concerned with the theses that moral claims are relative in some way to societies or cultures and relative in some other way to individuals.

9.3 Taxonomy of Views

Moral realism is the view that moral claims are objective: there is a fact of the matter about moral issues, and these moral facts do not systematically depend on individually held or culturally shared beliefs and values; that is, whether an act is right or wrong does not depend on whether it conforms to anyone's beliefs and values. Moreover, moral claims characterize the moral facts and can do so accurately or inaccurately. Suppose, for example, that Olivia takes $50 from Tristan's wallet without his knowledge. According to moral realism, there is a fact of the matter about whether Olivia's behaviour was morally appropriate that is not determined by Olivia's beliefs and values or by those shared by members of her community. Moreover, the moral claim

> What Olivia did was wrong

either accurately or inaccurately characterizes in its own right the moral nature of Olivia's act; it does not do so only relative to some further unmentioned yet essential feature of that act. It is worth mentioning that moral realism does not entail that all acts of a certain kind are morally the same, that is, that they are all right or all wrong. A realist could consistently claim that the rightness or wrongness of promise breaking, for example, depends on details of the situation in which it occurs and hence that while certain acts of promise breaking are wrong, others are morally appropriate. Moreover, moral realism is compatible with a certain amount of indeterminacy on moral questions. A moral realist could argue, for example, that there are moral facts concerning the appropriateness of homicide, assault, promise keeping and promise breaking, lying and truth-telling, and so forth, but that there is no fact of the matter regarding whether abortion is wrong. As a result, while moral claims regarding homicide, assault, and the like are either accurate or inaccurate on this view, moral claims regarding matters such as abortion are not.

Moral anti-realism is the denial of moral realism and, in particular, of the view that moral claims are objective. If moral claims are not objective, then they are either empty or relative. Moral anti-realism can, accordingly,

"True-For" Morality

A common response to discussions of moral skepticism is to say that although you believe that certain acts are right or wrong, it is simply your opinion or simply true for you. So, for example, Fred might say, "I believe that killing except in self-defence is always wrong, but that is just true for me." Although such statements are normally intended to express adherence to some form of moral skepticism, it is far from clear that they actually do so or that those who say such things are actually moral skeptics. The problem is that the first part of such statements seems to presuppose moral realism. After all, that it is always wrong for anyone to kill in self-defence is something that only a realist would believe. In order for this to count as a version of moral relativism, to say that it is only true for you must be to say you believe that the prohibition against killing except in self-defence applies only to you, and that as far as you are concerned, there is nothing inappropriate about killing not in self-defence on the part of other parties. A better interpretation of why people say such things is that although they are moral realists, they want to communicate that they consider their moral beliefs to be fallible, perhaps in order to avoid offending those with differing beliefs.

take two basic forms: moral nihilism, according to which moral claims are empty; and moral relativism, according to which they are relative. We will consider each in turn. **Moral nihilism** is, as above, the view that moral claims are empty. There is simply no fact of the matter on moral questions. On this view, homicide, assault, honesty, charity, and so on are neither right nor wrong because there is no such thing as moral rightness or wrongness. Rightness and wrongness have the same status as ghosts, unicorns, and leprechauns. And since there is no such thing as rightness or wrongness, moral claims cannot accurately characterize actions as right or wrong. But, as above, even though moral claims are empty, the nihilist can nevertheless acknowledge that claims about moral beliefs—what individuals or groups believe to be right or wrong—are objective. **Moral relativism** comes in two basic varieties: social relativism and subjectivism. These views differ in what they take morality to be relative to: social groups or individuals. According to **social relativism**, whether an act is right or wrong depends on whether it conforms to the shared moral beliefs of the group and, in particular, the group to which the person who performed the act—the agent—belongs. According to **subjectivism**, in contrast, whether an act is right depends on whether it conforms to the moral beliefs of the agent herself.

9.4 Social Relativism

As noted above, **social relativism** is the view that moral claims are relative to social groups; in particular, whether an act is right or wrong—or a claim morally evaluating that act is true or false—depends on whether it conforms to the shared moral beliefs of the agent's social group. In effect, moral facts can be viewed as a kind of social fact: facts about the shared values and membership conditions of social groups. Consider Laurel, who took $50 from Marcus without his permission or knowledge. Now suppose that Laurel and Marcus belong to a social group in which all wealth is shared communally and private property is scorned. According to social relativism, Laurel's act would be right in such circumstances exactly because it conforms to the shared moral beliefs of her community. Moreover, the moral claim

What Laurel did was wrong,

considered in its own right, is neither accurate nor inaccurate. But when considered relative to Laurel's social group, it is false. One might, of course, consider the claim relative to some other social group with different shared moral beliefs, but insofar as Laurel is not a member of this other group, their beliefs place her under no moral obligations.

It is worth emphasizing, however, the distinction between descriptive and normative social relativism. Descriptive social relativism is just the view that social groups can and often do differ in their shared moral beliefs and values. A descriptive social relativist might, for example, note the differences in moral attitudes toward homosexuality in different social groups. And this is something even a moral realist can accept. Normative social relativism, in contrast, is the view that one's moral obligations are to conform to the shared moral beliefs of one's group: to so conform is to act rightly, whereas to fail to do so is to act wrongly. And although one might think that normative social relativism follows from its descriptive cousin, descriptive relativism is in fact compatible with moral realism and thus cannot be used in any straightforward way to establish some kind of moral skepticism. One might worry that to endorse moral realism in the face of cross-cultural variability in shared moral beliefs is to be guilty of ethnocentrism: the view that only the moral beliefs of one's own social group are correct and that other societies whose moral beliefs differ from those of one's own are, to that extent, morally defective. But although the ethnocentrist may be a kind of moral realist, taking moral claims to be objective does not require any kind of partiality in favour of the beliefs of one's own moral group: a moral realist could consistently judge that the moral beliefs of her own group are systematically wrong.

> ## Agent-Based vs. Appraiser-Based Social Relativism
>
> According to agent-based social relativism, which is presented above, the truth or falsity of a moral judgment depends on whether it conforms to the shared moral beliefs of the agent's social group: the person whose behaviour is being scrutinized. According to appraiser-based social relativism, in contrast, the truth or falsity of a moral judgment depends on whether it conforms to the shared moral beliefs of the appraiser's group: the person evaluating the action. And since different appraisers can be from different social groups—with different shared moral beliefs—the truth or falsity of a judgment evaluating a single action can vary from appraiser to appraiser on this view. For example, the judgement that abortion is morally wrong might be true if the appraiser was a member of a conservative religious denomination but false if he or she was a member of an abortion-rights organization.

In addition to worrying about whether there are any good reasons to accept social relativism, there are a number of worries about the view itself. First, there are several open questions about how the view should be formulated, each of which can affect whether it entails of any given act that it is right or wrong. One question is what conditions need to be satisfied in order for an individual to count as a member of a given group. Some groups require that one be born in a certain geographical area, while others require that one's biological parents already be members. Some groups require that one voluntarily join as an adult, while others require that certain initiation procedures be satisfied. But insofar as the morality of one's actions requires conformity to the beliefs of one's group, a general account of exactly which group or groups one counts as a member of is required. A second formulation question concerns exactly what beliefs count as the shared moral beliefs of one's group. Within any group there will be a variety of different moral opinions. And these opinions will vary along at least two different dimensions: how widely they are shared, and how deeply they are held. What is required are principled grounds to determine how widely shared and deeply held a belief needs to be in order to count as one of the shared moral beliefs of a social group. A third formulation question concerns which of the many groups a person is a member of counts as her social group for the purpose of determining whether she acts rightly or wrongly. Given that we are all members of multiple social groups, many of which differ in their shared moral beliefs, an account of which group is the authoritative one on moral matters is required.

Even if the formulation questions can be adequately addressed, a number of serious difficulties arise for social relativism. First, it is not clear how to morally evaluate interactions between people who are members of different social groups on this view. Suppose that an agent from one group treats someone from another group, the patient, in a certain way; for example, the agent breaks a promise she made to the patient. And suppose that the agent's group considers this kind of action to be morally appropriate while the patient's group considers it to be morally wrong. Since the agent's behaviour conforms to the shared moral beliefs of

> ### Case Study 9.3:
> ### Taylor's Vasectomy
>
> Suppose that Taylor had a vasectomy while a member of a minority religious group that believed birth control to be deeply wrong. Later, he left the group, and he now identifies as a member of a secular community in which all forms of birth control are considered to be morally permissible.
>
> **QUESTION**: Has the moral status of Fred's act changed since he left the minority religious group?

her group, she did nothing wrong according to social relativism; but since how he was treated violates the shared moral beliefs of his group, social relativism also entails that the patient was wronged. The upshot is that social relativism entails that someone can be wronged by means of an act that itself is not wrong, which may not be intelligible. Second, social relativism seems to run afoul of some serious counter-examples. For example, insofar as the permissibility of slavery counts as a shared moral belief of the inhabitants of the American South during the slave era, which it arguably was, at least among the members of white populace, then social relativism entails that no acts of enslavement that occurred in that region during that era were morally wrong. But slavery was then and always has been wrong regardless of the views of the populace on that issue. Third, within groups there are often minority subgroups whose moral views differ from those of the majority. Social relativism seems to entail that such minority moral beliefs are erroneous simply because they are in the minority and that, for similar reasons, acts by members of such minority subgroups that conform to their beliefs are automatically morally wrong. Moreover, since what it is for an act to be morally appropriate is for it to conform to majority opinion, social relativism seems to entail that moral criticism of majority opinion is conceptually impossible. However, not only is minority moral opinion not automatically erroneous but criticism of majority opinion is also both possible and sometimes appropriate.

9.5 Subjectivism

As noted above, **subjectivism** is the view that moral claims are relative to individuals: whether an act is right or wrong, or a claim evaluating it is correct or incorrect, depends on whether it conforms to the agent's individual moral beliefs. Moral facts, on the subjectivist picture, can be viewed as a kind of psychological fact rather than as a kind of social fact: facts about the beliefs and values of individual subjects. Consider again Laurel, who took $50 from Marcus without his knowledge and permission and who belongs to a social group whose members approve of acts of this kind. Suppose that Laurel nevertheless believes that others are entitled to private property and that taking this property from them without their consent is wrong. Because her behaviour fails to conform to her own moral beliefs, her act was wrong according to subjectivism. Moreover, whereas considered in its own right, the claim

> What Laurel did was wrong

is neither accurate nor inaccurate, considered relative to Laurel herself it is true.

As with social relativism, we can distinguish between descriptive and normative versions of subjectivism. Descriptive subjectivism consists in the observation that individuals differ in their moral beliefs. A descriptive subjectivist might, for example, note the differences in moral attitudes toward recreational drug use among different individuals. And as with descriptive social relativism, this is something a moral realist can acknowledge. Normative subjectivism, in contrast, is the view that one is morally obligated to conform to one's own moral beliefs, so whether one acts rightly or wrongly depends on whether one's actions conform to such beliefs. It is worth emphasizing that people do not automatically act morally on the subjectivist picture; it is, after all, often quite difficult to live up to one's own moral standards. It is also worth emphasizing the distinction between subjectivism and ethical egoism. Ethical egoism is a version of moral realism according to which one's obligations are to pursue one's own self-interest and one acts rightly to the extent that one does so. What your obligations are according to subjectivism, in contrast, depends on your moral beliefs. If you believe that one ought morally to pursue one's self-interest then you are obligated to do so. But if you believe that one is morally required to sacrifice one's own

Moral Skepticism and Moral Beliefs

One's views about the status of moral claims as objective, relative, or empty puts constraints on the kinds of moral beliefs one can consistently hold. Suppose, for example, that one is inclined to sincerely claim that killing except in self-defence is always wrong. If one is a moral realist, one can thereby express the belief that all instances of non-self-defence killing are wrong, no matter who commits them. If one is a social relativist, however, all one can consistently believe is that the wrongness of non-self-defence killing is included among the shared moral beliefs of one's own community and that only such acts committed by members of that community are wrong. If one is a subjectivist, all that one can consistently believe is that the wrongness of non-self-defence killing is included among one's own moral beliefs and that only such acts committed by oneself are wrong. Finally, if one is a moral nihilist, one does not believe there is such a thing as rightness or wrongness, so one cannot believe that any acts of non-self-defence killing are wrong. By means of one's claim that killing except in self-defence is wrong, one can consistently only express personal disapproval toward acts of that kind.

interests for the sake of the interests of others, then you are not obligated to pursue your own interests.

There are, as one might expect, a number of concerns about subjectivism. First, as with social relativism, some questions of formulation need to be addressed. An individual's moral beliefs can vary in terms of how stable they are and how deeply held they are. As a result, the subjectivist requires principled grounds for deciding whether relatively fleeting moral beliefs, or just those that are stable and to which the subject is deeply committed, form the moral standard against which his or her acts are evaluated. Second, subjectivism runs afoul of what might be called the **innocent person problem**. If an agent performs an act that conforms to her moral beliefs, then she acts rightly and is thus, at least in this instance, an innocent person. But if someone else believes acts of that kind to be morally wrong and, moreover, worthy of punishment, then according to subjectivism it would be morally appropriate for this latter person to punish the original agent. But this entails that it can be morally appropriate to punish an innocent person, contra the widely held view that punishing the innocent is seriously wrong. And third, subjectivism runs afoul of serious counter-examples. In particular, it entails that as long as an agent is true to herself in the sense that her behaviour conforms to her moral beliefs, she can do no wrong. But this means acts of torture, pedophilia, and the like are morally appropriate just as long as the torturer or pedophile believes this to be the case.

9.6 Moral Nihilism

In a nutshell, **moral nihilism** is the view that there are no moral facts and that, as a result, moral claims designed to characterize such facts are empty. No actions of any kind are morally right or wrong because there is no such thing as moral rightness or wrongness, and claims intended to attribute moral features to actions in fact attribute nothing to them whatsoever. If this is correct, however, then extremely widespread patterns of behaviour and deeply held attitudes toward this behaviour are simply ill-conceived and misguided. Suppose once again, for example, that within a certain society there is a widespread pattern of promise keeping: people generally do the things they commit to doing. And suppose that the reason most people are inclined to engage in this behaviour is because they believe it is morally right to do so. But if there is such a thing as moral rightness, then these people in fact have no reason for behaving as they do. Given the radical nature of this implication, moral nihilism is in need of strong motivation. The central goal of this section is to assess whether any such motivation is forthcoming.

One possible reason to endorse moral nihilism is that moral realism requires some kind of **transcendental element**—a supreme being or abstract moral law—but there is no more to reality than the **immanent**, empirical world we inhabit. If, for example, what is morally right is what is commanded by God and what is wrong is what is prohibited by God, then if God does not exist to make such commands, there are no moral facts. As a result, any claims purporting to describe such facts are empty. There two central ways of responding to this sort of argument. First, one might argue that God, or some other kind of transcendental element, does in fact exist and so can serve as the basis of objective morality. The existence of God, however, is a substantial issue in its own right and considering it here would take us too far afield (but see Chapter 7). In any event, second, one might argue that moral realism does not require commitment to the existence of any kind of transcendent reality and that a basis for moral facts can be found in the immanent, empirical world we inhabit. For example, rather than taking morality to consist in conformity to the commands of a supreme being, one might instead take the rightness or wrongness of certain actions to stem from the impact of those actions upon the interests of other immanent beings. And rather than taking our motivation to act morally to stem from fear of punishment at the hands of a supreme being, one might instead take it to be the product of our capacity to empathize with beings similar to ourselves.

A second motivation for moral nihilism might be the worry that there is an insurmountable fact/value gap, and as a consequence, any moral facts would have to be irreducibly non-physical. The fact/value distinction is the distinction between value judgements—concerning things being good or bad, right or wrong, beautiful or ugly, and so forth—on the one hand, and factual judgements—concerning things having observable or measurable properties—on the other. And the idea here is that value judgements cannot be identified with or understood in terms of factual judgements; as a result, if there are features of the world described by value judgements, these features are of a fundamentally different kind from the physical facts of the world. But, the argument goes, ours is a purely physical world that does not contain any non-physical facts; hence, there are no moral facts. In response, one might, of course, reject the purely physical picture of reality; but our focus here will be on the fact/value gap. Although the putative existence of an insurmountable fact/value gap is a complicated issue, there is some reason to believe that any such gap is surmountable. In particular, it seems clear that **prudential or rational normativity** is compatible with a physical picture of reality; and if this is right, it suggests there is no in principle reason why moral normativity is not compatible as well. By prudential or rational normativity what is meant is what you should or ought to do in order to achieve your desires or goals or to satisfy your interests. For example, it could well be true that if Fred wants to travel in Europe next summer, he should get a part-time job and save his earnings. And what is important to note is that the truth of this claim does not seem to require any non-physical facts: it is compatible with Fred being a complex physical object whose desires are simply further physical states of his. In lieu of any positive reason to believe that moral normativity is distinct from prudential normativity in this regard, we have at least grounds to be optimistic that moral realism is compatible with a physical picture of reality.

A third motivation for moral nihilism is that most people's moral beliefs are the product of a process of enculturation and that such beliefs vary from culture to culture. But if morality were objective, we would expect people to derive their moral beliefs directly by means of apprehending the moral facts and we would expect there to be little variation among the shared moral beliefs in different social groups. The difficulty with this argument is that the objectivity of morality is compatible both with the fact that moral beliefs are acquired through enculturation and with cross-cultural variability. First, scientific claims are the paradigm example of objective claims, but for most of us at least, they, like moral claims, are acquired through enculturation. Few of us form our scientific beliefs on the basis of hypothesis formation, experimentation, and the like; instead, most of us learn the science we do in school and simply accept as true what our science teachers tell us. And second, there is and has historically been cross-cultural disagreement on issues that are clearly matters of objective fact. There has, for example, been historical disagreement about the shape of the planet: some people have thought it to be flat while others have thought it to be spherical. Despite this disagreement, there is a fact of the matter about the shape of the planet, and those who have thought it to be flat—or continue to do so—are now and have always been simply wrong.

9.7 Emotivism

Even if one thinks that moral nihilism is well motivated, it runs into difficulties in its own right. Moral discourse makes up a very large proportion of human discourse as a whole. People constantly talk about the rightness and wrongness of actions, events, institutions, and so on. But if moral nihilism is correct, all this talk is essentially meaningless. In particular, insofar as moral talk consists in the use of what are grammatically subject-predicate sentences to attribute moral properties to actions of various kinds, speakers who use moral sentences do not successfully say anything. Consider, by way of analogy, the sentence

What Fred ate is red.

This sentence consists of a subject—"what Fred ate"—and a predicate—"is red"—and is used to attribute redness to a certain foodstuff. If, however, Fred did not in fact eat anything, then the speaker would not successfully say anything by means of it. Moreover, if the predicate "is red" did not in fact pick out any real colour, the speaker's utterance would again be meaningless. Consider, now, the moral claim

What Mary did is wrong.

This sentence consists of a subject—"what Mary did"—and a predicate—"is wrong"—and is used to attribute the property denoted by the predicate to the action denoted by the subject. But if moral nihilism is true, then the predicate does not denote any property and hence nothing is successfully said by means of the moral sentence.

Although much has been written about this difficulty, one particular response will be considered here: **emotivism**. According to emotivism, moral sentences are not used to attribute moral properties to actions; in fact, they are not subject-predicate sentences at all, despite their superficial similarity to them. Although they do contain subject terms that pick out actions, moral sentences are used to express approval or disapproval of those actions, rather than to attribute properties to them. Moreover, they function more like exclamations—"Hurray," "Boo," and the like—than as statements of approval or disapproval; that is, they are more on the order of

> What Mary did—boo!

than

> I disapprove of what Mary did.

In fact, on the view in question, they are not used to make statements at all.

Although emotivism does reconcile the meaningfulness of moral talk with the absence of moral facts, there is some reason to be dissatisfied. One objection is that it is incompatible with genuine moral reasoning. Consider, for example, the following argument:

> PREMISE 1: Lying is wrong.
> PREMISE 2: What Fred did was lie.
> CONCLUSION: What Fred did was wrong.

This argument is deductively valid: the conclusion follows from the premises in the strong sense that it is not even possible for the premises to be true and the conclusion false. But consider the emotivist construal of it:

> PREMISE 1: Lying—boo!
> PREMISE 2: What Fred did is lie.
> CONCLUSION: What Fred did—boo!

This is not even an argument at all—neither Premise 1 nor the conclusion is even a statement—let alone one that is valid. The upshot here is that emotivism does not seem to be compatible with genuine moral reasoning.

In this chapter, we have considered a variety of arguments for skepticism about morality, as well as a number of anti-realist moral theories. Although many of the views we considered ran into serious difficulties, skeptical attitudes toward morality remain very common.

Reading Questions

1.   Why is it beneficial to have a good reputation?

2.   What does it mean to say that a claim is empty?

3.   What are the two basic forms of moral skepticism?

4.   What does it mean to say that there is a fact/value gap?

5.   What reason is there to think that the objectivity of morality is compatible with the fact that, for most of us, moral beliefs are acquired through enculturation?

6.   What is the difference between a statement and an exclamation?

7.   What is moral ethnocentrism?

8.   Why does the fact that people are members of multiple social groups pose difficulties for social relativism?

9.   What is the difference between subjectivism and ethical egoism?

10. What is the innocent person problem that arises for subjectivism?

Reflection Questions

1.   Think of a variety of kinds of actions that in your opinion are morally right or wrong. What, in your view, makes those actions right or wrong? What would it take to convince you that your opinions are simply incorrect?

2.   Think of a number of different social groups of which you are a member. Think of some of the ways in which your moral opinions differ from the views of the members of those groups. What, if anything, do these disagreements tell you about your own moral opinions?

Further Reading

General introduction to moral skepticism:
David Lyons, *Ethics and the Rule of Law* (Cambridge: Cambridge UP, 1984), ch. 1.
John Mackie, *Ethics: Inventing Right and Wrong* (London: Penguin, 1977).

Moral nihilism:
Richard Joyce, *The Myth of Morality* (Cambridge: Cambridge UP, 2001).

Emotivism:
A.J. Ayer, *Language, Truth, and Logic* (London: Gollancz, 1936).

Social relativism:
Robert Audi, *Moral Value and Human Diversity* (New York: Oxford UP, 2007).

Subjectivism:
David Wiggin, "A Sensible Subjectivism?," *Needs, Values, and Truth* (Oxford:
    Blackwell, 1987), pp. 185–214.

10

MORAL REALISM

Moral realism is the view that there are facts of the matter about the rightness or wrongness of actions, which are independent of the moral beliefs of individuals or groups and which can be characterized accurately or inaccurately by moral claims. Moral facts are, however, a species of normative facts, facts about what should or ought to be done; after all, to say an act is morally right is to say that one ought morally to perform it, and to say it is wrong is to say that one ought to refrain from performing it. As a result, the moral realist is faced with the challenge of explaining how it can be a fact that one ought to behave in various ways.

A moral theory is designed to determine which acts are right and wrong, as well as to explain why they are so. This involves identifying those features that make an act right, as well as those that make an act wrong. In addition, what is required is an account of why the possession of such features obligates us to perform or refrain from performing certain acts. In this chapter, we will consider various accounts of moral rightness and wrongness, as well as the relation between God and morality.

CHAPTER CONTENTS:

- a taxonomy of types of moral realism is developed;
- the relationship between God and morality is explored;
- utilitarian approaches to morality are evaluated;
- the notion of moral rights is introduced; and
- the question of moral motivations is addressed.

10.1 Varieties of Realism

Realist accounts of morality can take a variety of different forms, and at least some
of the objections to moral realism stem from the failure to recognize this fact. In
particular, there is a tendency to argue from the difficulties that arise for one form
of realism to the conclusion that moral realism itself must be false. For example,
one of the reasons some people balk at moral realism is because of their objections
to what might be called moral absolutism. **Moral absolutism** is the view that morality
consists in a number of simple, exceptionless moral rules. Such rules offer a uniform
moral assessment of all acts of a certain kind. Examples of absolute rules include

> Killing human persons is always morally wrong

and

> Truth-telling is always morally required.

The trouble with moral absolutism is that there always seem to be exceptions to
relatively specific moral rules of this kind. This sometimes involves circumstances
in which following a moral rule would result in serious harm to oneself or others.
Cases of killing in self-defence or to protect innocent third parties, for example, are
often thought to be exceptions to the general prohibition against killing. This can
also involve circumstances in which the only way to follow one moral rule is to fail
to follow another. For example, I may have to lie to Mary about Fred's whereabouts
in order to fulfill my promise to Fred to keep his whereabouts a secret. Now while
it is certainly true that moral absolutism is one kind of moral realism, it is not the
only kind. As a result, even if such exceptions show moral absolutism to be false,
they give no reason to suppose that moral realism itself is erroneous.

Realist alternatives to moral absolutism include both moral particularism and
other species of moral universalism. **Moral universalism** is the view that there are
general moral principles that determine the rightness or wrongness of actions. But
unlike moral absolutism, not all varieties of moral universalism entail that all acts
of any given relatively specific kind are morally equivalent. Consider, for example, the principle that one ought to always do what produces the most happiness.
Although in most circumstances this requires truth-telling and refraining from killing human persons, in some circumstances it might require lying or killing. Moral
particularism, in contrast, is the view that the rightness or wrongness of actions
is not determined by general rules or principles. Rather, it is wholly a function of
features of the situation in which the act occurs. A particular act of lying or killing, for example, might be morally appropriate, but this depends on things such as
the agent's motivations, the moral character of the victim, the consequences of the
action, and so on. The fact that the act in question is an instance of some general
principle or other is morally irrelevant. It is worth emphasizing that moral particularism counts as a version of moral realism. After all, particular actions count as

right or wrong on this view. But types of action are neither right nor wrong, so claims to this effect are always false.

We can also distinguish between versions of moral realism according to which moral questions always have determinate answers and those according to which these answers are sometimes indeterminate. To say that moral questions are fully determinate is to say that for any given action, there is a fact of the matter about its rightness or wrongness—even if the moral qualities of an act are controversial, it nevertheless is either right or it is wrong. And to say that moral questions are partially indeterminate is to say that in the case of at least some actions, there is no fact of the matter regarding their rightness or wrongness. So even if killing human persons, except in self-defence, is always wrong, and truth-telling, except to prevent harm to others, is always right, abortion when the life and health of the pregnant woman is not at risk, for example, might be neither right nor wrong.

> ### Permissible or Required
>
> To say that an act is morally wrong is to say it is prohibited: it is something that ought not to be done. But to say that an act is morally right can mean that it is either permitted or required. To say an act is permissible is to say that it may be done—one does not do wrong if one performs it—but it is not true that it must be done—one does no wrong if one refrains from performing it either. To say that an act is required, however, is to say that it must be done, and that one does wrong if one does not perform it. It is worth emphasizing that an act's being permissible but not required is not the same as its being neither right nor wrong; rather, it is to say that it is, in one sense, morally right.

10.2 God and Morality

One very common realist view is that some kind of superior being or god is the source of morality. Although this view can take many forms, we will focus here on the **divine command theory**, according to which a superior being—let's call it "God"—created the universe and everything that exists within in it, including human persons. Moreover, human persons have free will, which means that they have a certain degree of control over the actions they perform. God, however, commands that they perform some of these and refrain from performing others. And if someone complies with God's commands, they act rightly, whereas if they violate one of these commands, their action is morally wrong. So, for example, if God commands that we refrain from killing other human persons except in self-defence and Mary kills someone when she is not at risk of harm from her victim, then she acts wrongly according to the divine command theory. And if God commands that we always speak the truth and Fred speaks truly, then Fred's act of truth-telling is right.

There are two further issues that a moral theory needs to address to which the divine command theory has superficially plausible answers. The first issue is that of moral epistemology. **Epistemology**, in general, is concerned with knowledge and justification. **Moral epistemology**, then, is concerned with knowledge of morality and, in particular, how we know what is morally required and prohibited. According to the divine command theory, moral knowledge of this kind requires knowledge of God's commands. And often advocates of views of this kind take God's commands to be found in certain religious texts, such as the Christian Bible. After all, these texts are supposed to be records of experiences of their authors in which the commands of God, among other things, were directly revealed to them. The second issue concerns **moral motivation:** what reason do we have to act morally? The divine command theory offers two separate answers to this question. First, insofar as God commands us to act in certain ways, and does not merely ask or suggest that we do so, God intends to subject us to some kind of punishment should we fail to comply. And as long as the punishment God intends to apply is sufficiently unpleasant, fear of being subjected to it may sufficiently motivate at least most of us to comply with God's commands. So, for example, if God commands us to keep our promises and intends to subject us to eternal damnation should we fail to do so, our fear of eternal damnation should motivate us to keep our promises. Second, given that God created us and the universe we inhabit, we are under an extreme debt of gratitude to God. After all, we owe gratitude to those who provide us with aid in times of need; giving us both existence and a world to inhabit counts as exceptional aid. Therefore, this debt of gratitude we owe God obligates us to obey God's commands.

Freedom and Responsibility

In order to be morally responsible for your actions, you have to have the ability to act otherwise. Suppose, for example, you see a child drowning in the water but you do not jump in to save him or her because you yourself are unable to swim. In such circumstances, you cannot be held responsible for your failure to save the child—even if God commanded that you help those in need—exactly because you lacked the ability to do so. As a result, unless you want to acknowledge a systematic disconnect between rightness or wrongness, on the one hand, and moral responsibility, on the other, your moral theory needs to presuppose that human persons have at least some degree of free will.

Case Study 10.1: The Moral Atheist

Suppose that Fred is an atheist: not only does he refrain from believing in the existence of any particular god but he also positively believes that no gods exist. And suppose that he is certain that he could kill his nephew without being caught by human authorities, and if he does so he stands to inherit a substantial fortune. Nevertheless, he refrains from doing so because he believes it would be wrong.

QUESTION: Is Fred's disbelief in the existence of gods compatible with his belief in the wrongness of killing his nephew? Even conceding the wrongness of this act, could he have any good reason to refrain from performing it?

The divine command theory consists of three distinct but related elements:

- an account of how we know what is right or wrong;
- an account of why we are motivated to act morally; and
- an account of the nature of rightness and wrongness.

Each of these elements, however, runs into serious difficulties. Consider, first, the account of moral knowledge. According to the divine command theory, our moral knowledge comes from divinely inspired religious texts. Now even supposing that God exists and inspired certain texts, there are numerous difficulties with the suggestion that moral knowledge can be acquired from such texts. First, in order to acquire moral knowledge in this way, we need to be able to determine which religious texts were divinely inspired and which were not, and it is not clear how we could make this determination. Second, many of the texts we currently have access to are the products of a series of sometimes slipshod translations between languages which have themselves undergone significant changes in grammar, spelling, vocabulary, and meaning. As a result, even if the original text provided a reliable record of the commands of God, the texts we currently have access to are not so reliable. And third, there are multiple ways of interpreting any given religious text, each of which could yield a different account of exactly what God commanded. For example, in interpreting a text, one needs to determine what should be taken literally and what should be taken metaphorically, and interpretations that disagree about the status of different sentences can easily yield different accounts of morality. One might respond that we can fix upon the correct interpretation by appeal to the intentions of the author: the correct interpretation of a religious text is that which accords with what God intended. But although this might help in the case of non-religious texts, it is unlikely to do so in the case of religious texts. After all, the only evidence we have of God's intentions is the religious texts themselves.

Consider, second, the account of moral motivation which, recall, claims that we are moved to comply with God's commands either due to fear of punishment should we fail to do so or out of gratitude for God's having created us. Either way, however, the divine command theory runs into difficulty. Although fear of punishment may well motivate us to act morally, it is a defective kind of moral motivation. Not only is the threat of some kind of severe punishment itself morally suspect, but people who need some such threat in order to be moved to act well are also themselves morally suspect. They are the kind of people who would act wrongly if they thought they could get away with it. Moreover, it is unclear whether we are under a debt of gratitude to God for creating us—or, more modestly, would be if such a being existed and did so—and equally unclear that gratitude would require compliance with any commands that God happens to make. If someone provides you with desired aid in a time of need, you may owe her gratitude. But this does not obligate you to do whatever she happens to want. Rather, it obligates you to be ready to help out should your benefactor find herself in need of aid.

Consider, finally, the account of rightness and wrongness: an act is right just in case it conforms to the commands of God. There are, however, two ways of understanding this view, each of which runs into serious difficulties: right actions are right because they are commanded by God; and right actions are commanded by God because they are right. On both interpretations, the class of morally right actions coincides with the class of actions that we perform. The difference is that on the first interpretation, God's commands are what make the actions right. Not only do they not become right until God commands that we perform them, but had

God commanded differently or made no such commands at all, they would also not now be (or ever have been) morally right. On the second interpretation, in contrast, the moral status of the actions in question is independent of God's commands; they would have been right had God not commanded we perform them and even had God commanded that we not do so. In effect, God commands us to perform actions because he recognizes that such actions are independently right and he wants us act rightly.

On either interpretation, however, the divine command theory runs into serious difficulties. Consider the first interpretation. If what makes an action right is that God commands that we perform it, then whatever God commands would be morally required. As a result, if as a matter of fact God commanded that we refrain from killing innocent people, then it would follow that killing innocents is wrong. But if God had instead commanded that we kill innocent people, then killing innocents would be morally required. One might, of course, respond that God wouldn't command us to kill innocents and so the problem here doesn't arise. But given that there is no fact of the matter concerning the rightness or wrongness of killing innocents independent of God's command according to the theory at issue, God had no moral reason to command one way rather than the other. Hence, there is no good reason to think, according to the divine command theory, that God has any more reason to command us to refrain from killing innocents than he has to command us to kill innocents. Second, if God commands us to perform right actions because they are right, then such actions would have been right even had God refrained from commanding us to perform them. As a result, God's commands are irrelevant to the moral status of right actions, and hence God has no role to play in an account of the nature of morality. The upshot is that God's commands are either morally arbitrary or morally irrelevant. So even if God exists and commands that we act in various ways, these commands do not offer an adequate basis for morality.

> ### Case Study 10.2:
> ### The Malevolent Creator
>
> Suppose that the universe and its contents were created by a supremely malevolent being. And suppose that this being commanded that we refrain from helping others in need. Moreover, suppose that this being intended to subject those of us who disobeyed to severe eternal torment. Finally, suppose that Mary provided a starving child with food.
>
> **QUESTION**: Would Mary's act be right or wrong in such circumstances?

10.3 Act Utilitarianism

Although there is a wide variety of non-religious alternatives to the divine command theory, one simple and compelling view is **utilitarianism**. On this view, what determines the rightness or wrongness of acts is the value—or utility—of the consequences of those acts. As such, utilitarianism yields an attractive account of moral motivation: the basic idea is that one is obligated to produce whatever is good and refrain from producing whatever is bad. Two important utilitarian approaches to morality are act utilitarianism and rule utilitarianism. The difference between these two approaches is whether the primary focus is on the moral status of particular actions or the moral status of types of actions. On the **act utilitarian** approach, each action is evaluated individually in terms of its particular consequences. On the **rule utilitarian** approach, in contrast, social rules prohibiting, permitting, or requiring the performance of various kinds of actions are evaluated in terms of their consequences; individual actions are evaluated only derivatively, in terms of whether they involve violating or conforming to a social rule that has valuable consequences. For illustrative purposes, we are going to focus on a simple version of act utilitarianism here. In order to develop this view, we will need a theory of value—of what, as a matter of fact, is good—as well as a theory of rightness—of exactly what our obligations are with respect to producing goodness.

The goal of a **theory of value** is an account of what is good or valuable. There are, however, a number of different senses in which something can be valuable: it can be economically valuable, having a high market price; aesthetically valuable, having a high degree of beauty; historically valuable, that is, significant because of its connection to certain historical periods or events; or sentimentally valuable, evoking positive emotions or happy memories in an individual; and so on. The concern here, however, is with **moral value**: what makes certain circumstances morally better or worse than others. In addition, what is of interest is intrinsic rather than instrumental value. To say something is **instrumentally valuable** is to say that it is valuable, not in its own right, but because of what it can be used to achieve. For example, for most of us money is instrumentally valuable: we value it not for its own sake but rather for the things we can purchase with it. To say something is **intrinsically valuable**, in contrast, is to say it is valuable for its own sake: even if we could not use it to acquire something else we cared about, we would still value it. For example, for most parents their children are intrinsically valuable; parents value their children for their own sake and not for what they can acquire by means of them.

Although there are many different accounts of intrinsic moral value, one prominent view is that the only thing that is valuable for its own sake is happiness. **Happiness** is a psychological state of which human persons, at least, are capable and which certain psychologically complex non-human animals may be capable of as well. So, on this view, circumstances we think of as morally bad—famine, war, and oppression, for example—are so because of their impact on the psychological states of human persons and, in particular, the unhappiness they cause, while circumstances we think of as good—peace, justice, and the like—are so because of the happiness they produce. Now according to this view, the more happiness there is, the better things are, morally speaking. There are, at least, two ways of developing this idea: the greater the total number of happy people, the better things are; and the greater the total amount of happiness, regardless of how it is distributed, the better things are. In what follows, we will be assuming the latter and, therefore, we will be assuming that circumstances in which there are a lot of slightly happy people may

Intrinsic Mind-Dependent Value

Many people claim that goodness or value is **mind-dependent** in the sense that something can be valuable only in virtue of someone's valuing it and that it does not make sense to speak of something being valuable in its own right, independent of the value people place upon it. Even if this is right, however, it does not follow that all value is instrumental value. After all, among the things we value, we can distinguish between those we value for their own sake and those we value for their consequences.

be worse morally than circumstances in which there are a few very happy people

As noted above, a **theory of rightness** morally evaluates actions in terms of the value of the circumstances they produce. There are three different ways in which a theory might go about doing this. First, a theory might simply look at the value of the circumstances produced by an action: if it produces circumstances that are good or valuable, then it is right; but if it produces circumstances that are bad, then it is wrong. The trouble with this suggestion is that it entails that you could act rightly even if your actions made things worse rather than better, morally speaking. After all, as long as the outcome is circumstances that are good, the fact that you made things less good than they were before is irrelevant on this view. Second, a theory might compare the value of the circumstances that an act produces with how valuable the circumstances were before the act was performed: if an act produces circumstances that are better than they were before, then it is right; if an act produces circumstances that are worse than they were before, then it is wrong. The trouble with this suggestion is that you might find yourself in circumstances in which anything you could do, including doing nothing, would result in circumstances being worse than they currently are. But one might think that if you make things the best they can be in such circumstances, then you are acting rightly, even if the best things can be is worse than they were before. Finally, a theory might compare the value of the circumstances an act produces with the value of the circumstances that would have ensued had the agent acted instead on her other options: if an act produces circumstances that are better than would have been produced by any of the agent's other options, then it is right; if an act produces circumstances that are worse than would have been produced by at least some of the agent's other options, then it is wrong. On this view, an act that produces circumstances that are worse than they were before can be right as long as these consequences are better than would have ensued had the agent acted on her other options. In what follows, this latter theory of rightness will be assumed.

Combining the theory of value and the theory of rightness yields the **greatest happiness principle**: an act is morally right just in case it produces more total happiness than any of the agent's other options. Suppose, for example, that Fred finds Mary's wallet, which contains her ID, so he can easily contact her, as well as $50 in cash, which Mary needs to buy food for her five starving children. And suppose that rather than return the wallet to Mary, Fred throws it away and keeps the money for himself. In order to determine whether Fred's act was right, according to the greatest happiness principle, we need to compare the total amount of happiness produced by his act with the amount of happiness that would have been produced had he acted on his other options, that is, had he returned the wallet to Mary. Finally, suppose that Fred uses the money to download some videos and buy a six-pack of Pilsner Urquell, his favourite imported beer, and spends a pleasant evening watching videos and drinking beer, but that had he returned the wallet to Mary she would have used the money to feed herself and her children. Fred's act of keeping the wallet resulted in his being a little bit happy but also resulted in Mary and her children being quite unhappy. Had he returned the wallet instead, he would have been less happy but Mary and her children would have been substantially happier. As a result, since one of his other options would have produced more total happiness than what he actually did, Fred's act was wrong according to the greatest happiness principle. It is worth emphasizing, however, that if Mary would have used her money on something other than food for herself and her children if Fred had in fact returned her wallet, it might have turned out that Fred's act of keeping the wallet was right.

Despite its many attractions, there are a number of reasons to object to the greatest happiness principle. First, in order to assess the rightness or wrongness of an action, on this view, we need to be able to determine the total amount of happiness it produces. But it is far from clear that there is any genuine way to measure quantities of happiness, especially when we consider the happiness of a number of different people. Second, the application of the greatest happiness principle to a given action requires that we be able to determine which consequences are attributable to that event; but what occurs as a result of an action is the complex product of numerous distinct factors, often including the actions of other people. Third, the application of the greatest happiness principle requires determining not only the consequences attributable to an act that was performed but also what would have occurred had the agent acted on her other options. But there may simply be no determinate fact of the matter regarding what would have happened had the agent acted differently. And finally, by focusing only on the total amount of happiness produced and not the impact of actions on individual people, the greatest happiness principle fails to require that right action involves proper respect for moral persons, treating them instead as mere valueless receptacles of valuable psychological states.

Case Study 10.3: The Perfect Donor

Suppose that Fred goes into the hospital for a routine cosmetic procedure. And suppose that also in the hospital that day are five patients in urgent need of organ transplants: one needs a new heart, one needs a pair of lungs, one needs a liver, and two need kidneys. Routine pre-operative testing surprisingly reveals that Fred is a perfect match for all of these patients. As a result, Fred's doctor, Mary, decides to harvest Fred's organs.

QUESTION: Supposing that Fred could have been expected to lead a life producing roughly the same amounts of happiness as each of the organ recipients if he had survived, is Mary's act wrong according to the greatest happiness principle? Do you think her act is right or wrong?

10.4 Rights

An alternative approach to morality, which avoids many of the objections that arise for the greatest happiness principle, is one that invokes the notion of **moral rights**. The basic idea is that people possess a number of rights, which entitle them to various forms of behaviour on the part of other people. And so, on this view, to engage in behaviour to which others are, by their rights, entitled is to act rightly, whereas to fail to so behave is to act wrongly. Someone who has a right to life, for example, is entitled to behaviour on the part of others that preserves his or her life. Hence, if you rescue someone with a right to life from life-threatening circumstances, you act rightly, whereas if you kill that person, you act wrongly. Rather than a complete alternative to the utilitarian picture, the invocation of rights can be understood as a supplement to it. In particular, one might view the obligation to maximize the total amount of happiness by means of one's actions to be constrained by the requirement that the rights of the affected parties be respected. Suppose, for example, that Mary is faced with the following options: she can hack into Fred's bank account and use the money to pay the rent for the homeless shelter she runs, or she can abandon her efforts to keep the doors of the shelter open. Utilitarian considerations favour the first option, especially if Fred would be inclined to use his money predominantly for his own benefit. But if Fred has property rights that would be violated were Mary to steal his money, then on the mixed utilitarian/rights picture, acting in this way would be wrong. In effect, rights can be viewed as trumps, overriding utilitarian considerations that count in favour of their violation.

To say someone has a right to something is equivalent to saying that others have an obligation to provide that person with whatever she has a right to or, at least, to refrain from depriving her of it. What it is for me to have a right to life, for example, is for others to have an obligation to refrain from killing me. An important distinction, on this picture, is between positive and negative rights. Someone has a **negative right** to something just in case others have an obligation to refrain from depriving her of it; someone has a **positive right** to that same thing just in case others have an obligation to provide her with it. To have a negative right to free speech is for others to be obligated to refrain from preventing you from expressing your views; to have a positive right to free speech, in contrast, is for others to be obligated to aid you in expressing your views, perhaps by providing you with a certain kind of forum. And not only are positive rights typically more controversial than negative rights but they also normally place obligations only on a narrower class of people: while everyone is obligated to refrain from killing you, only health-care and other professionals are obligated to save your life. The reason for this is because in order to be under an obligation to engage in a certain course of action, someone needs both the ability and opportunity to do so. In order to be under an obligation to rescue you from life-threatening circumstances, I need to have the relevant skill set to do so, I need to have the relevant tools, and I need to be in the right proximity. If your appendix is about to burst, I can be under an obligation to try to save you only if I have surgical training and adequate medical equipment, and I can get to you in order to apply my skills. But except under extraordinary circumstances, it takes no special skills to refrain from killing you; and anyone anywhere can so refrain.

As with act utilitarianism, there are a number of reasons to worry about the theory of rights. First, the picture according to which rights trump all other moral considerations is far too simple: not only are there arguably exceptions to all rights—that is, circumstances in which they are appropriately disregarded—but different rights can also come into conflict with one another. Consider, for example, killing in self-defence and circumstances in which the only way to respect one person's right to privacy is to restrict another person's right of free speech. Ultimately, a theory of rights

> **Case Study 10.4:**
> **The Partisan Station Manager**
>
> Suppose that Fred runs a local television station that has a segment in which various people express their political views. And suppose that Mary, a local blogger, applies to appear in this segment. Upon reading Mary's blog, Fred discovers that he strongly disapproves of her political views. Although Fred does nothing to interfere with Mary's blog, he refuses to allow her to appear on his station.
>
> **QUESTION**: Does Fred violate Mary's free-speech rights? What if any difference does it make if Fred's network receives a subsidy from the government?

requires an account of the conditions under which it can be morally appropriate to violate or disregard the rights of others, as well as an account of the conditions under which competing rights have priority over one another. Second, different sorts of entities might have a positive or negative right to a range of different things, some of which are more controversial than others. For example, one might wonder whether all human persons have a right to an education, whether convicted felons have a right to vote, and whether unborn humans and certain non-human animals have a right to life. What is required is a general account of who has what kinds of rights to what, and why. Finally, one might wonder exactly what a right is in the first place, especially given that the possession of a right places others under obligations to uphold it. One might suppose that rights are naturally occurring intrinsic features of certain entities, like having a particular chemical makeup. The trouble with this is that none of the intrinsic physical properties possessed by creatures we think of as possessing rights by themselves suffice to place others under obligations to them. As a result, this strategy seems to entail that rights are mysterious non-physical features of their bearers. Alternatively, one might take rights to be conventional in the sense that one has a right to something only because others have agreed to provide one with it or refrain from depriving one of it. The trouble with this is that it could turn out that the members of certain relatively powerless minority groups lack rights to basic goods simply because the majority does not agree to provide them. One might, instead, formulate things in terms of the hypothetical agreements of idealized agents rather than the actual agreements of real people, agents who would not deny basic goods to powerless minority groups. But one still might wonder why the hypothetical agreements of ideal agents place real people under any sort of obligations.

10.5 Moral Motivations

The question of **moral motivation** is the question of why one should act morally or do the right thing. Suppose, for example, that it would be morally wrong for Fred, who has found Mary's wallet, to keep it for himself and morally right for him to return it to her, and that Fred knows this. The question is what motivation Fred has for returning the wallet to Mary, especially if he would be personally better off keeping it for himself, at least if no one found out. One possible answer is that the fact of its being the right thing to do itself might motivate Fred to return the wallet. Some people are simply generally motivated to do what is right, and so, if they come to believe a particular course of action is right, they will simply be moved to engage in it. Another possible answer is that his care for the impact of his actions on Mary might motivate Fred to return her wallet. Some people care about the impact of their actions on others and, as a result, are generally moved to perform acts that benefit others and refrain from performing acts that harm them. As a result, insofar as right actions are those that benefit others and wrong actions are those that harm them, such people will be moved to act rightly.

Some people, however, are motivated neither by moral duty nor by care for others, but rather are motivated solely by self-interest. And if Fred is one of these people, does he have any motivation to do the right thing and return Mary's wallet? More generally, is acting morally in one's self-interest? The answer is that it depends. Although Fred might on this one occasion do better by acting immorally and keeping Mary's wallet, doing so could have a negative impact on his reputation and, as a result, undermine his attempts to achieve his goals later. In order to achieve their goals, people often need to secure the cooperation of others. But people with bad reputations are often unable to secure the cooperation they need and thus find their goals frustrated. After all, unless we are desperate, most of us will not enter into agreements with people who cannot be trusted. So unless one can avoid the impact of immoral behaviour on one's reputation, acting morally will generally be in one's long-term self-interest. But, of course, one will do best by maintaining a good reputation while acting immorally when it is in one's interest to do so. If I can convince people I am trust-

Case Study 10.5: The Prisoner's Dilemma

Suppose Mary and Fred are arrested on suspicion of having committed an armed jewellery-store heist. The police do not have enough evidence to convict them of this crime but they do have enough evidence to convict them of another less serious charge. As a result, the police separately offer each of them the following deal: if one testifies against the other while the other does not, then the defector goes free and the other gets a 10-year sentence; if both testify against the other, they each get a 5-year sentence for armed robbery; and if neither testifies against the other, they each get a 1-year sentence for the minor charge.

QUESTION: Assuming that Fred and Mary are each concerned only with lessening their own jail time, and that they have no access until after the fact to what the other has done, what would it be rational for them to do?

worthy despite breaking my agreements when there is profit in doing so, perhaps by keeping my victims silent, then I will continue to be able to enter into beneficial agreements in the future.

A separate question from what motivations people might have to act morally is whether an account of what morally right action consists in can be given in terms of motivations. The basic idea underlying this approach is that what it is for an action to be morally appropriate is for it to be the product of the relevant kinds of motivations. And a central question here is exactly what sort of motivation is the relevant kind, the kind that is constitutive of morally appropriate action. One answer that will not do here is that the motivation to do the right thing is constitutive of morality. After all, to say that what it is for an act to be morally right is for it to be motivated by the desire to act in a way that is morally right is entirely uninformative. What one needs instead is a motivation whose goal or object makes no mention of morality, such as the desire to promote the interests of other people or something along these lines. However, even if one can come up with a defensible account of morality-constituting motivations, there are problems with this whole approach to morality. The basic difficulty is that the moral status of a person and the moral status of his or her action can come apart: a person can do the right thing for the wrong reasons or the wrong thing for the right reasons. Consider, for example, someone whose sole motivation for helping a person in need is to impress a potential romantic partner, or someone, motivated by charity, who provides a person with something seriously harmful to him or her. The upshot is that while having the right kinds of motivations may be constitutive of being a morally virtuous person, having the right motivations is neither sufficient nor required for morally right action.

In this chapter we have considered a number of realist moral theories, as well as a number of accounts of moral motivation. Despite the objections to them, utilitarian and rights-based moral theories are still widely discussed in the philosophical literature, and religious accounts of morality remain very popular. For advocates of moral realism, the question of the nature of morality remains to be resolved.

Reading Questions

1.   What is the relation between moral absolutism and moral universalism?

2.   What reasons do we have for being moral, according to the divine command theory?

3.   According to the divine command theory, what has to be true in order for an action to be morally wrong?

4.   What is a theory of moral epistemology designed to tell us?

5.   What is the difference between intrinsic and instrumental value?

6.   What is the greatest happiness principle?

7.   What is the difference between positive and negative rights?

8.   Why can't rights be intrinsic physical properties of individuals?

9.   Why is it important to maintain a good reputation?

10.   Why can't the desire to do the right thing be constitutive of morality?

Reflection Questions

1.   Think of a number of different actions you think of as morally right. What
      sort of consequences do those actions typically have? If some of these con-
      sequences were different, how would that affect your moral assessment of
      them?

2.   Think of a number of cases in which you consider yourself to have done the
      right thing. Think about whether doing the right thing made you better off
      or worse off in those cases. What was your motivation for doing the right
      thing in the cases in which doing so made you worse off? Was your motiva-
      tion different in the other cases?

Further Reading

General introduction to realist moral theories:
Wilfrid J. Waluchow, *The Dimensions of Ethics: An Introduction to Ethical
      Theory* (Peterborough, ON: Broadview P, 2003).

God and morality:
"Euthyphro," in *Plato: Five Dialogues: Euthyphro, Apology, Crito, Meno, Phaedo,*
      ed. John Cooper (Indianapolis: Hackett Classics, 2002).

Act utilitarianism:
John Stuart Mill, *Utilitarianism,* ed. Colin Heydt (Peterborough, ON:
      Broadview P, 2010).

Rights-based morality:
Tom Campbell, *Rights: A Critical Introduction* (London: Routledge, 2006).

Moral motivation:
John Mackie, *Ethics: Inventing Right and Wrong* (London: Penguin, 1977).

11

JUSTICE

Justice is one of our most fundamental moral concepts. To characterize something as an injustice is to brand it as seriously wrong, and the demand for justice is a deeply compelling call to action. Nevertheless, the notion of justice is a problematic one. One difficulty is that the concept gets applied in a seemingly disparate collection of domains. People talk about just individuals, economic justice, and criminal justice, among other things, and it is not clear to what extent the sense of justice is the same in each case. Moreover, it is not entirely clear in any given case what justice requires and why.

The central concern of this chapter is whether justice has any kind of unified nature and, if so, what this nature is. To this end, we will consider what justice means in the various domains in which the concept is applied, and whether there is a common core shared across these domains. In particular, we will explore whether the various applications of the concept of justice are unified by an overarching concern with fairness.

CHAPTER CONTENTS:

- the relationship between justice and morality is explored;
- the sense in which justice is a virtue of individual people is examined;
- various accounts of justice in the distribution of goods are evaluated; and
- the question of criminal justice is addressed.

11.1 Justice and Morality

The first question that needs to be addressed is the connection between justice and morality more generally. One view might be that justice and morality are the same thing: for something to be just is simply for it to be morally right; and for something to be unjust is for it to be morally wrong. The trouble with this suggestion is that there are grounds for thinking that something can be morally right without its being just; similarly, something can be wrong without being an injustice. Someone might argue, for example, that giving resources—food, clothes, money, and so on—to someone in need is the right thing to do, but if the beneficiary of one's charitable actions is not entitled to these resources, if he has not been unfairly deprived of these or similar resources, then one's act is not required by justice. Similarly, if someone provides unwarranted offence to others, perhaps by displaying pornographic material on a public billboard, then although her act is wrong, she arguably has not committed any kind of injustice against those she has offended. After all, she has not treated them unfairly nor has she deprived them of anything to which they are entitled.

A second view is that justice is simply one dimension of morality in the sense that being just is simply one way of being morally right and being unjust is simply one way of being wrong. So right actions include, for example, acts of justice, charity, kindness, and the like, while wrong actions include such things as acts of injustice, offense, and harm. Although an improvement over the previous view, this suggestion also runs into some difficulty. In particular, it seems that something can be both just but, all things considered, wrong, as well as unjust but, all things considered, right. Take as a first example a case in which punishing someone for a crime he has committed would result in extreme suffering for a large number of people who are dependent on him. One might argue that although punishing someone in such circumstances would be just, it might nevertheless be wrong. Consider, second, a case in which someone is passed over for a position for which she is best qualified in favour of a less qualified candidate on the grounds that the latter is a member of a group that has been historically discriminated against. One might argue that although favouring the less qualified candidate is the right thing to do, all things considered, the more qualified candidate has nevertheless been treated unjustly.

A third view is that justice is one dimension of morality, not in the sense of being one way of being right among others, but rather in the sense of being one moral consideration among others. The idea here is that in assessing whether something is right or wrong, one marshals a number of distinct moral considerations: what the harms and benefits are, the impact on the rights of various parties, any offence that might be caused, and so on. And justice is just one of these considerations. As noted above, these considerations might point in different directions in a given case: considerations of justice might suggest that an act is right, whereas consideration of harm and benefit might suggest that it is wrong, or vice versa. Whether an act is right or wrong, all things considered, is a function of the various moral considerations counting for or against it. Finally, on this view, the fact that an act is just or unjust does not by itself determine that it is right or wrong; it is just one factor that plays a role in this determination. And this is the view that will be adopted for the remainder of the chapter.

As we are assuming that justice is not simply identical to morality, we must also assume that justice is definable in its own right—that there is something in particular that justice consists in. The central question of this chapter, then, is in what justice consists: what features something has to have in order to count as just or unjust. This is complicated by the fact that there are a number of very distinct sorts of bearers of justice, that is, things capable of being evaluated as just or unjust. One kind of bearer of justice is a person. We characterize certain people as just and others as unjust. When applied in this way, justice is treated as a virtue: a morally significant character trait. Another kind of bearer of justice is an economic system. Certain ways of distributing economic goods and resources are thought of as just, whereas others are thought to be unjust. For example, an economic system in which most of the wealth generated ends up in the hands of a small minority—the so-called "one per cent"—might be thought of as unjust. A third kind of bearer of justice is the treatment of criminal wrongdoers. If someone is guilty of a serious crime, justice in this sense requires not only that he be convicted of that crime but also that he be subjected to a suitable punishment for it. The final kind of bearer of justice is a procedure. Questions of procedural justice concern whether legal processes of various kinds, such as criminal trials, are just or unjust. Despite the differences among the various bearers of justice, one possible unifying factor among the corresponding senses of justice is a connection between justice and fairness. In the remainder of this chapter, we will explore the relation between fairness and justice in the case of each of the various ways of applying the concept.

11.2 Justice as a Virtue

The first sense of justice at issue is the justice of individual people. When one says of a person that she is just, one is attributing a virtue to her. A **virtue** is a morally significant character trait. And a **character trait** is a behavioural disposition: a **disposition** to engage in a certain range of behaviour. To say something is disposed to behave in a certain way is to say that if it is subjected to the right kind of conditions it will behave in that way. For example, what it means to say that salt is water-soluble is that if it is placed in water, then it will dissolve; and what it means to say that glass is fragile is that if it is struck with sufficient force, it will shatter. It is important to note that something can have a disposition without ever engaging in the behaviour in question, as long as the relevant conditions never occur. A piece of glass, for example, can be fragile even if it never shatters, as long as it is never struck with sufficient force.

As with other dispositions, to have a character trait is to behave in a certain way when subjected to the right sorts of conditions. To be charitable, for example, is to give aid if one encounters someone in need; and to be stubborn is to refuse to change your attitude or behaviour if someone attempts to make you do so. And as with dispositions more generally, one can have a character trait without ever engaging in the relevant sort of behaviour. You could, for example, be charitable without ever giving aid, as long as you never encountered anyone who was in need. It would, however, need to be true of you that if you were to meet some such person, you would offer him aid. In at least some cases, exactly what character traits you have is a product of your psychological states. So, for example, a charitable disposition might be explained by a deeply held desire to aid those in need. Moreover, because the existence of such psychological states does not depend on the conditions that trigger the behaviour in question, they can explain why the character trait can exist in the absence of the behaviour. If a charitable disposition is explained by a desire to help others in need, then I can have that character trait in the absence of any aid-giving behaviour as long as I retain the desire to help others.

Some character traits are **morally neutral** in the sense that, other things being equal, possession of them does not make one a morally better or worse person. Consider, for example, stubbornness. Although stubborn people may be difficult to deal with, they are not morally defective for that reason. Moreover, in any given instance, stubbornness can be morally praiseworthy, morally blameworthy, or neither, depending on what one is stubborn about. Other character traits are morally significant in the sense that, other things being equal, possession of them does make one a morally better or worse person. Those character traits that make one a better person are virtues. Examples of virtues include such things as honesty, generosity, courage, and justice. And those character traits that make one a morally worse person are vices. **Vices** are often thought of as opposites of virtues. So, for example, the opposite of honesty is dishonesty, the opposite of generosity is stinginess, the opposite of courage is cowardice, and the opposite of justice is injustice. In addition to opposites, there are also **exaggerated counterparts** of at least some virtues, that is, an excess of the traits that make one virtuous. Consider, for example, courage. To be courageous to is to be disposed to subject oneself to a certain amount of risk of harm in order to achieve a greater good. A courageous person might, for example, run into a burning building in order to rescue someone trapped inside. Consider instead, however, someone willing to subject herself to a risk of harm in order to achieve some relatively trivial good, such as running into a burning building in order to rescue a six-pack of beer rather than a person. We would consider such a person reckless, not courageous. And unlike courage, recklessness is no virtue.

What remains to be done is to provide an account of the virtue of justice in particular. Assuming, as suggested

Case Study 11.1:
The Morally Neutral Person

Suppose that Fred and Mary have a dispute over the moral character of their friend Jane. They both agree that Jane lacks the virtues of courage and honesty. Fred argues that this by itself establishes that she has the corresponding vices of cowardice and dishonesty. Mary argues, in contrast, that Jane could lack these virtues without having the corresponding vices, that she could in effect be a morally neutral person.

QUESTION: Is vice merely the absence of virtue or something substantial in its own right?

above, an intimate connection between justice and fairness, a just person is some-one who is fair in his dealings with other people. Of course, one might worry that one can be just or unjust in one's dealings with non-human animals, and even the environment, and not just people. This is, however, a matter of some controversy. As a result, for simplicity we will focus on human-centred justice here. The ques-tion, then, is what counts as dealing fairly with others. There are two sorts of cases worth treating separately here: cases in which the interests of a just person compete with those of other people; and cases in which the just person is adjudicating the competing interests of other people.

Although just people may never be called upon to adjudicate conflicts between others, how they would go about doing so is instructive regarding how they would navigate the conflicts in which they might find themselves with others. Suppose, for example, that Fred and Mary both desire a certain valuable object or sum of money and Jane is called upon to determine which of them, if either, should receive it. Now the first thing to note is that if justice consists in fairness, and fairness requires **impartiality**, then it would seem that a just person is one who would not play favou-rites when adjudicating a disagreement. If, for example, Fred is a friend of Jane's, or if Mary is someone she dislikes, this should play no role in Jane's decision. Now, of course, the requirement of impartiality does not entail that no decision in favour of one party can be made, only that it cannot be based on the personal biases of the adjudicator. Moreover, impartiality by itself does not ensure fairness. If Jane bases her decision on a coin toss, the result would be unfair if, for example, Mary wins the coin toss but the object is Fred's property.

Although no exact formula can be given of fair dispute adjudication, a couple of principles can be delineated here. First, the adjudicator needs to take into account the various entitlements of the competing parties. So, for example, if the object in question belongs to Fred, or if its owner has promised it to him, then this counts toward a decision in his favour. But if Fred has an unpaid debt to Mary, this counts toward a decision in her favour, even if the object belongs to Fred. Second, if consid-erations of entitlement are indecisive, then considerations of need might come into play. If, for example, neither Fred nor Mary has a unique entitlement to the object they both desire, but Mary needs it, perhaps to protect herself or her family from harm, whereas for Fred it is a mere luxury item, then this counts toward a decision in Mary's favour. Finally, it is worth noting that in order to count as a just adjudi-cator, Jane does not need to "get it right" in some objective sense, but rather needs only to be guided by the right sorts of considerations in her decision-making process.

Consider now the more common case in which the interests of a just person compete with those of other people. The question is under what conditions a just person ought to pursue her interests at all and how she ought to go about doing so if she does pursue them. Suppose, for example, that rather than adjudicating between Fred's and Mary's competing claims for some valuable object, Jane herself desires the same object as Fred. Now if, as above, justice requires fairness and a minimal requirement of fairness is impartiality, then, in the case at hand, this means that the just person should give no undue favouritism to her own interests over those with competing interests. For example, the fact that Jane cares more about herself than she cares about Fred should play no role in how she resolves her dispute with him, at last insofar as she is a just person.

In addition to being impartial, the first thing a just person needs to do is to determine who, if anyone, is entitled to the satisfaction of their interests. For example, if Jane determines that Fred is entitled to the object they both desire, she should renounce her claim to it. But if she determines that that she is entitled to it, she can insist upon receiving it and take the necessary steps to ensure she does so. Second, if a just person determines that neither she nor her competitor is entitled to the satisfaction of their interests, then she must determine if one party needs to have his or her interests satisfied. For example, if Jane determines that neither she nor Fred is entitled to the object they both desire, but also determines that Fred needs this object while she merely wants it, then again she should renounce her claim to it. But if she determines that she needs it and Fred merely wants it, then although she cannot insist upon receiving it, she is nevertheless within her rights to vigorously pursue it. Finally, if a just person determines that neither he nor his competitors are entitled to the satisfaction of their interests and that none of them uniquely needs their interests satisfied, then he is free to competitively pursue his interests. But there are constraints on how he goes about doing so. In particular, he must pursue his interests fairly. Suppose the object Jane and Fred are competing for is a house they both what to buy. Under the conditions in question, Jane is free to make a bid on the house and moreover to make the kind of bid she believes will enable her to both secure the house and do so at a favourable price. But what she may not do, if she is just, is treat Fred unfairly in the bidding process. So she may not do such things as prevent Fred from making a bid at all, illicitly attempt to discover what he is bidding, or falsely accuse him of being unable to make good on his offer.

> **Case Study 11.2:**
> **Love and War**
>
> Fred, in his romantic pursuit of Mary, lies about the intentions of his romantic competitor, Jane. Jane complains that this behaviour is unfair and hence incompatible with Fred's claim to being a just person. Fred counters that his behaviour is not unfair because in the pursuit of love anything goes.
>
> **QUESTION**: Is all fair in love and war?

Finally, it is worth saying a few things about the relation between virtuous character traits and **virtuous actions** in general. As a first pass, we might take this relation to be governed to by the following bi-conditional:

> A person has a virtue if and only if whenever the right sorts of conditions occur, she engages in the relevant behaviour.

So, for example, Fred is charitable, on this view, if and only if whenever he encounters someone in need, he provides that person with aid; and Mary is courageous if and only if whenever an important good can be achieved by subjecting herself to a non-trivial risk of harm, she engages in that risky behaviour. As it stands, however, this characterization of the relation between virtuous character and actions is too tight. In particular, there are a couple of reasons for thinking that someone might refrain from engaging in the relevant behaviour under the conditions in question despite having the virtue. First, one might not realize that the right sorts of conditions obtain. Fred might, for example, fail to provide aid to someone he encounters because he fails to realize that this person needs assistance; and Mary might refrain from running into a burning building to perform a rescue because she fails to realize that there is anyone trapped inside. Minimally, the account will have to be adjusted to require that a virtuous person engage in the requisite behaviour only if she believes that the triggering conditions obtain. Second, for whatever reason even virtuous people occasionally do not act virtuously. Fred might on one occasion realize that someone is in need and, perhaps even out of momentary selfishness, refrain from providing aid; but if he normally provides aid in such circumstances we would still judge him to be charitable. Similarly, Mary might, perhaps even out of momentary fear, refrain from running into a burning building despite realizing that someone is trapped inside; but if she normally risks harm to herself to perform a rescue in such circumstances, we would still judge her to be courageous. As a result, the account will have to be adjusted to require only that a virtuous person normally or typically engage in the requisite behaviour when she believes that the triggering conditions obtain, not that she always do so.

11.3 Distributive Justice

Let us turn now to the issue of distributive justice. The concern of **distributive justice** is how the goods that a society produces should be distributed among the citizenry. Collectively a society produces a number of goods. These include basic necessities such as food, clothing, and housing, as well as luxury items of various kinds—cars, computers, television sets, and the like. In different economic systems, not only are different goods produced but these goods also get distributed in different ways among the populace. And the question of distributive justice is what kind (or kinds) of economic system is (or are) just. For the sake of simplicity, we will focus here only on the question of how the goods that are produced should be distributed and not on the question of what goods should be produced and how they should be produced. We will simply assume that businesses are free to produce whatever goods they choose and that individuals are free to choose whether to start their own business or work for someone else's business (or neither). Moreover, we will assume that what is primarily distributed is some form of currency and that individuals are free to use this currency to purchase whatever goods they choose.

One theory of distributive justice is **egalitarianism**. According to this view, the economic goods produced in a society should be distributed equally among the members of a society. In order to fully understand this view, it is helpful to distinguish between equality of opportunity and equality of result in the distribution of resources. If there is **equality of opportunity,** then certain positions or jobs may have higher compensation than others. But everyone has the same opportunity to acquire these higher-paying positions; that is, no candidates for such positions are unfairly discriminated against. If there is **equality of result**, in contrast, then the compensation is the same for all positions. As a result, everyone ends up with the same quantity of goods—or, as above, the same purchasing power—regardless of what position they occupy. And it is the latter—equality of result—that the egalitarian takes to be required for distributive justice. The basic motivation for egalitarianism is that fairness requires treating everyone the same, and treating everyone the same requires giving them the same amount of resources.

With respect to objections to an egalitarian account of distributive justice, we can distinguish between those focused on issues of efficiency and those focused more directly on fairness and other moral issues. There are two efficiency-based objections we will

> ### Case Study 11.3: Won't Somebody Please Think of the Children?
>
> Fred and Mary are both members of an egalitarian society. Fred, however, has seven children while Mary has none. Fred argues that his family should receive eight units of resources to Mary's one on the grounds that to do otherwise would involve treating his children unfairly. Mary counters that not only would this provide Fred's family with more than they need but it would also force her and other single people to subsidize those who decide to have children.
>
> **QUESTION:** In an egalitarian system, should each family/household receive the same share of resources, or should families/households receive resources according to the number of members they have?

consider here, as well as two moral objections. First, distributing resources equally does not ensure that they go where they are needed. Different people have different needs. Compare, for example, someone with a serious medical condition that is very expensive to treat and someone who is in good health. If they each receive the same share of resources, the person with the serious medical condition may have little, if anything, left over after she pays the medical bills, and may not even have enough for that. As a result, egalitarianism is not an efficient way of ensuring that everyone gets what they need. Second, increased compensation is probably the most effective way to motivate people to be more productive. Hence, if every position comes with the same compensation, the people occupying those positions are likely to be less productive and the total amount of goods to be divided among the populace is likely to be lower. But if more productive people receive higher compensation, this may make everyone better off by generating a much higher pool of resources to be distributed.

Let us turn now to the moral objections to egalitarianism. First, one might argue that because some people try harder or are more productive than others, they deserve a greater share of societal resources than do others. As a result, because it entails that everyone should receive the same compensation, egalitarianism is unfair to those who deserve more. And second, if people are free to exchange their resources as they like, there are inevitably going to be winners and losers; that is, some people are going to end up with a greater share of societal resources than others. As a result, in order to sustain an equality of results, the state will have to place severe restrictions on people's liberty to do what they want with their possessions.

One alternative to egalitarianism is a **desert-based principle**. On this view, as a result of their actions certain people—in particular, those who are more productive—deserve more resources than others. And according to desert-based principles, such people should in fact receive the share of societal resources that they deserve. If, for example, one of my colleagues spends every spare minute writing and publishing philosophy papers while I spend my time lazing around in my underpants watching televised game shows, then a desert-based principle would entail that my colleague should be better compensated than I am. There are a number of different ways of measuring how many resources individuals deserve, but for our present purposes we will focus on two of them: productivity and effort. **Productivity** is a function of how many goods a person actually produces or, equivalently, her contribution to the total amount of societal resources. According to productivity versions of desert-based accounts of distributive justice, one's share of societal resources should be proportional to one's productivity: the more productive someone is, the more goods she should receive. **Effort** is a measure of how hard one tries to produce goods, whether or not one is successful in so doing. And according to effort versions of desert-based theories, one's share of societal resources should be proportional to one's effort: the harder one tries, the more one should receive. It is worth emphasizing that although in many cases effort and productivity go hand in hand, this is not universally the case: some people are highly productive with relatively little effort while others are relatively unproductive despite their extreme exertion.

Now the desert-based approach to distributive justice does better than the egalitarian approach in a number of respects. First, unlike egalitarianism, desert-based approaches reward behaviour designed to increase productivity and, hence, the total amount of societal goods available to be divided among the populace is likely to be higher. And second, because goods are distributed on the basis of desert, desert-based approaches avoid the charge of unfairness that egalitarianism faces.

Nevertheless, desert-based approaches do still run afoul of a number of difficulties. First, as with egalitarianism, it does not ensure that resources go where they are needed. After all, less productive people may have greater needs than others. And in some cases, lower productivity is in fact due to someone's greater needs. For example, someone with serious mobility difficulties may be less productive than others if she or he occupies a position in which mobility is required for productivity. Second, as with egalitarianism, since free exchanges are likely to result in distributions of goods which are not proportionate to productivity or effort, the state will have to place severe restrictions on people's liberty to do what they want with their possessions in a desert-based system. And third, it is not clear that the productivity version of the desert-based approach is as fair as advertised. How productive one is is due largely to advantages or disadvantages one does not deserve. People with certain innate abilities—intelligence, strength, dexterity, and the like—are typically more productive than those who lack abilities. And people raised in environments more amenable to the possession of certain sorts of skill sets—financially secure environments in which education and industry are valued, for example—are again more likely to be productive than those who are not. But being born with innate abilities and being raised in advantageous environments are a matter of luck rather than desert. Hence, to the extent that productivity is based on such things, it too is a matter of luck rather than desert. One might, of course, retreat to the effort version of the desert-based approach. But in so doing one would lose some of the advantages claimed for the approach. After all, not only is effort much harder to measure than productivity, but effort by itself also does not have to be particularly productive. As a result, effort versions of desert-based theories may not avoid the charge of inefficiency that egalitarianism faces.

Finally, we will consider **libertarian** or **market-based** approaches to distributive justice. On the libertarian approach, what determines whether an economic system is just is not the outcome, that is, who ends up with what, but rather the process by which this outcome is achieved. In particular, what is required for distributive justice is that goods be distributed on the basis of free-market exchanges. As long as what each of us has is the product of voluntary and unrestricted trades we make with one another of our labour or possessions for other goods, then the resulting distribution of goods is just, even if certain people come out ahead of others in these trades. Moreover, any mandatory redistribution of goods from winners in free-market exchanges to losers on the part of the state is unjust because it involves taking from people what they acquired justly. As it stands, the libertarian theory runs into some obvious difficulties and needs to be adjusted accordingly. First, the outcomes of fraudulent or otherwise defective exchanges are not just. If, for example, you take my money but do not provide me with what you promised, then I can reasonably argue that you owe me my money back. The upshot is that the libertarian needs to require that the market exchanges themselves are fair or just, where this minimally requires that each side provide the other with whatever they agreed to. And second, even if I subsequently engage only in fair market transactions, if the goods I start out with were stolen or otherwise unjustly acquired, then the share of goods I end up with is unjust as well. The upshot here is that the libertarian needs to require that the initial distribution of goods, prior to any market exchanges, be just. It should be noted that most libertarian theories incorporate some additional restrictions on just distribution to avoid worries of these kinds.

> ### Case Study 11.4:
> ### A Den of Thieves
>
> Suppose there was a community consisting of the descendants of thieves and the descendants of their victims. And suppose that this community decided that goods would from now on be distributed by means of fair market transactions.
>
> **QUESTION**: How would the possessions of the members of this community have to be initially redistributed in order for libertarian distributive justice to ensue?

There are a number of advantages to the libertarian account of distributive justice. First, unlike both egalitarianism and desert-based approaches, libertarianism places minimal restrictions on people's liberty to do what they want with their possessions. As long as they meet relatively minimal conditions of fair dealing, they may do as they like with their property. And second, since the more productive one is, the more goods one has to exchange with others for what one wants, libertarianism promotes the profit motive and the increased efficiency that comes with it.

Nevertheless, libertarianism runs into some serious difficulties. First, allowing the markets to determine how goods and resources are allocated will result in many people lacking what they need. After all, there is no reason to believe that in general, people with greater needs will either start out with enough goods to satisfy these needs or generate enough goods through successful market transactions to do so. Second, because people cannot survive without basic necessities such as food, water, and shelter, those without extra resources lack the option of walking away from transactions designed to secure these things for them. As a result, for some people market transactions are in an important sense coerced rather than free. And third, some people through no fault of their own are excluded from the market altogether; they lack any goods anyone is willing to trade for and have no marketable skills whatsoever. But one would be hard-pressed to claim that it would be fair if such people received no share of societal resources, not even to cover basic necessities.

11.4 Criminal Justice

The final concern of this chapter is criminal justice. It may prove fruitful to distinguish between substantive and procedural justice. Suppose someone has been charged with a criminal act of some kind. **Substantive justice** is concerned with a fit between what the person in fact did on the one hand and the person's treatment by the state on the other: that is, whether the person is convicted or acquitted of having committed the criminal act, and whether and how the person is punished by the state for it. Suppose, for example, Fred is charged with assault and did, in fact, commit the crime. If he is convicted of committing the assault and receives a punishment appropriate for his act, then his treatment by the state is substantively just. But if he is not convicted, or if he is convicted but receives an inappropriate—that is, too harsh or too lenient—punishment, then his treatment by the state is substantively unjust. **Procedural justice**, in contrast, is concerned with whether the process by which a person's guilt or innocence is adjudicated is fair. If, for example, Mary was charged with fraud and was convicted after being deprived of adequate legal counsel, the criminal proceedings against her were procedurally unjust, regardless of whether she did in fact commit the crime she was charged with. But if the criminal charges were brought against her only after a fair and thorough police investigation, she received adequate legal

> **Case Study 11.5: The Lucky Investor**
>
> Suppose that Mary, a shrewd negotiator, convinces Fred to pay a hefty price for shares in a company that makes clothes for pet iguanas. And suppose that due to an extremely unlikely upswing in the lizard accessory market, Fred is able to resell his shares for a huge profit.
>
> **QUESTION**: Is there any sense in which Fred deserves his new-found wealth?

representation, no prejudicial evidence was brought before the jury, the judge's instructions to the jury were appropriate, and so on, then the proceedings against her were procedurally just. And this would be true even if she was convicted of a crime she did not commit.

Substantive criminal justice concerns how people who violate the law deserve to be treated by the state for those violations. For simplicity we will focus on laws that place justifiable restrictions on liberty and, in particular, restrictions on liberty designed to prevent harms to others. For example, laws prohibiting physical assaults may restrict my liberty to punch random strangers, but they are justified by the need to prevent us from harming one another. And the idea here is that if I nevertheless punch a random stranger, I consequently now deserve punitive treatment by the state. Consider by way of analogy someone who helps out someone else in a time of need. If she subsequently finds herself in need, then arguably, because of her earlier behaviour she deserves aid from the beneficiary of her earlier assistance. Similarly substantive criminal justice presupposes that because of their acts, criminal lawbreakers deserve **punishment**: treatment harmful to their interests inflicted by the state. More to the point, someone who commits a criminal act deserves to be charged, convicted, and punished appropriately for that crime. Hence, if one is treated in this way, one's past criminal act justifies this action against one on the part of the state. It is worth emphasizing that similar treatment by the state can be justified on a different basis than justice and desert. **Preventative detention**, like punishment, can involve incarcerating someone for an extended period of time. But preventative detention is not justified by what someone has done but rather by what the states feels that person will do if left to her own devices: she as of yet has done nothing that warrants punishment; incarcerating her is instead justified by the need to protect society from what evidence suggests she is likely to do in the future. Similarly, **mandatory rehabilitation**, such as court-ordered drug treatment, may involve incarceration but is not justified by desert. Even if prompted by past criminal behaviour, therapy designed to prevent someone from engaging in criminal activity in the future is justified by its impact on the subject herself and on society more generally. Any punitive effect this treatment has on the subject is merely incidental to its central purpose.

Two central questions about substantive criminal justice are worth raising at this point: why past criminal behaviour justifies any kind of punishment by the state at all, that is, why criminals deserve to be punished; and exactly what kind and severity of punishment are appropriate for a given crime. We will consider each in turn. First, ordinarily it is wrong for the state to punish people—to fine, incarcerate, or execute them. But, on the view at issue, because of their past actions, criminal lawbreakers deserve to be punished, so the state is justified in so doing. But it is not entirely clear why the criminal's past action results in his subsequently deserving any kind of treatment at all, even if the state might be well advised to punish him whether he in any sense deserves it at all. The question is similar to the one discussed above concerning desert-based distributive theories. And similarly, there are a variety of accounts both of what sort of treatment criminal wrongdoers deserve and of why. One might argue that by their actions criminals incur a debt to society that they repay through punishment. But debts are normally incurred when someone accepts something on the understanding that she will return it or provide something else to her beneficiary down the road. And not only do criminal acts not typically involve accepting something from someone, but they are also rarely performed with the understanding that the victim will be repaid. And even if criminals do incur debts to society through their actions, it is far from clear why punishment is an acceptable currency in which this debt may be paid. Second, one formula for the appropriate punishment for a criminal act is the familiar "eye for an eye" slogan. On this view, a criminal should be subjected to the same treatment as was the victim of her crime. So, for example, a murderer should be executed and someone guilty of assault should be beaten. The main trouble with this view is that it entails the state being involved in unacceptable behaviour such as raping rapists and torturing torturers. But the state should do no such thing. An alternative would be to take the appropriate punishment to be a function of the amount of harm caused in the criminal act—the greater harm a criminal causes the more severe her punishment—without requiring that the punishment involve the same kind of treatment as the original criminal act. So, for example, one might adopt the view that all crimes deserve a period of incarceration, with more harmful crimes resulting in a longer period behind bars and less harmful crimes resulting in a shorter prison term. These sorts of considerations will be developed in more detail in Chapter 14.

Let us turn now to the question of procedural justice. As outlined above, the issue is whether the process by which a person's guilt is adjudicated is fair. There are two central senses in which a process of this kind might be thought to be unfair: it might not allow the accused to present an adequate defence against the criminal charge she faces; or it might violate the accused's rights. In order for a process to be fair in the first sense, one must have adequate representation, one must be made aware of the charges one is facing and the evidence to be presented must be made available in a timely fashion, one must have the opportunity and the resources to both rebut the prosecution's case and offer other exonerating evidence, among other things. To the extent that a process is lacking in any these respects, it is unfair because it increases the likelihood of conviction beyond what is warranted by the evidence. In order for a process to be fair in the second sense, no evidence can be used against the accused that was acquired in a way that violated his rights. Suppose, for example, that the members of the accused's society have a right to privacy that entails that the state cannot access personal information about them unless it has been established that there is a compelling reason for so doing. And suppose that the state acquires personal information about the accused without having a compelling reason for so doing and uses this information as evidence in the criminal proceedings that have been brought against him. In such circumstances the process would be unfair because the state is using information about the accused to which it is not entitled.

Now one might think that substantive justice takes priority over procedural justice in the sense that an unjust criminal process can be tolerated as long as the outcome is substantively just. Suppose, for example, that the accused in a criminal trial in fact committed the crime with which he has been charged. On the view at issue, a guilty verdict would be morally unproblematic even if the process followed in the trial was unfair. There are, however, a number of problems with this view. First, it presupposes that there is a method of discerning the guilt or innocence of someone charged with a crime that is independent of and more reliable than the criminal trial itself. However, even the best method of ascertaining guilt will fall short of perfect reliability, so a certain number of judgements of guilt made on the basis of it will inevitably be false. And given that just procedures are designed in part to make the likelihood of conviction match what is warranted by the evidence, alternative methods of discerning guilt may ultimately be less rather than more reliable. As a result, tolerating procedural injustice in the name of substantive justice may lead to people being convicted of crimes they did not commit. Second, it might be argued that prohibiting the use of evidence acquired in a way that violates the accused's rights results in a likelihood of conviction that is lower than what is warranted by the evidence; hence, substantive justice ought to take priority over at least this second sense of procedural justice. The trouble with this argument is that, insofar as the state is permitted to violate the rights of the citizenry in order to acquire evidence for criminal prosecution, the right itself is undermined. If, for example, the state is free to acquire private information about the citizenry without requiring a compelling reason to do so, whenever it wants to build a criminal case against them, then there is no sense in which there is a genuine right to privacy in the society in question. Ultimately, there are grounds for thinking that procedural justice should actually take priority over substantive justice, rather than the reverse. In particular, even if the accused is in fact guilty of the crime with which she has been charged, her conviction ought to be thrown out if the criminal trial that led to it was unfair.

In this chapter we have considered a number of domains in which the concept of justice is utilized: virtuous character, the distribution of goods, and criminal wrongdoing. And we have explored the extent to which these various uses of the concept could be unified through their connection with fairness. Although the connection between justice and fairness remains controversial, it nevertheless yields a promising strategy for elucidating this concept.

Reading Questions

1. What are the two senses in which justice might be a dimension of morality?

2. What is a character trait? What makes a character trait a virtue?

3. What is the difference between courage and recklessness?

4. What does it mean to be an impartial adjudicator?

5. What is the egalitarian theory of distributive justice?

6. What are the two versions of the desert-based approach to distributive justice?

7. What are two advantages of the libertarian approach to distributive justice?

8. What is the difference between substantive and procedural justice?

9. What is the difference between punishment and preventative detention?

10. What are the two senses in which criminal proceedings might be thought to be unfair?

Reflection Questions

1. Think of a number of character traits that you or people you know possess. Do you consider any of these character traits to be virtues or vices? What kinds of impacts does the possession of these character traits have on other people?

2. Think of a number of things that you possess that others, who desire those things, lack, or that others possess but that you both desire and lack. How did it come to pass that you were able to acquire these things but others were not, or vice versa? Is there anything morally problematic about this outcome?

Further Reading

General introduction to theories of justice:
David Schmidtz, *Elements of Justice* (Cambridge: Cambridge UP, 2006).

Justice as a virtue:
Plato, *Republic*, trans. R.E. Allen (New Haven, CT: Yale UP, 2006).

Egalitarian theories of distributive justice:
Kai Neilsen, "Radical Egalitarian Justice: Justice as Equality," *Social Theory and Practice* 5 (1979): 209–26.

Desert-based theories of distributive justice:
George Sher, *Desert* (Princeton, NJ: Princeton UP, 1987).

Libertarian theories of distributive justice:
Robert Nozick, *Anarchy, State, and Utopia* (New York: Basic Books, 1974).

Justice and punishment:
David Boonin, *The Problem of Punishment* (Cambridge: Cambridge UP, 2008).

Procedural justice:
C. Steiker, "Punishment and Procedure: Punishment Theory and the Criminal-
    Civil Procedural Divide," *Georgetown Law Journal*, 85 (1997): 775–820.

12

LIBERTY

Liberty is widely held to be one of the most important political values. Having the freedom to pursue one's goals is generally thought to be necessary for leading a fulfilling life. And political systems are often measured by the extent to which they promote liberty and, in particular, free speech. Nevertheless, it is clear that there ought to be at least some restrictions on liberty: after all, we ought not to be free to subject others to violent assaults. Moreover, it is unclear to what extent commitment to liberty requires that the government intervene on behalf of those who lack the ability to successfully pursue their own goals.

The central concern of this chapter is what the appropriate limits of liberty are; that is, exactly what range of actions can a government legitimately prevent its citizens from engaging in? To this end we will need to consider exactly what political liberty is and whether it can be restricted for any reason other than preventing harms to others. Moreover, we will consider whether there are any reasons at all for restricting speech.

CHAPTER CONTENTS:

- the concept of liberty is elucidated;
- the question of the limits of liberty is raised;
- the harm principle is explored;
- paternalistic theories are considered;
- legalizing conventional morality is evaluated;
- the limits of free speech are discussed; and
- the relation between art and pornography is addressed.

12.1 The Concept of Liberty

Before attempting to address the limits of liberty, it is important to clarify exactly what liberty is. The first thing to note is that political rather than metaphysical freedom is at issue here. **Metaphysical freedom** concerns whether we ever have control over what we do. The issue of metaphysical freedom normally arises in discussions of free will and determinism: if we are simply complex physical objects whose behaviour is wholly governed by the laws of nature, is anything we do under our control? It is important to note that the issue of metaphysical freedom is independent of that of political freedom: one could in principle be metaphysically free without being politically free, and vice versa. The former possibility is fairly obvious: you could, after all, have control over what you do but nevertheless find yourself in a political system in which a wide range of activities are regulated by the state. The latter possibility is, perhaps, less obvious, but all that it requires is that you lack control over what you do while at the same time there is relatively minimal state interference in your actions.

In order to clarify the notion of **political freedom**, it is important to note two ways in which someone can interfere with your actions: **prevention** and **coercion**. Someone prevents your actions if she actively undermines your ability to perform them. Suppose, for example, I want to throw a rock through a picture window. Someone could prevent me from doing this by taking the rock away from me or holding my arms down. Someone coercively interferes with your actions if, rather than actively preventing them, she threatens to subject you to some kind of sanction if you perform them. So, for example, if, rather than taking the rock away or holding my arms down, you threaten to physically assault me if I throw a rock through a picture window, then you are attempting to coerce me into refraining from doing so. It is worth emphasizing that whether an attempt to coerce someone is successful will depend on the nature of the threatened sanction and whether the subject thinks the threat is credible. If, for example, I do not particularly mind being physically assaulted—or if I think that the benefits of throwing the rock through the window outweigh the costs—then I am unlikely to be deterred by the threat of an assault. Moreover, even if the prospect of an assault would normally deter me, if I do not think the person who made the threat intends to carry it out, or would be able to do so if she tried, then again the threat would likely have no effect.

As a first pass, we might say that political freedom is a measure of the extent to which the state actively prevents the citizenry from performing actions of various kinds or coerces them into refraining from performing these actions. If it is my neighbour who actively prevents or coerces me from throwing a rock through a picture window, it does not follow that I lack the political freedom to do so. But if it is an agent of the state who prevents or coerces me from doing so, typically a police officer, then I lack the relevant kind of political freedom. Of course, the fact that the person interfering with your actions is an agent of the state does not suffice for your lacking the political freedom to perform such actions. After all, an off-duty police officer could prevent you from performing actions you are legally entitled to engage in. What is minimally required in addition is that the person in question be acting in her capacity as an agent of the state and, moreover, that she is engaging only in the kind of interference she is authorized to interfere in.

One might worry that, in a practical sense, you can lack the political freedom to engage in a course of action even when agents of the state are not authorized to interfere with it. I have in mind two sorts of cases here. First, agents of the state might themselves systematically interfere with acts of that kind even though they are not authorized to do so. If, for example, it is legal to consume alcohol in public parks but the police constantly harass people who do so, then in a practical sense you lack the political freedom to do this. And second, the state might be unwilling or unable to prevent a group of private vigilantes from systematically interfering with actions that the state itself does not regulate. If the police do not prevent private vigilantes from constantly harassing people who consume alcohol in public parks, then you lack the political freedom to engage in such activity, again in a practical sense, even if such conduct is strictly legal.

It is worth emphasizing that political freedom comes in degrees. How politically free a society is depends on exactly what sorts of activities the state interferes with and what sorts of procedures they use to do so. A state that prevents or coerces its citizens from both public actions, such as speech and assembly, and private actions, such as recreational drug use and certain sorts of sexual activities, is less free than a society in which the state prevents only those actions that cause a more or less direct harm to others, such as assault and homicide. And a society in which the state enforces its prohibitions against actions of a certain kind by means of violence, arbitrary arrest, and secret trials, is less free than a society in which the state enforces its prohibitions by means of non-violent sanctions imposed only after fair and transparent judicial processes.

Finally, we might distinguish between positive and negative liberty. A person has **negative political liberty** to pursue a desired course of action just in case neither state nor anyone else attempts to prevent or coerce her from doing so. But even if you have the negative liberty to engage in this course of action, you may still be unable to do so due to certain limitations you face. You might, for example, lack the economic resources to join a private club or even to buy groceries for your family; you might lack the intellectual abilities to get into medical school or even to read; or you might lack the physical abilities to play professional sports or even to get from place to place. Now in some cases, there is little the state can do to enable its citizens to pursue goals for which they lack the intellectual or physical abilities: short of weakening medical-school admission standards or subsidizing its own professional sports league, the state cannot help those who are not smart or athletic enough to pursue medicine or professional sports on their own. But in other cases there is a lot the state can do: it can provide literacy programs for those who struggle with reading and provide public transportation for those who struggle to get around. Moreover, it can provide financing for those citizens who lack the economic resources to pursue their goals. **Positive political liberty** can therefore be viewed as a measure of the extent to which the state does things along these lines to enable its citizens to overcome the limitations they face in pursuing their goals. It is worth noting that the amount and kind of aid the state ought to provide its citizens to overcome the limits on their ability to pursue their goals are matters of some controversy. The primary focus in this chapter will, however, be on negative liberty.

12.2 The Limits of Legal Coercion

The central question of this chapter concerns the appropriate limits of political liberty; that is, in exactly what sorts of activities on the part of the citizenry ought the state to interfere. Now one answer might be that the state ought not to interfere at all: citizens ought to be able to do whatever they want without fear of punishment by the state. Few people, however, find such a position palatable. After all, in the absence of state coercion, criminals would be free to prey on the weak without fear of punishment. Someone might argue that this worry could be alleviated by the existence of private security firms that individual citizens could hire for protection, but even so, such arrangements would leave those without the resources to hire such firms vulnerable. One motivation for the view that there ought to be no state restrictions on individual liberty is that it would maximize individual liberty. The trouble with this suggestion is that given the inevitable conflicting goals that would arise among the citizenry, even though strictly speaking a complete absence of state restrictions would maximize political liberty, it might even reduce the overall liberty in a society in a more general sense. If, for example, I desire to take your car and you need to use your car to satisfy your desire to go on a vacation in the mountains, then my freedom to take your car would undermine your freedom to go on your vacation.

At the other extreme, one might argue that the state ought to have widespread control over the activities of its citizens—perhaps because the state is better placed than individuals to know what is in their interest—and hence there ought to be quite severe state restrictions on liberty. There are, of course, reasons to object to this suggestion as well. First, even if it is true that the state is better placed than the individual to know what is in her interest, it might be argued that **autonomy**—the ability to make one's own choices—is fundamentally valuable in its own right, even if the exercise of autonomy makes one worse off. As a result, such a political system would deny its citizens something of primary importance. And second, there are reasons to think that in most cases the individual rather than the state is better placed to know what is in her own interest. What makes one better off is arguably a function of one's personal desires, interests, and goals. And the individual is better placed to know what these are than the state in any given case. In the end, a balance will have to be found between the interest of the state in furthering the interests of its citizens and the interests of individual citizens in setting and pursuing their own goals.

12.3 The Harm Principle

What sorts of state restrictions on the individual liberties of citizens are justified? One common answer is that the state is justified in restricting liberty in order to prevent harm to others. Typically advocates of the **harm principle** take the prevention of harm to be both sufficient and necessary for the justification of restrictions on liberty. To say that the prevention of harm to others is a **sufficient** justification for restricting liberty is to say that the fact that state-imposed regulation prohibits harms to others by itself renders that regulation morally appropriate, even if it interferes with individual freedom. So, for example, the harm principle entails that laws prohibiting assault and murder are justified because they interfere with actions that harm others. To say that the prevention of harm to others is **necessary** for the justification of restrictions on liberty is to say that any regulation that interferes with individual freedom but that does not prohibit behaviour which harms others is not morally justified. So, for example, laws prohibiting marijuana use are not justified, according to the harm principle, because they restrict behaviour that at worst harms only marijuana users themselves.

The motivation for the harm principle—here understood as the view that the prevention of harm to others is both necessary and sufficient for the justification of restrictions of liberty—is twofold. First, the sufficiency claim is motivated by the wrongness of harming others together with the obligation of the state to protect its citizens. Insofar as harming others is wrong, it ought to be prevented. And insofar as the state has a duty to protect its citizens, it is the state that ought to prevent such harms. And this is exactly what the sorts of restrictions of liberty at issue are designed to do. And second, the necessity claim is motivated by the fundamental importance of autonomy. Given the importance of autonomy to human flourishing, it ought to be promoted except when it interferes with the autonomy of others. And limiting restrictions on liberty to the prevention of harm to others does exactly that.

In order to get clearer on the implications of the harm principle, we need to clarify the sense of harm at issue. In its narrowest sense, harm refers exclusively to **physical damage** to the body. In this sense, if I am killed or beaten or disfigured then I am harmed, but if I am traumatized or my house is burned down I am not. Most advocates of the harm principle, however, accept a broader conception of harm. One dimension in which the concept can be broadened is to allow it to include certain sorts of **psychological damage** in addition to physical damage. In this broader sense, acts such as threats or bullying that do not result in physical damage can nevertheless count as harms if they result in serious depression, panic attacks, nightmares, emotional detachment, and the like. It is worth emphasizing that acts that merely cause offence do not count as harms on even this broader definition. So, for example, if public nudity offends you but does not result in any kind of psychological trauma, then seeing me walking around without my clothes on does you no harm. A second dimension in which the concept of harm can be broadened is to allow it to include **damage to things** other than the person herself. In this broader sense, I can be harmed if my house is destroyed or my money is stolen even if I do not undergo any physical or psychological damage. It is worth emphasizing that, in this broader sense, only acts that impact my property, or things to which I am otherwise entitled, count as harms and not acts that more generally undermine my interests. After all, I may have an interest in getting a new job, but your getting it instead does not count as a harm to me in the relevant sense. Finally it is worth emphasizing that only the more or less **direct consequences** of your actions count as harms for the purposes of the harm principle. Even if actions of a certain kind can cause serious physical or psychological damage to others, regulations restricting such acts would not be justified by the harm principle if the harms in question were only an **indirect consequence** of the actions. Consider, for example, the difference between killing someone by stabbing him yourself and causing his death by telling a friend of a friend of a violent felon that the victim was planning to report the felon to the police.

As it stands, however, the harm principle may have to be modified somewhat to avoid certain troubling implications. First, consider, for example, actions like drunk driving. Since in most cases driving drunk does not result in actual harm, the harm principle does not seem to entail that restrictions on this activity are justified. But the reason that we think that drunk driving ought to be prohibited is not because it always results in harm but rather because it poses an unacceptably high, and unnecessary, risk of harm. As a result, the natural solution to this is to modify the harm principle to include acts that risk harm to others in addition to those that cause it. Second, certain people, such as children, do not know what is in their own best interest, and if left to their own devices they would probably engage in behaviour seriously detrimental to their interests. But as long as they do not harm others, the harm principle entails that the state restrictions on their activity are unjustified. The best response to this worry is to restrict the harm principle to the actions of competent adults and permit state interference in the actions of those who are not competent, at least insofar as this interference is designed to protect them from harm. And third, there are certain actions one could take—such as selling oneself into slavery—that permanently undermine one's own autonomy. After all, someone who sells herself into slavery is no longer free to set and pursue her own goals. But since the motivation for the harm principle is the protection of individual autonomy, because it allows individuals to cede their own autonomy, the harm principle seems to be in some sense self-refuting. The obvious solution to this worry is to allow the actions the state can justifiably restrict to include both those that harm others and those that undermine the agent's own autonomy.

Despite its many attractions, the harm principle is nevertheless subject to a number of objections. First, although it is less controversial than the necessity claim, there are some grounds to resist the sufficiency claim—that the prevention of harm to others is sufficient for the justification of restrictions of liberty. Consider, for example, cases in which you harm someone in order to protect yourself from being harmed by that person. According to the sufficiency claim, the fact that acts of self-defence harm others entails that state regulations prohibiting self-defence would be justified. But as a matter of fact such restrictions may well be unjustified. Second, there are a number of reasons to resist the necessity claim as well—that the prevention of harms to others is necessary for the justification of restrictions of liberty. One reason is that engaging in acts that directly harm yourself can also indirectly harm those toward whom you have obligations. If, for example, I use dangerous recreational drugs, it can undermine my ability to support my family. But since I directly harm only myself, the harm principle entails that the state cannot justifiably restrict my use of such drugs. Another reason to resist the necessity claim is that certain acts that harm only yourself nevertheless have high societal costs. Consider, for example, riding a motorcycle without a helmet. If you have an accident while riding without a helmet and suffer a serious head injury which, let us say, could have been prevented had you been wearing a helmet, then society will incur high additional costs of treating you. And such costs arguably justify restrictions on your liberty to ride without a helmet even though doing so does not harm anyone else. A final reason to resist the necessity claim is that, given that the sufficiency claim is in part motivated by the fact that the state has an obligation to protect its citizens from others, this same obligation seems to require that the state protect citizens from themselves. And this seems to entail that restrictions on liberty designed to protect citizens from harming themselves are justified, contra the necessity claim.

12.4 Paternalism

Paternalism is the view that the state can justifiably restrict individual liberty in order to protect people from harming themselves or undermining their own interests. Most paternalists accept that the state can also justifiably restrict liberty in order to prevent harm to others. As a result, paternalism should be understood as a claim to the effect that the prevention of people from harming themselves is sufficient but not necessary for the justification of restrictions on liberty. So, for example, because riding a motorcycle without a helmet, or using certain recreational drugs, can be harmful to the person who does it, paternalism entails that regulations prohibiting such activities, such as mandatory helmet legislation or illicit drug bans, are justified. For the sake of consistency, we will assume here that, as with the harm principle, the sense of harm at issue includes both physical and psychological damage to the agent, as well as the loss or destruction of her property. One might worry that including property damage as a harm renders paternalism implausible; after all, the argument might go, people are entitled to do with their property as they will. But the loss of property can have a negative impact on a person's mental or physical health with which the state is properly concerned. So, for example, given that we need economic resources to maintain our physical well being, the state might place paternalistic restrictions on gambling in order to protect those resources. Finally, it is worth emphasizing that the motivations for paternalism are, as above, the societal costs of actions that harm only the agent him or herself and the obligation of the state to protect its citizens from themselves as well as others.

There are weaker and stronger versions of paternalism. According to **strong paternalism**, the state should substitute its own judgement over that of the individual regarding what goals she should pursue or, more generally, what counts as human flourishing, or even what sort of life she ought to lead. And the state places restrictions on individual liberty designed to ensure that the citizenry achieves these goals. If, for example, the state judges that longevity is something that its citizens ought to pursue, then strong paternalism entails that restrictions on activities that pose a serious risk of shortening one's life, such as cigarette smoking, are justified. According to **weak paternalism**, in contrast, the state should defer to the goals individuals set for themselves. But they should restrict liberty in order to protect individual citizens from the kinds of harms that would prevent them from achieving their goals. So, for example, since a serious head injury would prevent most people from achieving their goals, weak paternalism entails that legislation requiring that motorcyclists wear helmets would be justified.

There are, as one might expect, a number of objections to paternalism. First, there is reason to believe that paternalistic restrictions will make people worse rather than better off. Not only is an individual better placed than the state to know what is in her interest, but some individuals may also simply value the behaviour prohibited by the paternalistic restrictions. For example, I might value the experience of wind blowing though my hair while riding a motorcycle more than anything else that would be forestalled by a serious head injury. And second, even if paternalistic restrictions do happen to make people better off, one might still object to them on the grounds that they interfere with individual autonomy, which is of fundamental importance in its own right. What it is to be a person, as opposed to a mere thing, is to have autonomy in the sense of setting and pursuing one's own goals. By placing paternalistic restrictions on its citizens—interfering with their liberty for their own good—the state fails to treat them with the respect due to them as persons.

12.5 Legal Moralism

Legal moralism is the view that that the state can justifiably restrict liberty in order to prevent people from violating the shared moral standards of the community. Suppose, for example, that in a given community it is believed that prostitution or recreational drug use is morally wrong. According to legal moralism, in that community regulations prohibiting prostitution or drug use would be justified. At first glance, this view may seem to justify only the same set of restrictions as are justified by the harm principle or paternalism. What is important to note, however, is that, according to legal moralism, restrictions on the freedom to engage in activities that violate community standards are justified even if they harm neither the agent nor anyone else. Suppose, for example, that marijuana use is in the relevant sense harmless: it causes no significant physical or psychological damage to those who smoke it, or to anyone else for that matter. According to legal moralism, laws prohibiting its use would still be justified as long as recreational drug use was believed by the members of the community to be wrong. As with paternalism, legal moralism should be understood as a claim to the effect that the prevention of behaviour that violates community standards is sufficient but not necessary for the justification of restrictions on liberty. After all, most moralists would accept that restrictions on harmful behaviour are justified even if the members of the community at issue consider that behaviour to be morally permissible. Moreover, it is worth noting that legal moralism and paternalism are independent: one could endorse legal moralism while rejecting paternalism, or vice versa.

Although one might have a number of reasons for endorsing legal moralism, the central motivation for the view is a **utilitarian** one: a community with laws restricting behaviour that violates community moral standards is better off than a society that lacks such restrictions. The basic idea is that being part of a community is highly beneficial, providing such things as security, access to food, shelter, and other necessities, aid in times of need, human fellowship, opportunities for personal fulfilment, and the like. And a society that has restrictions on behaviour that violates community standards is more likely stable and cohesive and, as a result, more likely to be able to continue to provide such benefits. But a society that lacks such restrictions is likely to lack cohesion and thus risk a kind of societal breakdown that would undermine the benefits of community.

However, one might have a number of reasons for rejecting legal moralism. First, one might argue that the utilitarian argument that serves as the basic motivation for the view is flawed. In particular, one might argue that the failure to restrict behaviour that violates community moral standards but that does not directly harm anyone is unlikely to lead to any kind of significant societal breakdown. Moreover, even if one concedes that individual autonomy could justifiably be restricted to prevent substantial social costs, such restrictions would not be justified if they served only to prevent the minor social costs that might reasonably be expected to ensue if citizens were permitted to engage in behaviour that violates community standards. Second, it is not entirely clear how it can be determined exactly what the shared moral standards of a community are. Within any community there will be a variety of moral views, differing in how widely they are shared and how deeply they are held. In the absence of principled grounds to determine how widely shared and deeply held a moral belief needs to be in order to count as a community moral standard, legal moralism offers no criterion for determining whether any given restriction on individual liberty is justified. And third, even assuming that community moral standards can be determined in a principled way, within a community there will often be minority subgroups whose moral views diverge from these standards. Legal moralism seems to entail that the liberty of any given member of some such group to act on her conscience can be curtailed simply because she is in the minority. But this seems to be no more than discrimination against the members of the minority group.

12.6 Free Speech

The focus of the final two sections of this chapter will be on the expression of thought. That there should be no restrictions on one's freedom of thought is more or less uncontroversial on both principled and pragmatic grounds. Since merely thinking something, without in any way acting on it, does no harm to either the thinker or anyone else, neither the harm principle nor paternalism can be used to justify any restrictions on thought. And although certain thoughts, such as coveting the goods of others, might contravene the shared moral standards of some community, thinking such thoughts, again without acting on them, is unlikely to result in the kind of social breakdown that is appealed to in the defence of legal moralism. Moreover, even if restrictions on freedom of thought were justified, such restrictions could not practically be enforced. Although the state can prevent the expression of certain thoughts—such as criminalizing Holocaust denial—it can do little to prevent thinking those thoughts without expressing them. Things are different, however, with the expression of thought. Not only does the state have the power to regulate the expression of thoughts but there may well also be principled grounds for restricting the expression of certain thoughts, as well as restricting certain ways of expressing thoughts. In this section, we will focus on the expression of thoughts by means of speech; in the next section we will focus on the artistic expression of thoughts.

Speech here will be understood to include the use of both written and spoken language. Moreover, it will be understood to be communicative in the sense of being directed toward at least one other person. There is, after all, little reason to believe that your freedom to talk to yourself, or to write something that only you will ever read, should be ever be curtailed.

Case Study 12.1: Fighting Words

Some of the things we might want to say are extremely insulting to those we are inclined to say them to. In some circumstances, saying such things might be likely to provoke a violent response and, a result, might be thought to count as a way of harming oneself. As a result, someone with paternalistic inclinations might argue in favour of legal restrictions on insulting speech in contexts in which the risk of a violent response against the speaker is unduly high.

QUESTION: Should free speech ever be restricted on paternalistic grounds, that is, to protect the speaker from harm?

Now it is widely believed that there should at least be minimal restrictions on **free speech** to prevent more or less direct harm to other people. The classic example is of yelling "Fire!" in a crowded movie theatre. Because of the likelihood that someone will get seriously hurt in the ensuing rush in the dark to escape the theatre, the harm principle entails that the state could justifiably restrict your freedom to yell "Fire!" in those circumstances, in the absence of an actual fire. On similar grounds, one might also concede that speech designed to incite violence would also be justifiably restricted by the state.

As above, advocates of the harm principle claim that the prevention of harm is both necessary and sufficient for the justification of restrictions of liberty. In this case, although speech that is likely to cause more or less direct harm to others may be restricted, speech that is unlikely to be directly harmful may not be restricted. In addition to the general motivations for the harm principle, there is a specific motivation for it in the case of speech. In particular, the reason the state ought not to restrict speech that is offensive, unpopular, inconvenient, for instance, but not harmful is twofold. First, if the speech in question is true, then the benefit of having truths stated outweighs the costs of any offence or discomfort it might cause. So, for example, if it were the case that the average temperature of the planet is not rising and, hence, speech denying anthropogenic global warming were true, then such speech could make us better off by preventing futile and costly policies designed to prevent global warming. And second, even if the speech in question is false, it is nevertheless valuable because permitting and repudiating, rather than restricting, false speech results in the actual truth being held on the basis of evidence and not merely as dogma. So, for example, allowing speech denying anthropogenic global warming and explaining why it is false, rather than preventing such speech altogether, can result in the populace understanding the evidence for global warming rather than simply being forced to accept the authority of experts.

There are, however, potential counterexamples to both the thesis that the prevention of harm is sufficient for the justification of restrictions on speech and the thesis that it is necessary. First, speech designed to terminate romantic relations, for example, may be seriously psychologically harmful to the person to whom it is directed, but few would say that the state ought to prevent people breaking up with one another. This suggests that by itself the prevention of harm is not a sufficient basis for restricting speech. And second, **hate speech**—speech designed to instil hatred toward the members of an identifiable group—does not cause any direct harm to others, but many people still think that it ought to be restricted. If this is right, then the prevention of harm is not necessary for the justifiable restriction of speech.

One strategy for justifying restrictions on hate speech would be to broaden the harm principle so that it includes both direct and indirect harms. Although the only likely direct consequence of hate speech is increased hatred on the part of the audience toward the group targeted by the speech, this hatred can subsequently lead to violence against members of the targeted group. If, for example, a speaker incites hatred toward university professors on the part of an audience of students, this hatred might subsequently result in violence against professors by these students. As a result, hate speech itself can indirectly harm members of the group targeted by it. And if restrictions on speech can be justified by the prevention of both direct and indirect harms, then prohibiting hate speech can be justified on this basis. The trouble with this approach is that it would justify too broad a range of restrictions on speech. After all, more or less anything we say can ultimately result in harm to others. Even seemingly innocuous speech defending the display of roses might result in indirect harm by hardening attitudes against or in favour of the display of carnations rather than roses. One might, of course, distinguish between hate speech and more innocuous forms of (indirectly) harmful speech in terms of its content. But this would involve a departure from harm as the only basis for restricting speech.

A second strategy might be to invoke the **offence principle**, according to which the prevention of offence is sufficient for the justification of restrictions on speech. On this view, both speech that is harmful and speech that is offensive can be justifiably restricted. And since many people are offended by hate speech, it can be justifi-

> ## Case Study 12.2: Political Dirty Tricks
>
> Suppose that during a political campaign, a rogue political operative rigs up a number of voice-activated bombs designed to go off when the local NDP candidate says, "Vote NDP." Moreover, suppose the rogue operative plants these bombs at various locations where NDP election rallies are scheduled to take place.
>
> **QUESTION**: Should the NDP candidate's freedom to say "Vote NDP" during campaign rallies be restricted under such circumstances?

ably prohibited on this basis. The trouble again is that the offence principle would justify too broad a range of restrictions on speech. Different things offend different people, and almost anything that might be said will offend someone. As a result, taking offensive speech to be speech that in fact offends someone would have the effect of justifying restrictions on almost all speech. Alternatively, one might take offensive speech to be not speech that does offend but rather speech that should offend. This opens up the possibility that in many cases people are in fact offended by speech that should not offend them, as well as cases in which people are not offended by speech that should. But it is not clear that an uncontroversial account of what should offend people is forthcoming.

One final strategy would be to distinguish between regulations prohibiting speech and regulations ensuring that it is avoidable—that is, ensuring that those who do not wish to listen do not have to. After all, my freedom to say what is on my mind does not entail that you have to listen to me. On this view, only speech that is directly harmful to others ought to be prohibited by the state. As a result, the state may not justifiably prohibit speech, like hate speech, which is not directly harmful to anyone but is offensive or indirectly harmful instead. Nevertheless, the state may justifiably place restrictions on speech so that those offended by it, or those dangerously susceptible to it, can avoid having to listen to or read it. Such restrictions may include explicit warnings about the content of the speech or the requirement that it occur only in certain designated locations, among other things. Now as above, since almost all speech is offensive to someone, restrictions ensuring that it is avoidable should be enacted only when the speech is likely to seriously offend a significant number of people. But since hate speech is seriously offensive to many people, restrictions making it easily avoidable would presumably be justified.

12.7 Art and Pornography

The final issue to be addressed is artistic expression. Just as you can express your thoughts using language, you can also do so by means of producing art objects. Although **art objects** include things as diverse as paintings, films, sculptures, performances, and musical compositions, the focus here will be on pictures: paintings and photographs. Just as you can express the thought that, for example, Donald Trump is bigger than a breadbox by saying "Donald Trump is bigger than a breadbox," one can also do so by producing and displaying a picture of Trump standing next to a somewhat smaller breadbox. As with speech, some pictures are offensive in the sense that many people are likely to be seriously offended by them. And again as with offensive speech, rather than prohibit offensive pictures, the state may justifiably impose restrictions on their display so as to ensure that those who are offended by them can avoid seeing them. But if the pictures in question count as art objects, it is widely thought that they ought to be subject to fewer restrictions than if they were not considered to be art objects. For example, offensive pictures that are not art objects can be justifiably excluded from public art galleries, whereas offensive art should not be so excluded.

For simplicity we will focus on pictures with sexual content—depicting people engaged in sexual acts of various kinds. We will also assume that no one was harmed or exploited in the production of the pictures and that the depictions are of consenting adults engaged in activities that are neither physically nor psychologically harmful to them. Finally, we will be considering pairs of pictures that are intrinsically identical—that look exactly the same—but nevertheless differ in that one is an artwork and the other a pornographic picture. The first question that needs to be addressed is exactly what makes one picture **art** and the other **pornography**. One answer might be that it is simply a matter of what the picture looks like. If it depicts certain sorts of sexual activity—or depicts any sexual activity in the wrong kind of way—it is automatically pornographic. As a result, on this view it is simply not possible for an art object to be intrinsically identical to a pornographic picture. The trouble with this suggestion is that artists can make whatever pictures with whatever content they like, and by displaying them in the right sort of venues can get them accepted as art objects by the art community. To nevertheless deny that such pictures count as art objects sounds like an arbitrary stipulation. Another answer might be that what determines whether a picture is art or pornography are the intentions of the person who made it. In particular, if the maker intends that its primarily purpose is sexual arousal on the part of those who observe it, then it counts as pornography; but if the maker instead intends that its primary purpose is artistic appreciation—that observers attend to such things as its formal features, its conceptual content, and how it fits into the art-historical context in which it was produced—then it counts as an art object. If this is right, then pictures that look exactly alike can nevertheless differ in their status as art or pornography as long as they were made with different intentions. One might, of course, worry that this allows anything whatsoever to count as an art object as long as the maker has the requisite intentions. But given the variety of things that do count as art objects in the contemporary art scene, this may be a virtue rather than a vice of the view.

The central question here is whether the state can justifiably pose more substantial restrictions on pornographic pictures than on intrinsically identical pictures that count as art objects. In particular, the question is whether the state can justifiably exclude the former, but not the latter, from publicly funded venues. For example, one might wonder if the state may justifiably permit an art show in a publicly funded gallery but prohibit a pornography show displaying identical images in the same gallery. The first thing to note is that at issue here is positive not negative liberty. We are assuming that as long as the material is avoidable by those who might take offence, and is not directly harmful, then the state ought not to restrict the liberty of either an artist or a pornographer to produce such pictures. The issue rather concerns positive liberty: whether the state ought to aid artists, but not pornographers, in the expression of their thoughts by subsidizing venues in which their work can be displayed. Moreover, the issue is whether the state ought to place any restrictions on the kind of art it promotes. Although a full argument for the justification of unrestricted state aid to artists but no aid to pornographers cannot be presented here, a sketch of the general strategy might go as follows. The availability of artefacts designed for artistic appreciation enriches the community, so the state has an interest in making such objects available; but the availability of artefacts designed for sexual arousal does not enrich the community, so the state has no interest in making pornographic pictures available. Moreover, the communal benefits of art appreciation are diminished when the state intervenes and tries to control which sorts of pictures it makes available to the public. The obvious questions, of course, are exactly what benefits the community receives from the availability of art objects and exactly why state restrictions on which objects it makes available undermine these benefits. But these questions will have to be left to another time.

> ### Case Study 12.3: Pornography and Discrimination
>
> Suppose that the display of certain kinds of pornographic pictures results in widespread negative attitudes toward women, even if these pictures are easily avoidable by those who take offence at them. Moreover, suppose these attitudes result in unjust discrimination against women in the workplace and elsewhere.
>
> **QUESTION**: Should the display of these kinds of pornographic pictures be prohibited altogether by the state?

In this chapter we have considered a number of potential bases for restricting liberty, including the prevention of harm to others, the prevention of harm to oneself, and the violation of community moral standards. In addition, we have considered conditions under which the expression of thought ought to be prohibited, regulated, or promoted. The freedom to do or say what you choose is a crucial component of human flourishing. As a result, the question of the appropriate limits on freedom has important implications for all of us.

Reading Questions

1.   What is the difference between political and metaphysical freedom?

2.   What is the difference between positive and negative liberty?

3.   Why, according to the harm principle, are laws prohibiting marijuana use unjustified?

4.   What are two ways in which someone can be harmed by an action?

5.   What is the difference between paternalism and the harm principle?

6.   What is the difference between strong and weak paternalism?

7.   What is the difference between legal moralism and paternalism?

8.   What reasons are there for thinking there should be no restrictions on one's freedom of thought?

9. What is hate speech? Why isn't it prohibited by the harm principle?

10. What are two ways of distinguishing art from pornography?

Reflection Questions

1. Think of some different kinds of behaviour that are currently or have in the past been legally prohibited. What impacts do these behaviours have on the people who engage in them, as well as on other people? Do you think some of these behaviours should not be criminalized? Are there other currently legal behaviours that you think should be prohibited?

2. Think of a variety of things you might want to say but others might object to. What different reasons might people have for objecting to your speech? What reasons would it take to convince you to remain silent?

Further Reading

The issue of liberty in general, and the harm principle in particular:
J.S. Mill, *On Liberty*, ed. Leonard Kahn (Peterborough, ON: Broadview P, 2014).

Paternalism:
Gerald Dworkin, "Paternalism," *The Monist* 56 (1972): 64–84.

Legal moralism:
Patrick Devlin, *The Enforcement of Morals* (Oxford: Oxford UP, 1965).

Limits of free speech:
Joel Feinberg, *Offense to Others: The Moral Limits of the Criminal Law* (Oxford: Oxford UP, 1985).

Art and pornography:
Andrea Dworkin, *Pornography: Men Possessing Women* (London: The Women's P, 1981).

13

ABORTION

In this chapter we will apply some of the moral principles developed in Chapter 10 to a specific moral problem: the problem of abortion. In addition to being interesting and important in its own right, the topic of abortion has been chosen here because it effectively illustrates a number of arguments and views that are applicable in other contexts. These include such things as the difference between utilitarian and deontological reasoning, the importance of definitional and conceptual issues, and the extent of moral standing. At its core, the question of abortion is quite straightforward: is having (or performing) an abortion morally permissible, or is it morally wrong? And, at least in the public discourse, the main answers to this question are deeply entrenched. According to the pro-life position, an unborn human has the same right to life as you or I do; hence, insofar as abortion involves the intentional killing of the unborn, it is as wrong as murder. And according to the pro-choice position, the right to determine

CHAPTER CONTENTS:

- a taxonomy of principles and procedures is introduced;
- the question of moral standing is raised;
- the personhood argument is considered;
- early-personhood, late-personhood, and moderate accounts of the right to life are evaluated;
- potentiality arguments against abortion are explored; and
- the significance of bodily rights is discussed.

what happens in and to one's body is essential to autonomy; hence, the impermissibility of abortion is incompatible with the genuine freedom of women.

As we shall see, the question of abortion is an extremely difficult one. One standard way of approaching it is in terms of competing rights: the rights of pregnant women and the rights of unborn human beings. Framed in this way, the question of abortion hangs on exactly what sorts of rights pregnant women and unborn human beings have, and what sorts of obligations these rights place on (other) people. Moreover, insofar as pregnant women and unborn humans have competing rights—placing incompatible obligations on people—an account needs to be provided regarding which rights have priority under various circumstances.

13.1 Principles

The two rights that get invoked most frequently in the abortion debate are the bodily rights of pregnant women and the right to life of unborn human beings. As noted above, having **rights** places others under obligations to treat you in certain ways. And one way of characterizing rights is in terms of what sorts of behaviour they obligate people to engage in, as well as which people they obligate to behave in those ways. As a result, in order to evaluate a type of action in terms of rights, one needs to determine three things: what rights the affected parties have, what behaviours people are obligated to engage in as a result of these rights, and whether performing the type of action under consideration involves engaging in behaviour that conforms to or violates these obligations. So, for example, if one wanted to morally evaluate abortion in terms of the **right to life** of unborn humans, one would have to determine whether unborn humans have a right to life, what kinds of obligations other people would have toward unborn humans if they in fact did have a right to life, and whether an abortion would violate these rights. Similarly, if one wanted to morally evaluate abortion in terms of the **bodily rights** of pregnant women, one would have to determine whether pregnant women have bodily rights, what kinds of obligations toward pregnant women bodily rights would place on other people, and whether preventing women from having abortions would violate these obligations. A complication of adjudicating the problem of abortion in terms of rights is that the rights that get invoked are in direct conflict with one another. Insofar as bodily rights entitle a pregnant woman to determine what happens in and to her body, they entitle her to terminate her state of pregnancy. But since this results in the death of the unborn human inside her, her bodily rights entitle her to violate the unborn human's right to life. Similarly, since the unborn human's right to life entitles it to continued existence, it entitles it to have other people prevent the pregnant woman from having an abortion and thus to violate her bodily rights. It is therefore incumbent upon an advocate of a rights-based approach to abortion to give an account of how this conflict of rights is to be resolved. (Of course, as we will see below, one approach is to claim that unborn humans have no rights at all, in which case there is no conflict of rights to resolve.)

13.2 Procedures

The first thing to clarify is exactly what we mean by "abortion." After all, in order to adjudicate whether having or preventing an abortion violates anyone's rights, we need to know exactly what kind of behaviour abortion consists of. As a first pass, we might say that it is any procedure that has the effect of terminating a state of pregnancy. The trouble with this suggestion is that it is too broad; it includes procedures in which the termination of pregnancy is an unintended side-effect. Suppose, for example, that a heart surgery had the unintended consequence of terminating a state of pregnancy; we would not, for that reason, call the heart surgery a kind of abortion. A better characterization of abortion is that it consists of any procedure that has the effect of terminating a state of pregnancy that was designed and utilized for this purpose.

Although an improvement, this characterization blurs an important distinction between procedures designed merely to discontinue a state of pregnancy and procedures designed more strongly to prevent the existence of a human person who stands in a biological relation to the pregnant woman. In the former case, although the likely death of the as-yet-unborn human might be a foreseeable consequence of the procedure, it is not the point of the procedure: if this being were to survive its removal from the pregnant woman's body, the procedure would not be for that reason a failure. In the latter case, in contrast, the death of the unborn human is the point of the procedure: should it survive its removal from the woman's body, the procedure would be a failure.

Terminological Note

Frequently the terminology used in the abortion debate is loaded in the sense that it tacitly presupposes one or another moral position. So, for example, to refer to the entity destroyed during an abortion as a "child" or "baby" (and the woman who was carrying it as its mother) presupposes that abortion is morally equivalent to killing an already born baby or child. Similarly, to refer to this being as a "fetus" suggests that it is a mere thing, unentitled to any substantive moral protection. Although arguably no terminology is entirely free of such connotations, it is best to avoid them as much as possible. In this chapter, therefore, I will speak of the "unborn human" rather than the "child" or "fetus" (and the "pregnant woman" rather than the "mother").

Case Study 13.1: Partial Birth Abortion

A controversial abortion procedure is the so-called "partial birth abortion" or, more precisely, intact dilation and extraction. This procedure involves partially removing the unborn human from the pregnant woman's body before killing it in a way that is often designed to make its extraction from the woman's body less dangerous. Defenders of the procedure argue that it is sometimes medically necessary, while its detractors liken it to infanticide.

QUESTION: If an abortion procedure is designed to kill the unborn human, does it make any moral difference if the unborn human is killed before or after it is partially removed from the pregnant woman's body?

Finally, we can distinguish between procedures performed by the pregnant woman herself and those performed by a third party. Many abortion procedures are surgical or semi-surgical; as a result, a pregnant woman could perform them on herself only under highly unusual circumstances. But procedures that require only taking a pill, for example—such as the so-called "morning after pill"—can be performed by a pregnant woman without third-party assistance, although they currently can be used to terminate only very early-stage pregnancies. Moreover, it will be assumed here that third-party abortions are done at the behest of the pregnant woman and that the person who performs the procedure does so voluntarily. It is worth noting that neither of these conditions needs to be satisfied in any given case: a third party could perform an abortion without the consent of the pregnant woman, or could be coerced him or herself into performing the procedure.

13.3 Moral Standing

Before adjudicating on whether unborn humans have a right to life, it is useful to consider the more general question of whether they have any kind of moral standing. To say that something has **moral standing** is to say that how we treat it is morally significant: treating it in certain ways is morally appropriate, while treating it in other ways is morally wrong. We can draw a number of important distinctions among objects with moral standing. First, we can distinguish between direct and indirect objects of moral consideration. To say that something is a **direct object of moral consideration** is to say that its moral standing is an intrinsic feature of it: the reason treating it is certain ways is morally significant is because of the impact of that treatment on the object itself. Torturing kittens, for example, is wrong simply because of the suffering it causes them, and not merely because of the impact of such treatment on third parties. As a result, not only do kittens have moral standing but they are also, moreover, direct objects of moral consideration. To say that something is an **indirect object of moral consideration**, in contrast, is to say that its moral standing is a relational feature of it: the reason treating it in certain ways is morally significant is because of the impact of that treatment on third parties. Destroying a small child's favourite toy, for example, is not wrong because of the impact on the toy but rather because of the impact on the child. Hence, although the toy has moral standing, it is an indirect object of moral consideration.

Case Study 13.2: Indirect Objects

Suppose that contained within an adult human's body was something that was an indirect object of moral consideration, and that destroying it would have a negative impact on the interests of certain people other than the person whose body it inhabited. Moreover, suppose that removing this object from the body in question would result in its destruction. Finally, suppose that this object is the property of the person whose body it inhabits.

QUESTION: Would a person's decision to remove some such object from her body be morally problematic?

A second distinction concerns exactly what sorts of treatment of an object with moral standing are morally significant. For an object to have moral standing, there must be some ways of treating it that are either morally appropriate or morally wrong. But different sorts of treatment can be appropriate for different sorts of objects with moral standing. For example, because it is wrong to torture them, kittens, like normal adult humans, are direct objects of moral consideration. But although it is (almost) always wrong to kill normal adult humans, it is arguably appropriate in many circumstances to euthanize otherwise healthy kittens, at least as long as it is done painlessly. The central concern of the abortion debate is not whether the unborn human has any kind of moral standing, but rather whether it has the particular kind of moral standing that makes killing it, or, more modestly, depriving it of continued use of the pregnant woman's body—which it needs to survive—morally wrong.

Finally, we can distinguish between bearers of rights and bearers of duties. All direct objects of moral consideration are **bearers of rights**: if treating something in a certain way is morally required, then it has a right to such treatment; and if treating something in a certain way is morally prohibited, then it has a right to not be treated in that way. Since, for example, torturing kittens is wrong, kittens have a right not to be tortured. **Bearers of duties**, in contrast, are those things that have moral obligations to treat, or to refrain from treating, others in certain ways. Except, perhaps, in highly unusual circumstances, all normal adult humans have an obligation to refrain from torturing kittens. What is important to note is that classes of bearers of rights and bearers of duties do not coincide. To be a bearer of duties requires higher-order cognitive capacities and states of certain kinds, such as deliberation, the possession of moral concepts, and the like. Being a bearer or rights, in contrast, requires only that weaker standards be met, although what these standards are is exactly what is at issue in the abortion debate. Although both kittens and normal adult humans, for example, have a right not to be tortured, only the latter have an obligation to refrain from torturing others. Kittens, lacking the requisite cognitive states as they do, arguably do not have any obligations at all.

> ### Case Study 13.3: Rightless Duties
>
> It is widely believed that there are circumstances in which certain people have forfeited their right to life. If, for example, someone poses a serious threat to your life or health, or is guilty of a capital crime, or is participating in an unjust military action, many people believe it would not be wrong to kill that person.
>
> **QUESTION**: Suppose that in circumstances of these kinds a person would in fact lack a right to life. Would she nevertheless retain an obligation to refrain from killing others?

13.4 The Personhood Argument

The most common approach to the abortion issue involves the personhood argument. According to this approach, the whole issue hangs on whether the unborn human is a person with a right to life. Advocates of this basic approach typically share the following two presuppositions:

1. Normal adult humans have bodily rights
2. The right to life outweighs bodily rights

The first assumption is relatively straightforward. All adult humans, including pregnant women, have a right to control what happens in and to their bodies. And in the absence of any competing rights, this entitles them to subject themselves to any medical procedures they might like, among other things. The second presupposition is a little more complicated, however. Sometimes rights conflict in the sense that in order for you to exercise one of your rights you have to violate someone else's rights. Suppose, for example, that Mary has a right of free speech that entitles her to make public any information she possesses and Fred has a right to privacy that protects him from the dissemination of certain personal information. If Mary comes to possess such personal information about Fred, her right to express this information conflicts with Fred's right to keep it private. In an example of this kind, which right gets to be exercised may depend on the circumstances: whether Fred is a public figure, whether releasing the information fulfills an important public interest, and the like. But according to the second presupposition, the right to life is in a certain sense fundamental: whenever there is a conflict between someone's right to life and someone else's bodily rights, only the former can be exercised.

Given these presuppositions, whether abortion is morally permissible depends on whether the unborn human is a person with a right to life. After all, a right to life places other people under an obligation to refrain from engaging in behaviour that results in the death of the bearer of that right. And, as above, an abortion is a procedure designed either to kill the unborn human or to remove it from the pregnant woman's body, which in ordinary circumstances will result in its death. If the unborn human is a person, then, even though the pregnant woman has a right to control what happens in and to her body, this right is outweighed by the unborn human's right to life. Hence, it would be wrong for her to arrange or perform any procedure that would result in the death of the unborn human in her body. If the unborn human is not a person, then the pregnant woman's bodily rights take priority. As a result, it would be morally permissible for her to perform or arrange procedures that would result in the death of the unborn human.

It remains to be determined, of course, whether the unborn human is a person with a right to life. It is frequently claimed that because the unborn human is a living human organism, it is a person with a right to life, so killing it is morally wrong. But while it is uncontestable that the unborn is both living and human, it does not, in any straightforward sense, follow that it has any kind of right to life. Being human is a biological status, whereas having a right to life—or being a person—is a moral status. Although one might try to argue that all biological humans are moral persons, this is a substantial and controversial thesis that cannot simply be assumed. Three basic positions have been defended on this issue. According to the **early-personhood** position, the unborn becomes a person at (or shortly after) conception; hence, abortion at any stage of pregnancy is seriously morally wrong. According to the **late-personhood** position, human beings do not become persons until they are born or, perhaps, even some time after this event. As a result, abortion is no more morally problematic than any other medical procedure. And according to the **moderate** position, the unborn human starts out as a non-person at conception and gradually turns into a person throughout the course of pregnancy. Hence, early-stage abortions are morally permissible whereas late-stage abortions are seriously wrong. We will consider each position in turn.

THE EARLY-PERSONHOOD POSITION

A theory of personhood needs to give an account of what conditions are required or suffice for an entity to be a person with a right to life, as well as an account of why the satisfaction of those conditions are required or suffice. According to the early-personhood position, an unborn human is a person at or shortly after conception; hence, the criteria of personhood are properties possessed by newly conceived human beings. At this stage, the unborn human is merely an integrated cluster of biologically human cells; as a result, the early-personhood position is most naturally understood to take the criterion of personhood to be biological humanity—that is, all and only biologically human entities are persons with a right to life.

There are, however, a number of problems with this suggestion. First, to say that all and only biological humans have a right to life is both too inclusive and too exclusive. It is too exclusive because it rules out the possibility of non-human persons. Whether there are in fact intelligent aliens, there at least could be. But if they are not biologically human, the early-personhood position, as we have been construing it, entails that they could not be persons. Moreover, higher mammals such as dolphins and chimpanzees arguably are cognitively sophisticated enough to have some kind of right to life. But again, because they are not biologically human, the early-personhood position rules out this possibility. And it is too inclusive because there are biologically human entities that pretty clearly lack a right to life. Consider, for example, a cancerous tumour or a living human-tissue sample in a lab. Second, there is simply no adequate explanation for why being a biologically human entity is either sufficient or required for having a right to life. In order to defend a criterion of personhood, it is not enough to merely stipulate that all and only entities having a certain property are persons. One needs, in addition, an explanation of why the possession of this property confers a right to life upon its bearer. And what is lacking in the case at hand is an account of exactly why the property of biological humanity should do so.

One might attempt to shore up the early-personhood position by appeal to certain sorts of theological considerations. For example, one might argue that it is not biological humanity that confers personhood upon an entity but rather the possession of an immaterial soul, and one might therefore claim that the reason the unborn human acquires a right to life at or shortly after conception is that it acquires a soul that time. And since there is no reason to suppose that dolphins and aliens lack souls or that cancerous tumours have them, the charges of being too inclusive and too exclusive are thereby avoided. The trouble with this suggestion is that it relies on unverifiable claims about immaterial souls. First, there is no good evidence that there are such things as souls. Second, even if there are souls, there is no evidence that unborn humans acquire them at or shortly after conception. And third, even if they acquire them at that time, there is no good reason to suppose that the possession of a soul confers a right to life upon an entity.

Finally, it is worth emphasizing that, regardless of its theoretical underpinnings, if the early-personhood position on personhood is correct, then all abortions at any stage of pregnancy are seriously wrong, including those in which the pregnancy is the result of rape or incest. Many people who are opposed to abortions in most cases nevertheless make exceptions in these cases, due to both the woman's lack of responsibility for being pregnant and the psychological harm carrying the unborn to term might produce. But if the unborn human is a person with a right to life, and, as we have been presupposing, if the right to life trumps all other moral considerations, then the cause of pregnancy and the repercussions of continuing it are irrelevant: abortion even in the case of rape or incest is seriously wrong. This is an implication that even many people who self-identify as pro-life find untenable.

THE LATE-PERSONHOOD POSITION

According to the late-personhood position, the criterion of personhood is having higher-order cognitive states, such as sentience, self-consciousness, and the possession of various relatively sophisticated concepts. Since human beings do not normally acquire such states until after they are born, the late-personhood position entails that an unborn human is not at any time a person with a right to life. As a result, abortion is morally permissible at any time during pregnancy. The basic idea here is that an unborn human is, in intellectual sophistication, closer to a simple non-human animal than to a grown human; it lacks the social relations, the self-awareness, and the like. And since we don't ascribe a strong right to life to non-human animals of a similar level of sophistication, then we shouldn't with an unborn human either.

As with the early-personhood position, there are a number of reasons to object here. First, unlike some versions of the early-personhood position, the late-personhood criterion does not entail that a cancerous tumour has a right to life. But despite its more stringent requirements, it might be argued that the late-personhood criterion nevertheless remains too inclusive. In particular, it might be argued that there are humans who possess higher-order cognitive states but who lack a right to life. Insofar as it is not wrong to kill someone with the relevant states who poses a serious threat to your life or health, or is guilty of a capital crime, or is participating in an unjust military action, there are humans that the late-personhood criterion counts as persons who nevertheless lack a right to life. Second, although the late-personhood criterion does allow for the possibility of non-human persons, it might nevertheless be argued that it is too exclusive. In particular, it might be argued that there are humans who uncontroversially possess a right to life despite lacking the relevant higher-order states—newborn human infants are a particularly problematic example. And third, it might be argued that what the late-personhood criterion offers is an account of what it is to be bearer of duties, for which higher-order cognitive states are certainly required, rather than an account of what it is to be a bearer of rights and, in particular, the right to life. After all, while higher-order cognitive states are pretty clearly required in order to have obligations to other people and to be responsible for what you do, it is less clear that they are required in order for other people to have obligations toward you.

Unlike the early-personhood position, however, there is plausible and defensible justification for the late-personhood account of personhood. On this view, this reason it is wrong to kill a person is because it frustrates a central and deeply held desire: the desire for continued existence. The reason this desire is so important is that its satisfaction is a precondition of the satisfaction of all of the other desires a person might have. In order to satisfy one's desire to become a famous author, for example, one has to continue to exist long enough to do so. And in order to desire continued existence, an entity needs to have higher-order cognitive states. Minimally, it needs to be capable of having desires and to possess relatively sophisticated concepts such as that of a self and of persistence through time.

The trouble with this justification of the late-personhood criterion is that it renders it even more exclusive. Even an entity possessing higher-order cognitive states can lack a right to life if it fails to desire continued existence. Although it may not be entirely clear whether humans in temporary states of unconsciousness of various kinds retain their conscious desires, certain conscious adult humans—depressed or suicidal people, for example—can certainly fail to desire continued existence despite having a right to life. In light of such worries, an advocate of this approach might abandon the appeal to a desire for continued existence and invoke instead the possession of an interest in continued existence. Even someone who does not desire to continue existing can have an interest in doing so in the sense that continued existence will enable her to fulfill her future desires. The trouble with this manoeuvre, however, is twofold. First, someone whose future is sufficiently bleak may, as a result, have no interest in continued existence; nevertheless, it would still be wrong to kill her (at least without her consent). And second, this strategy may render the late-personhood criterion so inclusive that it entails the wrongness of abortion. After all, the newly conceived unborn human has future desires that can be satisfied only if it continues to exist, in more or less the same sense as a suicidal adult does. And if this is all that is required for a right to life, the unborn human has a right to life in the same sense in which a suicidal adult does. The challenge for the advocate of the late-personhood position is to articulate a sense in which beings with higher-order cognitive states are related to their future desires in ways in which entities lacking such cognitive states are not, which allows us to explain why the former but not the latter are persons with a right to life.

THE MODERATE POSITION

According to the **moderate** position, an unborn human being starts out as a non-person at conception but gradually acquires a right to life throughout the course of pregnancy. As a result, early-term abortions are morally unproblematic on this view, whereas late-term abortions are seriously wrong. In order to generate this result, the moderate criterion of personhood must be a feature that unborn humans have later in pregnancy but that newly conceived humans lack. Although there are a number of features that could potentially fill this role, the most common approach involves taking the criterion of personhood to be sentience: the ability to feel, perceive, and have conscious experiences. So on this version of the moderate position, all and only entities that are sentient are persons. And this entails that unborn humans during the later stages of pregnancy fall into the class of persons, but newly conceived humans do not. Moreover, there is a plausible justification for taking sentience to be the criterion of personhood. With sentience comes the capacity to experience pleasure and pain. Since causing unnecessary pain is uncontroversially morally wrong—and, in particular, because of the impact of pain on the subject rather than on interested third parties—it is reasonable to conclude that sentient beings are direct objects of moral consideration and, moreover, that acquiring sentience distinguishes such entities from those that are morally significant only in an indirect sense, if at all.

As above, one might worry that the moderate criterion—that all and only sentient beings have a right to life—is both too exclusive and too inclusive. First, it might be thought to be too exclusive because of the possibility of currently insentient beings—such as adult humans in reversible comas—who nevertheless possess a right to life. A possible reply would be to claim that what is required for a right to life is not actual consciousness but the basic capacity for consciousness, and to argue that although humans in reversible comas are not currently conscious, they nevertheless retain that capacity. Second, it might be argued that the moderate criterion is far too inclusive because there are huge numbers of sentient non-human animals that most of us believe lack any kind of right to life. Although the moral status of higher mammals may be controversial, most of us do not believe that insects and arachnids are entitled to the moral protection of adult humans. Nevertheless, they do possess at least rudimentary sentience in virtue of their perceptual capacities and, as a result, have a right to life according to the view on the table. A possible reply would be to suggest that since sentience comes in degrees, so does the strength of an entity's right to life: the more sentient, the stronger the right; the less sentient, the weaker the right. On this basis, one could argue that although insects do have a right to life, it is so weak that it is outweighed by the mere preferences of adult humans.

A perhaps more serious worry for the moderate position is the charge that it equivocates between being a direct object of moral consideration and having a right to life. In order for an entity to be a direct object of moral consideration, there must be ways of treating it that are morally wrong because of their impact on the entity itself rather than on third parties. But it does not follow from the fact that certain ways of treating an entity are morally wrong that killing it must be included among these forms of wrongful treatment. In particular, if an entity is capable of experiencing pleasure and pain but incapable of even conceiving of continued existence, let alone caring about it, it could be argued that while it is wrong to cause some such entity unnecessary pain, it is not wrong to kill it. And if sentient unborn humans are entities of exactly this kind, then aborting them would not be wrong as long as it was done painlessly.

13.5 Potentiality

Given the difficulties that beset attempts to define personhood, many theorists have abandoned the personhood argument altogether in favour of arguments centred on potentiality or bodily rights. The former style of argument is the focus of this section, while the latter will be taken up in the next. Rather than focusing on the current status of an unborn human, potentiality arguments focus instead on its future status. Although an unborn human may not currently be a person with a right to life, it is nevertheless potentially a person. In order to draw any conclusions about the morality of abortion from this fact about unborn humans, however, the **potentiality principle** needs to be deployed. Although there are many ways of formulating this principle, the following is fairly characteristic: if the possession of some property L confers a right to life upon an entity, it is seriously morally wrong to kill anything that potentially has L. The advantage of this principle is that it enables us to draw conclusions about the morality of abortion even if we do not know what the criterion of personhood is. All we need to know is that normal adult humans satisfy this criterion and that an unborn human is potentially an adult human; on this basis alone we can conclude that abortion procedures that kill unborn humans are seriously wrong.

The potentiality argument against the permissibility of abortion hinges upon the potentiality principle, but this principle is fraught with difficulties. First, it is not entirely clear how the principle should be formulated, that is, what it means to say that the unborn human is potentially a person. One suggestion is that for an entity to be potentially a person is for it to be possible for it to become a person. This sense of potentiality is far too weak, however. While it is true that unborn humans are potentially persons in this sense, it is true of lots of other entities as well that they could possibly become persons, many of which it would be morally unproblematic to destroy. After all, all that is required for an entity to be a potential person in this sense is for there to be some possible mechanism by means of which the transformation might occur. For example, it will, presumably, eventually become possible to create human sex cells out of their chemical elements in a laboratory setting, cells that could be subsequently combined to generate a person. As a result, once this becomes possible, this criterion would entail that it is actually seriously wrong to destroy the laboratory chemicals in question. An alternative suggestion is that for an entity to be potentially a person is for it to be sufficiently likely that it will become a person. However, not only is it unclear what degree of likelihood would be sufficient, but also, how likely it is in any given case that an unborn human will become a person will depend on external environmental factors that seem irrelevant to the moral appropriateness of killing it. For example, given that the likelihood that an unborn human will be born and reach adulthood depends on the pregnant woman's nutritional intake, this would entail that the wrongness of killing it depends on the quantity and quality of food in her environment. It might then be permissible for a woman to have an abortion if she has access to abundant nutritious food, but impermissible if she is impoverished and has little food; but that seems arbitrary and intuitively wrong. A third suggestion is that for an entity to be potentially a person is for it to be part of its purpose or function to become a person or for it to be true that it will become a person in the normal course of events. But it is unclear whether unborn humans or other entities have such functions or purposes, as well as whether sense can be made of the notion of one course of events but not another being normal.

Second, even if an adequate formulation of the notion of potentiality can be developed, it is far from clear that there is any good reason to accept the potentiality principle. In particular, it is not clear how it could be seriously wrong to kill something that lacks a right to life simply because, in some sense, it potentially has this right. It is not in general true that how it is appropriate to treat something is determined by what features it has potentially rather than actually. For example, all adult humans are potentially deceased, but it is nevertheless not morally appropriate to treat them as if they are already dead. Moreover, insofar as an entity is a direct object of moral consideration, whether it is appropriate to treat it in a certain way is, in general, a function of the impact of such treatment upon it. It is wrong to torture kittens, for example, because of the pain and suffering it causes them. But if the treatment did not have the relevant kind of impact at the time it occurred, and would only do so were it to occur somewhat later after the entity's potentialities were actualized, there would not seem to be any basis to suppose that the treatment is inappropriate. It is not wrong, for example, to here and now torture an entity incapable of undergoing pain and suffering simply because in the future it may be somewhat likely to be capable of undergoing suffering.

And third, because it focuses on the future status of an entity rather than its

---

Case Study 13.4:
Intelligent Cockroaches

Suppose there was to be a drug that causes cockroaches to acquire the higher-order cognitive states possessed by normal adult humans. Suppose, however, that no cockroach ever ingested this drug.

QUESTION: Would it be seriously wrong in such circumstances to kill cockroaches? What difference would it make if one cockroach ingested the drug?

Case Study 13.5:
The Artificial Womb

Suppose there was a machine carrying some sperm along a conveyer belt to an artificial womb containing a human egg cell. Suppose that once the sperm reached the womb a process would occur to make the fertilization of the egg by the sperm highly likely. And suppose that once fertilization occurred, it was also highly likely that a newborn human baby would emerge from the artificial womb in approximately nine months.

QUESTION: Would it be seriously wrong to turn off this machine before the sperm reached the artificial womb?

current status, the potentiality principle runs the risk of entailing the wrongness of birth control in addition to abortion, at least in certain sorts of circumstances. After all, if egg or sperm cells, or some combination of the two, come to potentially have a right to life, then to kill them is seriously wrong, according to the potentiality principle. Suppose, for example, that, but for the use of birth control, a particular sperm would have fertilized a particular egg and, moreover, that the method of birth control used, perhaps a spermicidal product of some kind, prevents fertilization from occurring by killing some of the sex cells involved. This would be a case of killing something that potentially has a right to life. But even many opponents of abortion would nevertheless consider use of such methods of birth control morally unproblematic.

13.6 Bodily Rights

One of the presuppositions of the personhood argument is that the right to life outweighs bodily rights. If this is true, then if the unborn human is a person, it follows that abortion is seriously wrong. If, however, this presupposition is false, then abortion may well be permissible even if the unborn has a right to life. One way to criticize the claim that the right to life always outweighs bodily rights is to argue that the right to life does not entitle someone to the **bare minimum** she needs to survive. Suppose, for example, that someone is dying of thirst in the desert and the only source of water is in another person's water flask, a person, let us suppose, who is also in need of the contents of the flask. Even though the bare minimum the former needs to survive is the contents of the latter's water flask, her right to life does not entitle her to it. Similarly, although the bare minimum the unborn human needs to survive is continued use of the pregnant woman's body, this need by itself does not entitle it to such use, even if it has a right to life.

> **Case Study 13.6: The Violinist**
>
> Suppose you wake up to find that while asleep you have been hooked up to a famous violinist whose circulatory system has been plugged into yours. Moreover, suppose you discover that the violinist needs to be attached to you for nine months and if unplugged in the interim will die.
>
> **QUESTION**: Would it be seriously wrong to disconnect yourself from the violinist?

Although in some instances one might not be obligated to provide another person with the bare minimum that the latter needs to survive, in other instances one might be so obligated. Parents of dependent children, for example, are obligated to provide them with what they need to survive or, at least, to ensure that someone else does so. The question is under what circumstances one is obligated to provide dependent persons with what they need to survive and under what circumstances one is not. The focus will be on cases in which one person, the patient, is dependent on another, the agent, for the bare minimum needed to survive in the sense that not only is the agent capable of providing the patient with what he needs but she is also the only person realistically able to do so in the circumstances. There are four different cases of interest:

1. The state of dependence of the patient on the agent was involuntary—it occurred against the agent's will.

2. Although the state of dependence of the patient on the agent was voluntary, providing the patient with what she needs to survive would pose a serious risk to the life or health, or more generally the well-being, of the agent.

3. The state of dependence of the patient was voluntary, and providing the patient with what he needs to survive would pose no serious risk to the well-being of the agent.

4. Although the state of dependence of the patient on the agent was not voluntary, she voluntarily engaged in another course of action that she knew might lead to some such state of dependence.

If we assume that the unborn human is a moral person, then the first category includes cases in which a state of pregnancy is the result of rape. Similarly, the second category includes cases in which the state of pregnancy is voluntary, but carrying the unborn to term would pose a serious risk of harm to the pregnant woman. The third category includes cases in which the state of pregnancy is voluntary, and carrying the unborn to term poses no unusual risks. Although there are interesting and controversial questions about the permissibility of abortion in each of these cases, the focus of our discussion here will be on the fourth category.

The question raised by cases that are included in the fourth category is whether we are responsible for the consequences of our actions if we neither intend nor desire those consequences but are nevertheless aware that they may occur. On the one hand, it might be argued that when a pregnancy is the result of voluntary sexual relations, the woman is responsible for the unborn human's state of dependence upon her and, as a result, is obligated to provide it with the continued use of her body: the bare minimum it needs to survive. On the other hand, it might be argued that because the woman did not consent to providing the unborn human with what it needed to survive—either explicitly or tacitly—she is under no obligation to provide it with the continued use of her body. This is often thought to be especially clear when pregnancy is the result of contraceptive failure: the use of contraception is a strong indicator of a lack of consent to provide for any unborn human that might ensue.

In addition to the lack of clarity about in exactly what sorts of cases it entails that abortion is permissible, the appeal to bodily rights runs into other difficulties. First, it entails at most that a pregnant woman has a right to remove the unborn human from her body but not secure its death: if the unborn were to survive removal from her body—and thus no longer required the use of her body to survive—its right to life would render subsequently securing its death seriously morally wrong. But for many women, the point of having an abortion is not merely to terminate a continued state of pregnancy, or even to avoid a life path encumbered by the responsibilities of parenthood; it is to prevent the existence of a human person to whom the woman stands in a special biological relationship. And second, many abortion techniques involve killing the unborn human rather than merely removing it from the pregnant woman's body. But since the bodily rights argument entails only that a pregnant woman may permissibly deprive the unborn of what it needs to survive—the continued use of her body—and not to kill it, it also places a severe restriction on the range of abortion techniques she may permissibly deploy.

> **Case Study 13.7:**
> **The High Ledge**
>
> Suppose that a ledge high up on a tall building belongs to you but that someone else has made his way down to it. And although the bare minimum he needs to survive is the continued use of your ledge, you would rather not share it with him.
>
> **QUESTION**: Assuming that it would be morally wrong to stab the interloper, would it nevertheless be permissible to deny him use of your ledge by pushing him off?

In this chapter we have considered a number of different arguments for and against the permissibility of abortion, including the personhood argument, the potentiality argument, and the argument from bodily rights. The question of abortion remains a highly significant one because of the impact on both pregnant women and unborn humans of policies regulating the procedure. And the permissibility of the procedure, as well as the appropriateness of regulations governing it, remains a matter of ongoing controversy.

Reading Questions

1. What is the problem with defining abortion as any procedure that has the effect of terminating a state of pregnancy?

2. What is the difference between a direct and an indirect object of moral consideration?

3. What is the difference between a bearer of rights and a bearer of duties?

4. What are the presuppositions of the personhood argument?

5. What does it mean to say that the early-personhood position on abortion is too exclusive?

6. According to the late-personhood position, what features does an entity need to have in order to be a person?

7. What does it mean to say that an entity is sentient?

8.   What is the potentiality principle?

9.   What is wrong with the suggestion that what it is for an entity to be poten-
      tially a person is for it to be possible for it to become a person?

10.   What is the bare minimum an unborn human needs to survive?

Reflection Questions

1.   Think of a variety of particular things that it is possible to damage or
      destroy. What would be the impact of damaging or destroying these on
      other parties? Would it be morally wrong to damage or destroy each of
      these things?

2.   Think of a number of different kinds of natural and artificial life forms.
      What features distinguish them from inanimate things, such as rocks and
      chairs? What are the important distinctions between different kinds of life
      forms?

Further Reading

General introduction to the issue of abortion:
Peter Alward, "Ignorance, Indeterminacy, and Abortion Policy," *Journal of Value
      Inquiry* 41 (2007): 183–200, preliminary section.
Jeff McMahan, *The Ethics of Killing: Problems at the Margins of Life* (Oxford:
      Oxford UP, 2002).

Early-personhood position:
John Noonan, "An Almost Absolute Value in History," *The Morality of Abortion:
      Legal and Historical Perspectives*, ed. John T. Noonan (Cambridge, MA:
      Harvard UP, 1970), pp. 51–59.

Late-personhood position:
Michael Tooley, "Abortion and Infanticide," *Philosophy and Public Affairs* 2.1
      (1972): 37–65.

Moderate position:
Wayne Sumner, *Abortion and Moral Theory* (Princeton, NJ: Princeton UP, 1981).

Potentiality arguments:
Don Marquis, "Why Abortion Is Immoral," *The Journal of Philosophy* 86 (1989):
      183–202.

Mary Anne Warren, "Do Potential People Have Moral Rights?," *Canadian Journal of Philosophy* 7.2 (1977): 275–89.

Bodily rights arguments:
Judith Jarvis Thomson, "A Defense of Abortion," *Philosophy and Public Affairs* 1.1 (1971): 47–66.

14

PUNISHMENT

In this chapter we will apply some of the principles developed in Chapters 10–12 to a specific problem in political philosophy: the justification of punishment. The criminal justice systems in most societies subjects certain people—those judged to have performed prohibited actions—to harsh treatment of various kinds: people who have committed traffic offences are forced to pay fines; those who commit property crimes are sometimes required to perform community service; those guilty of acts of physical violence are often incarcerated; and in some societies, people guilty of certain specified crimes are sometimes executed. In ordinary circumstances it is normally considered illegitimate for the state to treat its citizens in such ways, but when prohibited actions have been committed, this treatment is generally believed to be not only permissible but also required.

The central question of this chapter is exactly why the punishment of criminals by the state is appropriate or justified. To this end we will need to clarify in exactly what punishment consists, as well as the relation between punishment and previous criminal behaviour. In addition to considering why

CHAPTER CONTENTS:

- the concept of punishment is introduced;
- retributivist and utilitarian accounts of the justification of punishment in general are evaluated;
- the appropriateness of specific punishments is explored; and
- the question of capital punishment is addressed.

punishment in general is justified, we will also consider exactly what kind and severity of punishment are appropriate in any given case. Of particular concern is whether capital punishment is ever justified.

14.1 The Concept of Punishment

Before we can address the question of why punishment is justified, we need to get clearer about exactly what punishment is. The basic definition of **punishment** we will be working with here is as follows: punishment is a form of treatment imposed on an individual by the state that is motivated by previous criminal behaviour on the part of the individual and that is designed to be harmful to him, or to frustrate his interests. Note that even though there are other forms of punishment for non-criminal acts imposed by non-state entities—such as a parent punishing a child—the discussion here is limited to criminal punishment. As noted above, the forms of treatment range from fines and community service requirements to incarceration and execution. Although in most cases such treatment is detrimental to a person subjected to it, it is certainly possible for someone to benefit from legal punishment. Being forced to perform community service might, for example, affect someone's character in a beneficial way, and being incarcerated might enable someone to kick a drug habit or, perhaps, provide a refuge from threats they face on the outside. Nevertheless, punishment is designed to be detrimental whether or not in any given case it is so. One might object that the point of punishment is not to harm the interests of convicted criminals but rather to rehabilitate them, turning them into responsible citizens who are disinclined to commit criminal acts again in the future. It is worth emphasizing, however, that there is a distinction between punishing someone who has committed a criminal act and subjecting one to **therapy**— between making one pay or making one better—and it is the former that is at issue here. The state might, of course, take the opportunity to offer various forms of therapy to someone who is being punished, especially if the punishment in question involves a period of incarceration. And the state might impose mandatory therapy upon someone who has been judged not to be responsible for his or her criminal actions. But insofar as we are concerned with the nature and justification of punishment and not various kinds of therapy, we are

Case Study 14.1:
The Happy Convict

Suppose that Fred has been convicted of burglary for the third time and sentenced to two years in the local prison. But suppose also that Fred has an unusually happy disposition and enjoys his time in prison just as much as he enjoys his time on the outside. Finally, suppose that Mary, the warden, noticing Fred's enjoyment of his time spent in her prison, gives him all the worst duties in an attempt to ensure that he suffers during his time under her watch.

QUESTION: Does Fred's enjoyment of his time in prison prevent that time from counting as punishment? Is Mary's attempt to undermine Fred's enjoyment required to ensure that he pays for his crimes?

concerned with forms of treatment designed to be detrimental to the interests of convicted criminals.

According to the basic definition, in addition to being designed to be harmful, punishment has three central features: it is not voluntary, it is motivated by previous criminal behaviour, and it is imposed by the state. We will consider each of these in turn. First, although someone guilty of a criminal act might believe that they deserve the punishment to which she has been sentenced and might cooperate with the treatment, her consent and cooperation are not required. Rather, the treatment is mandatory in the sense that it is imposed whether or not the convicted criminal consents to being so treated. Second, to say that punishment is motivated by previous criminal behaviour is to say that the reason the person in question is being so treated is because of the belief that she has committed a crime that warrants such treatment. Normally this belief is based on the outcome of some kind of judicial process in which a verdict of guilty has been reached. It is, of course, possible for a person innocent of a crime to be punished for it; the verdicts reached in criminal proceedings can, after all, be erroneous. But in order to count as punishment, the person must at least have been found guilty. One implication of this is that preventative detention is not a kind of punishment. **Preventative detention** occurs when someone who has not engaged in criminal behaviour, or at least has not been convicted of so doing, is incarcerated because the authorities have good reason to believe that the subject is likely to do so if allowed to remain free. But since the subject need not, at the time of her incarceration, have committed a crime, there is nothing to punish her for. Hence, any justification there might be for treating the subject in this way is independent of the justification of punishment. And third, in order for harmful treatment motivated by past criminal behaviour to count as punishment, it must be imposed by authorized agents of the state. If, for example, a private citizen on his own authority imprisons someone he believes to be guilty of a crime, not only does it count as revenge rather than punishment but it is also a criminal act that may itself warrant punishment by the state.

> ## Case Study 14.2: Punishing Conspiracy?
>
> Suppose that Fred and Mary hatch a plan to blow up the CN Tower to protest the actions of the government. And suppose that after attempting to purchase explosives from an undercover RCMP officer, they are arrested, charged, and convicted of criminal conspiracy and sentenced to be incarcerated for a period of ten years.
>
> **QUESTION**: Given that Mary and Fred never carried out their intended terrorist act, can incarcerating them be correctly viewed as a form of punishment?

14.2 Justification

The central question of this chapter is the moral or political justification of the punishment of convicted criminals. But a preliminary question is why punishment is in need of justification. After all, it might just seem obvious that criminals should be punished. The reason that legal punishment is morally problematic is because it involves treating people in ways that are harmful to them and, other things being equal, it is morally wrong to intentionally harm others. Taking money from someone, forcing her to engage in unpaid work, incarcerating her, or executing her is wrong unless there is a special justification in the case at hand for treating her in this way. But simply pointing to the person's own previous wrongful conduct by itself does not suffice as a justification. After all, one might rejoin with the old saw that two wrongs do not make a right. What is required is an account of why the person's previous wrongful conduct makes it permissible to subject him or her to harms to which it would be wrong to subject those who had not so behaved. Moreover, insofar as punishment is morally required and not merely morally permissible, an account of why it would be wrong to refrain from punishing a convicted criminal is also needed.

There are three separate questions that one might have in mind when discussing the justification of punishment. The first question—and the central question of this chapter—concerns why any sort of punishment is ever an appropriate way of treating those convicted of criminal offences. At its core, the question is why being guilty of wrongdoing in the past makes it permissible (or required) for the state to subject you to harmful treatment to which it is ordinarily wrong to subject people. The second question, which presupposes that punishment is at least sometimes morally appropriate, concerns exactly for what sorts of offences punishment is permissible. Since the threat of punishment for performing some act interferes with one's freedom to perform it, the fundamental question is what sorts of restrictions on liberty the state may justifiably impose. It is widely held that the state may restrict one's liberty to inflict harm upon others. More controversially, some people hold that the state may restrict one's liberty to harm oneself or even to engage in conduct that contravenes shared societal standards. This issue was discussed in detail in Chapter 12. The third question—which assumes that some form of punishment is appropriate for the conduct at issue—concerns exactly what type and severity of punishment are appropriate for that conduct. Is it conduct for which a fine, community service, or incarceration is appropriate, and how big a fine, how many hours of community service, or how much jail time is warranted?

14.3 Retributivism

There are two basic approaches to the justification of punishment: retributivist approaches and utilitarian approaches. The difference between them is that retributivist approaches are backward-looking—locating the justification of our current treatment of convicted criminals in their previous criminal behaviour—whereas utilitarian approaches are forward-looking—locating the justification of our treatment of criminals in the positive consequences that come from treating them so. We will consider each approach in turn. According to the **retributivist** approach, a person's past criminal behaviour makes the subsequent act of punishing him or her morally appropriate. In effect, the idea is that because of his previous bad behaviour, the person in question deserves to be punished. But the question remains exactly why previous bad behaviour makes one deserve a form of treatment that it is normally morally wrong to inflict upon someone. And retributivist theories of punishment can be distinguished in terms of the answer they give to this question.

Although there is a wide variety of retributive theories of punishment, we will focus on two here: the fairness theory and the social contract theory. According to the **fairness theory**, criminal laws should be modelled on the rules of a game. Just as a game player who violates the rules thereby gains an unfair advantage over his fellow players in his attempt at winning the game, someone who violates the criminal law gains an unfair advantage over her fellow citizens in her attempts to achieve success in her various enterprises. So, for example, if Fred steals money from Mary, he gains an unfair advantage over his fellow citizens in his attempt to acquire wealth. And just as it is appropriate to restore fairness to a game by penalizing a rule breaker—putting him in the penalty box, making him lose a turn, or the like—it is appropriate to restore fairness to the social game by punishing the lawbreaker.

Although it may well be morally appropriate to act to restore fairness when someone has gained an unfair advantage in some enterprise, it is far from clear that such considerations provide an adequate justification for punishing criminal wrongdoers. First, not every criminal gains an advantage from their act of wrongdoing. Crimes of passion, for example, often yield little advantage and in many cases are soon regretted. As a result, the obligation to restore fairness could not be used to justify punishment in such cases. Second, restoring fairness requires not only removing any advantage a rule breaker may have gained but also rectifying any disadvantage a victim of rule breaking might have suffered. And while punishing a law breaker might remove a criminal's unfair advantage, it does little to fix the unfair disadvantage suffered by the victim of her crime. As a result, the appeal to fairness seems better suited to justifying a requirement that the victims of crime be compensated rather than the requirement that perpetrators of crime be punished. And third, the fairness theory, in at least some cases, misses the point of punishment. For many crimes, we punish not because of the advantage the criminal has gained but rather due to the harm the victim of the crime has suffered. Even in games we find penalties imposed for both sorts of reasons: a hockey player, for example, might spend time in the penalty box for the unfair advantage she gained by hooking her opponent as well as for the harm, or risk of harm, she caused by high sticking. And the fairness theory seems ill-suited to offer any sort of justification for penalties of the latter kind.

Some philosophers ground ethics in the idea of an implicit "social contract" between all members of society. The idea is that, by choosing to live in a given society and thus benefitting from that society's social structures, criminal justice system, military protection, and the like, the members of that society have each individually agreed to behave in ways that are beneficial to that society. According to the **social contract theory** of punishment in particular, the members of a society are obligated to follow the terms of a contract according to which in exchange for the protection of the state, among other things, they agree to comply with the laws laid down by the state. Moreover, this contract specifies that non-compliance with the law will result in punishment of various kinds. Hence, just as it is appropriate to subject someone who has failed to comply with the terms of a contract he has signed to the penalties for non-compliance spelled out in the contract, it is appropriate to subject someone who violates the criminal code to legal punishment.

Although it is true that it is appropriate to hold someone to the terms of a contract she has signed, it is far from clear that punishment can be justified by appeal to some such contract. First, few if any of us have ever signed any such contract. And although we may be bound by the terms of a contract to which we have agreed, we are not bound by the terms of a contract to which we have not agreed. One might argue that by accepting the benefits offered by the state we have tacitly agreed to the terms of some such contract and, hence, are bound by it. But normally one can tacitly agree to a contract by means of one's actions only if there is a convention in force to the effect that performing actions of that kind counts as consenting to an agreement that one has been offered. It is far from clear that there is a convention to the effect that by accepting benefits from the government we agree to abide by the criminal code or face punishment. Second, it could be argued that although we never in fact agreed to the terms of the social contract specified above, the right kind of idealized agents in the right kind of hypothetical circumstances would have agreed to those terms. And because these ideal agents would have done so, we actual agents are bound by the terms of this contract. The trouble with this suggestion is that it is, again, simply unclear why the hypothetical agreements of ideal agents place real people under any sort of obligations.

> ## Case Study 14.3:
> ## No Good Will Come of It
>
> Suppose that several years ago, Fred injured Mary's daughter while driving drunk, and, after serving an appropriate sentence for his crime, he is released from prison. And suppose that shortly afterwards, Mary is convicted of assault for attacking Fred. Finally suppose that no good will come of punishing Mary for her crime: there is little likelihood that Mary will reoffend; Mary poses no threat to the general public; Fred has forgiven her for assaulting him; there would be no public outrage if she were not punished; and punishing her would be unlikely to deter others from committing similar assaults.
>
> **QUESTION**: Would it be appropriate nevertheless to punish Mary for her actions?

14.4 Utilitarianism

According to **utilitarianism**, an act or rule or institution is morally appropriate just in case it produces better consequences than the alternatives. As a result, utilitarian approaches find the justification for punishing criminal wrongdoers in the positive consequences that ensue from treating them so. And there are a number of different sorts of consequences of punishment that advocates typically appeal to. First, punishment is claimed to have both a specific and a general deterrent effect. A specific deterrent effect occurs when, as a result of being punished for an act of wrongdoing, someone is dissuaded from performing acts of that kind again in the future. Someone imprisoned for theft, for example, might be disinclined to steal again in the future for fear of being imprisoned again. A general deterrence effect occurs when people other than the punished criminal, who might otherwise have been inclined to commit the same crime she did, are dissuaded from doing so for fear of being treated in the same way. But either way, the expected result is a lower crime rate and, hence, a reduction in the harms produced by crime. Second, at least some forms of punishment result in the protection of the general populace from harm. As long as a criminal wrongdoer is incarcerated, then she is no longer free to commit crimes she might otherwise be inclined to engage in, thereby offering the general public protection from such harms. And third, punishing criminal wrongdoers can provide an outlet for social pressure for justice in the face of criminal acts and relieve social anxiety about crime. Criminal acts can leave the general public fearful, outraged, or both. And while fear of crime can interfere with the ability to lead fulfilling lives, outrage over crime can itself lead to violence. To the extent that punishing criminals alleviates such social phenomena, it can prevent the negative consequences that often come with them.

There are, however, a number of potential difficulties with the utilitarian justification of punishment. First, it is not entirely clear that the overall consequences of punishment are as positive as the utilitarian would have it. In addition to the positive consequences delineated above, there are a number of negative consequences of punishment as well. Not only does this include the impact of punishment on the criminal himself but it can also be harmful to the friends and family of the criminal, including those people who are dependent on him. In addition, the costs of certain sorts of punishment—incarceration in particular—can be quite high. And finally, isolating someone with a bunch of hardened criminals can increase, rather than decrease, the likelihood that he will engage in criminal activity upon his release. Given these negative consequences, it becomes less clear that punishment can be justified on utilitarian grounds. The utilitarian might, of course, rejoin that many of these negative consequences can be avoided by replacing incarceration with other forms of punishment. But it is worth noting that this might result in a corresponding weakening of the positive effects of punishment as well.

Second, there is no guarantee, on the utilitarian picture, that those who have engaged in criminal behaviour are those whose punishment would generate the best consequences. One such case involves someone who has in fact committed a criminal act but for whom punishment would not produce good consequences. Suppose, for example, that Fred is convicted of burglary, but not only is he unlikely to be deterred from doing it again by punishing him, given the particularly stupid way he bungled it and got caught, but other potential burglars are also unlikely to be deterred by his punishment from trying the same thing. Moreover, suppose that he is not a danger to the public at large, he is widely popular and so there is no public outcry for justice in his case, and he has numerous dependents who will likely go hungry if he is incarcerated. In such circumstances, the utilitarian view seems to entail that Fred ought not to be punished for his criminal activity. Another sort of case involves what is known as the innocent person problem. Such cases involve

circumstances in which the best consequences can be achieved by punishing someone for a crime she did not commit. Suppose, for example, that Fred has committed
a particularly heinous murder and successfully eluded the authorities. And suppose
that it is widely believed that Mary, an unpopular loner, committed the crime and
there will be riots in the streets if no one is punished for Fred's crime. In such circumstances, the best consequences can be achieved by punishing Mary for a crime
she did not commit, so the utilitarian
justification of punishment entails
that this would be the right thing to
do. But the punishment of an innocent person is seriously wrong, so, to
the extent that utilitarianism endorses
such actions, there are serious grounds
to be suspicious of the view.

Finally, it is worth noting that on
the utilitarian picture, an act is morally
justified just in case it produces better consequences than the alternatives.
Showing that punishing has better consequences than not punishing does not
show that it has better consequences
than any of the alternatives. After all,
there may be a form of treatment, distinct from punishment, that has even

> ## Case Study 14.4:
> ## The Anti-Crime Pill
>
> Suppose that the M&F Pharmaceutical
> Company has developed an anti-crime
> pill. The pill is designed to prevent those
> who take it from having any inclination to
> engage in criminal behaviour. And suppose
> that clinical trials have shown the anti-crime
> pill to be highly effective: 99 per cent of
> patients find themselves with no little or no
> inclination to engage in criminal behaviour
> for at least ten years.
>
> **QUESTION**: Would it be morally
> appropriate to force criminals to take this
> pill rather than punish them?

better consequences than punishment. One possibility here is some form of therapy
designed to rehabilitate the criminal rather than punish him. If, for example, rehabilitative therapy is more effective at preventing recidivism than the fear of being
punished again, then it and not punishment may be what is justified on the utilitarian
picture. The utilitarian might, of course, reply that, at least as things currently stand,
rehabilitative therapy is a more costly and less effective means of reducing crime than
punishment, so until things change, it is the latter and not the former that is justified.

14.5 Mixed Theories

Given the difficulties that arise for both the retributivist and the utilitarian approaches
to the justification of punishment, one might wonder whether a mixed theory, combining elements of both approaches, would be more successful. Although there are
many ways of going about combining these views, we will focus on one such combination of views here. Central to this view is the distinction between the justification of
individual acts of punishing, on the one hand, and the justification of the overarching
practice or institution of punishment, on the other. Individual acts of punishment—
the punishment of particular people for particular crimes—are justified on retributive
grounds: criminals are punished because of their previous acts of wrongdoing and
not because of the consequences that are likely to ensue in each case. But the general

practice of punishing individual criminals on a retributive basis is justified
by the positive consequences of having
such a practice: deterrence, protection,
and the like.

There are a number of advantages
of a mixed account of this kind over
both pure retributivist and pure utilitarian accounts. First, it avoids the need
to explain why criminals deserve to be
punished, that is, why previous bad
behaviour makes current harsh treatment appropriate. It is not presupposed
by the mixed approach that they in any
sense do deserve punishment; rather,
punishing them is appropriate because
of the social benefits of a practice or
institution of punishment. And second,

Case Study 14.5: The Innocent Person Practice

Suppose that due to public perception of increasing rates of unsolved crime, the government starts an institution that runs in parallel with the criminal justice system. The officers of this new system are charged with subjecting innocent people to harsh treatment when doing so has sufficiently positive social benefits, in particular when a crime has provoked social outrage, the actual perpetrator cannot be found, and a plausible "fall guy" is available.

QUESTION: Could this practice be justified on utilitarian grounds?

the mixed approach avoids the innocent person problem. Even if on a given occasion the best consequences can be achieved by punishing an innocent person, the mixed approach does not entail that punishing that person is morally appropriate. What is justified on utilitarian grounds is a practice according to which only guilty people are punished, a practice that rules out intentionally punishing the innocent.

Nevertheless, a number of difficulties remain even for the mixed approach, one of which we will focus on here. What is important to note is that the justification for punishment on offer here is entirely a utilitarian one. The only thing that is morally significant is the consequences of punishment. The view differs from the earlier utilitarian approach only in that it focuses on the consequences of practices rather than of individual actions. And the difficulty with this approach is that it renders considerations of desert and innocence entirely contingent. The reason criminal wrongdoers should receive the punishments they deserve and innocents should not be punished is that, as a matter of fact, a practice in which they are treated in this way is likely to have better consequences than one in which they are not. Nevertheless, if the consequences were different, a practice in which criminal wrongdoers did not receive what they deserved, and in which innocents could be punished, might be justified instead. But, the objection goes, desert and innocence are fundamental moral considerations whose status as such does not hang on the contingencies of outcomes in this way.

14.6 Specific Punishments

Let us turn now to the question of specific punishments. This question presupposes that it is appropriate to subject criminals to some kind of punishment; at issue is what kind and severity of punishment they should be subjected to. As with the justification of punishment in general, there are both retributivist and utilitarian accounts of which specific punishments criminals ought to receive. We will consider each in turn. One well-known retributivist approach to this question is the biblical **"eye for an eye"** punishment formula. According to this view, the criminal ought to be subjected to exactly the same treatment to which she subjected her victims. So, for example, someone guilty of assault ought to be beaten herself, and someone guilty of murder ought to be executed. Although this formula is quite popular, and often invoked in support of capital punishment, it is fraught with difficulty. First, there are crimes to which it cannot be reasonably applied. For example, if someone is guilty of multiple murders, he or she can only be executed once and no one else can be executed for his crime. And if someone is guilty of negligently or recklessly harming someone else, rather than intentionally doing so, it is not clear that the state can ensure that the criminal is negligently or recklessly harmed in response. Second, utilizing some such formula might have intolerable side-effects on third parties. Subjecting a criminal to the same treatment that his victims were subjected to requires that some particular person treat the criminal in this way. But a person given the responsibility of beating those guilty of assault or raping rapists could undergo serious psychological damage as a result. And third, there are limits to the severity of treatment to which the state should subject anyone that the "eye for an eye" formula simply ignores. The state simply should not rape or torture anyone, not even rapists and torturers.

A more plausible retributivist account takes the severity of punishment to which a criminal ought to be subjected to as being determined by her degree of blame-worthiness for her criminal act. **Blameworthiness** can be viewed as a function of how much harm the criminal did and her degree of responsibility for that harm. Someone who intentionally caused a certain amount of harm is wholly responsible for it, whereas someone who negligently or recklessly caused harm is less responsi-ble. And someone who caused harm entirely accidentally is not responsible at all for it and hence is not at all blameworthy. So, for example, someone who intentionally breaks someone else's leg and is thus wholly responsible for it should, on this view, be subjected to a punishment that inflicts the same amount of harm upon her as the broken leg caused her victim, someone who breaks another's leg unintentionally but negligently should face a punishment that inflicts a lesser degree of harm, and someone who breaks another's leg accidentally should face no punishment at all. Unlike the "eye for an eye" formula, this does not require that intentional leg break-ers have their own legs broken but only that they suffer the same degree of harm.

Although the blameworthiness formula is an improvement over "an eye for an eye," it does still run into serious difficulties. First, like the "eye for an eye" formula, it is insensitive to the limits of the severity of treatment to which the state should subject anyone. If someone intentionally commits particularly heinous crimes, the blameworthiness formula requires that he be subjected to the same amount of harm as he caused. But even though it does not require that he be treated in the same way that he treated his victims to the state, it does require some form of treatment that may fall beyond the limits of appropriate state behaviour. Second, the blame-worthiness formula is ill-suited to handle victimless crimes. Suppose, for example, that Fred successfully drives home drunk without hitting anyone or causing any property damage. Since Fred did not cause any harm, he is not blameworthy in the relevant sense and so should not be punished on this view. And third, there are strict liability offences—offences for which the punishment is the same whether or not they are committed intentionally. Typical strict liability offences include minor traffic violations. But since the blameworthiness formula ties punishability to one's degree of responsibility for what one does, it is incompatible with strict liability offences.

The alternative to the retributive approach to specific punishments is the **utilitarian approach**. According to this view, the degree and kind of punishment to which a criminal ought to be subjected are those that yield the best consequences. One might think that inflicting the most severe punishment—say life imprisonment—for any crime will always yield the best consequences. After all, doing so will arguably produce both the greatest deterrent effect and the greatest degree of protection from dangerous people, as well as relieving social-outrage anxiety about crime. But increasing the severity of punishment in this way can also have negative consequences. As outlined above, these may include such things as the impact on the criminal himself, as well as his family, friends, and any dependents he might have, and the increased costs of incarcerating so many people for the remainder of their lives. But moreover, handing out extremely long sentences for relatively trivial crimes might itself result in social outrage over the injustice of subjecting people to harsh treatment they are widely believed not to deserve and social anxiety about being convicted of a crime rather than being a victim. Finally, it is not clear that, at a certain point, the threat of longer prison sentences will result in a significantly stronger deterrent effect or whether once they reach a sufficiently advanced age, society needs any further protection from formerly dangerous criminals. Rather than recommending the most severe punishment in every case, the utilitarian approach to specific punishment recommends instead a severity of punishment that achieves the best balance of positive over negative consequences. In the case of relatively minor crimes, this balance is likely to favour a somewhat less severe punishment than the maximum.

There are, however, a couple of difficulties that arise for the utilitarian account here. First, we have a widely shared intuition that punishment should roughly map onto what one deserves: severe crimes deserve severe punishments and mild crimes deserve mild punishments. But because the severity of punishment is based on the consequences of such treatment and not on the nature of the previous criminal behaviour, the utilitarian account could entail that criminals should receive punish-

Case Study 14.6: Moral Luck

Suppose that Fred and Mary both attempt to murder their respective paternal grandfathers in order to receive large inheritances. And suppose that while Mary's attempt is successful, Fred, due to bad luck, does not succeed in killing his grandfather.

QUESTION: Given that the only difference between Mary's and Fred's actions is luck, is there any reason to believe that Mary deserves a more severe punishment than Fred does?

ments that differ significantly from what they intuitively deserve. If a severe punishment would yield the best overall consequences, the view might entail that a criminal should receive more harsh treatment than she deserves. And if a relatively mild punishment would yield the best consequences, the view entails that she should receive less harsh treatment than she deserves. The fundamental problem is that because it focuses only on the consequences of punishment, the utilitarian view delinks punishment from desert. And second, the consequences of punishing different people convicted of committing the same crime can be very different. There can be differences in the protection and the deterrent effects it yields, and differences in the impact on the criminal, her family, and her dependents, among other things. As it results, it could turn out, on the utilitarian picture, that different people convicted of the same offence ought to be subjected to very different punishments. But treating people who have committed the same offence differently is simply unfair.

14.7 Capital Punishment

The remaining question here concerns the upper limit on the severity of punishment and, in particular, whether or not for certain crimes it is appropriate for the state to execute people. Many people think that in the case of the most serious crimes—premeditated murder, for example—the perpetrators ought to be put to death. And both the "eye for an eye" and the blameworthiness accounts of specific punishment lend support to this view. But the question remains whether execution—like rape and torture—falls beyond the limits on the treatment to which the state ought to be able to subject its citizens, even those guilty of serious criminal offences. On the other hand, simply noting that killing human persons is normally seriously wrong will not resolve the issue: after all, incarcerating people for long periods of time is also normally seriously wrong, but most opponents of the death penalty advocate this form of treatment instead for those guilty of serious crimes. Three separate considerations relevant to this issue will be addressed here: the consequences of capital punishment, innocent people, and discrimination. We will consider each in turn.

First, one way of arguing that for or against the death penalty is by appeal to its consequences. In order to argue in this way, however, one needs to focus on a particular type of criminal act and to compare the consequences of imposing the death penalty for this type of act with the consequences of an alternative punishment. For our present purposes, let us suppose that the act in question is premeditated murder and that the alternative to the death penalty is a very long prison term. Now the consequences for the criminal and his friends, family, and dependents are normally worse if he is executed rather than incarcerated. And there may be psychological harms incurred by those hired by the state to carry out executions. Whether the costs of executing him are less than long-term incarceration will depend on things like the nature of the appeals process and the costs of a separate incarceration system for those scheduled to be executed.

The main issue, however, is whether execution provides a sufficiently greater deterrent effect than long-term incarceration, as well as sufficiently greater protec-

tion from dangerous criminals, to compensate for the increased negative consequences noted above. It is worth emphasizing that the difference in protection is
likely to be minimal. After all, an incarcerated criminal is no more dangerous to
the general population than one who has been executed. And even if the criminal
is eventually released, as long as the prison sentence was sufficiently long, she is
unlikely to pose much of a risk to others by that time. Whether the death penalty
produces a greater deterrent effect than long-term incarceration is ultimately an
empirical question. One would need to compare the rates of pre-meditated murder
in jurisdictions in which it is punished by execution with the rates in otherwise similar jurisdictions in which it is punished by long prison terms. And given the other
differences normally present between any two jurisdictions, reliable data of this
kind may be hard to come by. It is worth noting, however, that in order to expect
an increased deterrent effect from the death penalty, it would have to be true of a
significant proportion of people contemplating pre-meditated murder who would
not be dissuaded by the prospect of long prison sentences if caught that they would,
nevertheless, be dissuaded by the prospect of execution.

Second, given the fallibility of our criminal justice system, there will inevitably
be a certain number of innocent people convicted of crimes for which the death
penalty might be considered appropriate. Safeguards can, of course, be put in place
to reduce the occurrence of erroneous convictions, but inevitably some will occur.
As a result, if the death penalty is utilized, a certain number of innocent people will
likely be executed, and it is widely believed that executing an innocent person is one
of the most serious injustices the state can commit. As a result, there are grounds to
resist endorsing this form of punishment.

There are two possible responses that the death penalty advocate might offer at
this point. First, she might argue that subjecting an innocent person to an extremely
long prison term is also a serious injustice, so if worries about punishing the innocent count against the death penalty, they also count against long-term incarceration. This is sensible, but there is one important difference between the cases:
someone serving a long prison term for a crime she didn't commit can always have
her conviction overturned and her punishment rescinded; but once she is executed,
her punishment cannot be undone. And second, one might argue that the execution
of a small number of innocents is a cost worth paying in order to achieve justice
or the benefits of the death penalty in the overwhelming number of cases in which
those executed are guilty. Although there may be something to say in favour of this
suggestion, it would remain at best rather controversial.

Third, it has been argued that capital punishment is inevitably disproportionately applied to members of disadvantaged and/or unpopular minority groups
and, as a result, is discriminatory. There are three potential explanations for disproportionately higher minority-group capital-punishment rates: there might be
higher rates of capital crimes among the minority population; a higher percentage
of minority-group members charged with capital crimes might get convicted; and
a higher percentage of minority-group members convicted of capital crimes might
be subjected to the death penalty rather than some other form of punishment. And
each explanation might involve some unjust discrimination. Higher capital crimes

among minority crime rates might be the product of historical or continuing discrimination against the members of the group. Higher conviction rates might be the
product of conscious or unconscious bias against members of the group by those
charged with making a determination of guilt or innocence. And higher execution rates of those convicted of capital crimes might be explained by conscious or
unconscious bias against members of the group by those charged with determining
what punishment ought to be applied. But, the argument goes, if higher rates of
capital punishment among minority-group members are both inevitable and the
product of unjust discrimination, capital punishment itself is discriminatory and, as
a result, should not be utilized.

There are a number of responses the advocate of capital punishment might make
here. First, it could be argued that as long as each person subjected to the death
penalty is guilty of the crime for which she is punished, then the higher execution rates among the minority population do not constitute any kind of injustice;
after all, everyone who is executed gets what they deserve. However, to the extent
that higher minority execution rates are due to higher conviction rates, which are
themselves the product of bias, it is likely that there will be higher rates of innocent minority-group members executed than is found in the general population.
Second, it could be argued that the solution to disproportionately high minority-
group execution rates is not to eliminate the death penalty but to increase its use
on non-minority-group members convicted of capital crimes, perhaps by making it
the mandatory punishment for those convicted of such crimes. The trouble is that
although this may eliminate the effects of bias at the sentencing stage, it does nothing to eliminate it at the conviction stage. Finally, one might argue that the problem
is not the death penalty itself but rather discrimination against the minority group.
As a result, the correct response is not to reject the death penalty but rather to end
discrimination. The trouble is that discrimination is a quite intractable social phenomenon: the lingering effects of past discrimination against unpopular minorities
and continuing conscious and unconscious biases against them are very difficult to
change.

In this chapter, we have considered both utilitarian and retributive attempts to
justify the general practice of punishing criminal wrongdoers, as well as views combining elements of both approaches. In addition, we have considered the question
of what specific punishment criminals ought to be subjected to in particular cases
and whether capital punishment is ever warranted. As criminal activity continues
to evolve and the world increasingly seems to be smaller and more dangerous,
the questions of how we should treat criminal wrongdoers remains one of central
importance.

Reading Questions

1.   What is the basic definition of punishment?

2.   Why is legal punishment morally problematic?

CHAPTER FOURTEEN PUNISHMENT   245

3. What is the difference between a forward-looking and a backward-looking approach to justification?

4. Why, according to the fairness theory, is it appropriate to punish criminal wrongdoers?

5. Why, according to the social contract theory, do we have an obligation to obey the law?

6. What is the difference between a general and a specific deterrence effect?

7. What is the innocent person problem for utilitarianism?

8. How does the mixed approach to the justification of punishment differ from the utilitarian approach?

9. Why does the blameworthiness formula entail that drunk drivers should receive no punishment?

10. What does it mean to say that capital punishment is discriminatory?

Reflection Questions

1. Think of a number of things that you or people you know have done that you now consider to have been inappropriate. Do you think that you deserved to be punished for any of these actions? What would have been the impact of punishing you for those actions at the time?

2. Think of a number of cases in which, rightly or wrongly, your behaviour has undermined the interests of other people. Is there any sense in which your behaviour can be undone? If so, what would it take to undo it in the cases at hand?

Further Reading

General introduction to the issue of punishment:
David Boonin, *The Problem of Punishment* (Cambridge: Cambridge UP, 2008).
Michael Zimmerman, *The Immorality of Punishment* (Peterborough, ON: Broadview P, 2011).

Retributivist approaches:
Jeffrie Murphy, "Legal Moralism and Retribution Revisited," *Criminal Law and Philosophy* 1 (2007): 5–20.

Utilitarian approaches:
A. Ellis, "A Deterrence Theory of Punishment," *Philosophical Quarterly* 53
    (2003): 337–51.

Mixed approaches:
John Rawls, "Two Concepts of Rules," *John Rawls, Collected Papers*, ed. S.
    Freeman (Cambridge, MA: Harvard UP, 1999), pp. 20–46.

Specific punishments:
Richard Parker, "Blame, Punishment, and the Role of Result," *American
    Philosophical Quarterly* 21.3 (1984): 269–76.

Capital punishment:
M. Davis, *Justice in the Shadow of Death: Rethinking Capital and Lesser
    Punishments* (Lanham, MD: Rowman & Littlefield, 1996).

INDEX

From the Publisher

A name never says it all, but the word "Broadview" expresses a good deal of the philosophy behind our company. We are open to a broad range of academic approaches and political viewpoints. We pay attention to the broad impact book publishing and book printing has in the wider world; we began using recycled stock more than a decade ago, and for some years now we have used 100% recycled paper for most titles. Our publishing program is internationally oriented and broad-ranging. Our individual titles often appeal to a broad readership too; many are of interest as much to general readers as to academics and students.

Founded in 1985, Broadview remains a fully independent company owned by its shareholders—not an imprint or subsidiary of a larger multinational.

For the most accurate information on our books (including information on pricing, editions, and formats) please visit our website at www.broadviewpress.com. Our print books and ebooks are also available for sale on our site.

On the Broadview website we also offer several goods that are not books—among them the Broadview coffee mug, the Broadview beer stein (inscribed with a line from Geoffrey Chaucer's *Canterbury Tales*), the Broadview fridge magnets (your choice of philosophical or literary), and a range of T-shirts (made from combinations of hemp, bamboo, and/or high-quality pima cotton, with no child labor, sweatshop labor, or environmental degradation involved in their manufacture).

All these goods are available through the "merchandise" section of the Broadview website. When you buy Broadview goods you can support other goods too.

broadview press
www.broadviewpress.com

The interior of this book is printed on 100% recycled paper.